Italian-American Folklore

Italian-American Folklore

*Frances M. Malpezzi
and William M. Clements*

This volume is a part of
The American Folklore Series
W.K. McNeil, General Editor

August House Publishers, Inc.
LITTLE ROCK

Published by August House, Inc.,
P.O. Box 3223, Little Rock, Arkansas, 72203,
501–372–5450.

Printed in the United States of America

10 9 8 7 6 5 4 3 2 1

LIBRARY OF CONGRESS CATALOGING-IN-PUBLICATION DATA

Malpezzi, Frances M., 1946–
Italian-American folklore / Frances M. Malpezzi and William M. Clements.
p.   cm. — (The American folklore series)
ISBN 0–87483–279–9 (alk. paper) : $24.95 pb
ISBN 0–87483–278–0 (pbk. : alk. paper) : $14.95 hb
1. Italian Americans—Folklore. 2. Italian Americans—Social life and customs.
I. Clements, William M., 1945– . II. Title. III. Series
GR111.I73M35   1992
398'.08951073—dc20   92-19214

First Edition, 1992

Executive editor: Liz Parkhurst
Series editor: W.K. McNeil
Project editor: Tom Baskett, Jr.
Design director: Ted Parkhurst
Cover design: Byron Taylor
Typography: Lettergraphics / Little Rock

This book is printed on archival-quality paper which meets the
guidelines for performance and durability of the Committee on
Production Guidelines for Book Longevity of the
Council on Library Resources.

AUGUST HOUSE, INC.   PUBLISHERS   LITTLE ROCK

In memory of Francesca and Rocco Capello and Rose and Joe Capello—and for Albina, Pearl, and Guido Malpezzi

Contents

Acknowledgments

We have incurred many debts during the course of preparing this book. In addition to the interviewees named in chapter 1, we want to thank Patrick B. Mullen, Theresa A. Paladino, and Donna Partridge, all of whom suggested avenues of research that we might pursue; Wayne Narey and Lucia Peek, who shared the results of their own research with us; Jill Coe Butts and Elizabeth Stafford, who transcribed some of our interviews; Louise Gennuso, Sam Gennuso, Antoinette Giglio, and Ernesto Lombeida, who assisted in the translation of some Sicilian song texts; Tami Chandler, Carl Lindquist, and Norman Stafford, who helped with illustrations; and librarians in the Interlibrary Loan Department of the Dean B. Ellis Library, Arkansas State University, and in the Regional Studies Collection of the Charles C. Wise, Jr. Library, West Virginia University. We also appreciate the assistance of the following Arkansas State University administrators who facilitated our involvement in the institution's research reassignment program for one semester: Charles R. Carr, Chair of the Department of English, Philosophy, and Languages; C. Calvin Smith, Acting Dean of the College of Arts and Sciences; and Robert Hoskins, Vice-President for Academic Affairs. Finally, we are indebted to Tom Baskett, whose editing provided the necessary finish for our work.

Introduction

ITALIAN AMERICANS, like most ethnic groups that make up the population of the United States, have received relatively little attention from folklorists. Indeed, one of the best-known works dealing with Italian-American folklore, *South Italian Folkways in Europe and America,* was not written by a folklorist, but by a sociologist.

The reasons for this neglect are undoubtedly manifold, but a few speculations about the matter can be offered here. For one thing, the Italians are relatively recent migrants, and "new" arrivals generally have been of less interest to collectors and folklorists than the "more established" immigrants. Also important is the fact that these people are from a non-English-speaking background, and the native language remained strongest among the older Italian Americans, meaning that the lore was inaccessible to most American collectors. Throughout the history of folklore studies, fieldworkers have concentrated for various reasons on elderly informants. Most collectors were seeking survivals of old-country traditions, and older family members were deemed most likely to have preserved these.

Probably the slighting of Italian-American traditions in the late nineteenth and early twentieth century is mainly attributable to the narrow focus of most scholars of that time, an orientation that gave no consideration to the lore of most ethnic and cultural groups. A majority of folklorists then were occupied with the study of specific genres, such as the ballad, or with the traditions of "problem" groups like African Americans or American Indians.

Whatever the reasons for this neglect, it certainly wasn't because no one was aware of Italian-American folklore or of the need to collect it. In 1911 the First National Congress of Italian Ethnography approved a proposal submitted by Professor Lamberto Loria that called for research on Italian immigrant folklore.[1]

While Italian-American folklore was neglected, it was not entirely overlooked. Unless one counts such hysterical articles as "What Shall We Do with the Dago?: Prisons Should not be Comfortable,"[2] the earliest printed reference to the subject is a note in the July-September 1892 issue of the *Journal of American Folklore* pertaining to one Joseph Libertino, who claimed to possess supernatural powers but was arrested by New York City authorities as "an arrant fraud."[3]

This was followed by a small body of publications, most of them intended for popular audiences. Thus, Charlotte Kimball's "An Outline of Amusements Among Italians in New York" provides some interesting, useful accounts of traditional games and the typical situations in which they were played. Informative though it is, Kimball's article lacks much of the accompanying data modern folklorists prefer. Others, such as Elisabeth Irwin, concentrated on some of the more colorful aspects of Italian-American folklore.[4] Still others, like Adolfo Rossi, published relevant works of potential value that were little known primarily because they were issued in Italy and received little publicity in the United States.

Most of the publications on Italian-American lore issued before World War II were articles, and even they did not appear in huge quantities. Nevertheless, their number is sufficiently large that it would be impossible to discuss each one at length. There would not be much point in such treatment anyhow because the vast majority of these works are collections, often consisting of nothing more than unannotated texts with little or no accompanying data.

These early works concentrate on three aspects of Italian-American folklore: folk speech, festival days, and folk medicine. Worthy of mention in regard to the first topic is a two-part paper by Herbert H. Vaughan, "Italian and Its Dialects as Spoken in the United States" and "Italian Dialects in the United States, II," and one by A.G. Zallio, "Piedmontese Dialects in the United States," all of which appeared in *American Speech*.[5] Charles Speroni's "The Observance of St. Joseph's Day Among the Sicilians of Southern California" gives some examples of Sicilian dialect and provides bibliographic references.[6] Finally, Dorothy Gladys Spicer's "Health

Superstitions of the Italian Immigrant" is a brief, but very useful, early discussion of Italian-American folk medicine.[7]

Without question, though, the most important work on Italian-American folklore published prior to World War II was the already-mentioned *South Italian Folkways in Europe and America* (1938). Written by Phyllis H. Williams, a sociologist at Yale University, the book's purpose and intended audience are outlined in the subtitle, *A Handbook for Social Workers, Visiting Nurses, School Teachers, and Physicians.* In the 1930s it was unique, and even though a few comparative studies have appeared in the more than half century since it was published, it is still valuable. An early example of what might be called applied folklore, i.e., using folklore to facilitate some specific purpose, the book was well received by folklorists and sociologists and, as recently as 1970, was praised as the "only book on this subject."[8]

Yet Williams was no folklorist, nor did she claim to be; she was a good researcher. Her European examples were taken secondhand, but from a very valuable source, Guiseppe Pitre's twenty-five-volume *Biblioteca delle Tradizioni Popolari Siciliane* (1871-1913). American materials were "gathered entirely at first hand during eleven years of contact with more than five hundred Italian and Italian-American families drawn from practically all parts of Italy."[9] Apparently, this impressive amount of fieldwork resulted from a team collecting approach.

The book's twelve chapters cover a broad range of topics including employment, diet, housing, dress, marriage and the family, recreation, education, beliefs, folk medical practices, and death and funerary practices. These are not just dry listings of facts but well-written accounts enlivened with anecdotal material that places the folklore in context. For example, rather than just describing belief in the concept of the evil eye, Williams relates several instances like the following that dramatically demonstrate the hold such beliefs have on individuals:

> A group of women meeting at a friend's house to pass the afternoon noticed with misgiving that a childless woman, said to have the Evil Eye, was present. In America, as in Italy, it is considered dangerous to antagonize such a person. She is allowed to visit in the homes of

her neighborhood almost as freely as anyone and is treated like other guests. A young mother who had brought her six-month-old baby was especially uneasy and planned to leave as soon as she could without attracting attention. Everyone said something complimentary about the child, carefully adding "God bless it" afterwards. The childless woman did not say this, and the omission had such a depressing effect on the little party that in a short time they all went home. A few weeks later the baby died, and its death was attributed to the woman with the Evil Eye. Her malevolent influence had turned the child's blood to water. When the baby first began to ail, a doctor had been called in and had said that its diet needed changing, but the mother and her friends knew better. After what had happened, no diet would help. She followed the physician's advice only half-heartedly and depended more upon the counsel and practices of every *maga*[10] she could find. Lemons were stuck full of pins, and the heads cut off; strings were knotted; sacred cakes were baked and placed at the feet of the patron saint. All to no end. It was too late.[11]

South Italian Folkways was one of the first examinations of Italian folklore in both the Old World and the New, and it clearly demonstrated the value and relevance of such investigations. Probably without realizing it, Williams also mined an area of folklore in which she was an early prospector, namely, urban lore. In the past three decades it has become increasingly commonplace to write about the folklore found in American cities, but in 1938 it was a virtually unheard of type of research. One who wanted to find folklore automatically went to a rural area, preferably one that was extremely isolated and, thus, not typical of most rural regions. As recently as the 1950s, such a sophisticated scholar as Richard M. Dorson thought it necessary to make his first major field trip to a basically non-urban, out-of-the-way area.[12] Nearly two decades later, the same author asked the rhetorical question "Is There a Folk in the City?"—a query already answered in the affirmative by Phyllis Williams.

South Italian Folkways also was a pioneering American folklife study. Most folklore monographs concentrate on a single aspect of traditional culture, such as a genre. Williams, on the other hand, essays to cover the entire traditional life of Italian Americans. To be sure, hers was not the first book by an American scholar to adopt this approach. Earlier, Vance Randolph attempted similar kinds of studies in his *The Ozarks* (1931) and *Ozark Mountain Folks* (1932); but, while these books were lauded in their day, they have not stood the test of time nearly as well as Williams's 1938 volume.

The main difference between the way in which Williams's and Randolph's works are perceived today lies in the groups they studied. Both authors believed that most of the current lore found in the respective cultures they examined consisted of survivals, but Randolph dealt with a group whose ancestors migrated to America many generations ago, whereas Williams focused on a people who had migrated relatively recently. Therefore, the survivals she discussed seemed to belong to mainstream Italian-American culture; those Randolph treated seemed to be relics from an earlier time that had outlived their usefulness in mainstream society. In short, *The Ozarks* and *Ozark Mountain Folks* seem dated today while *South Italian Folkways* still seems relevant.

Good as it is, *South Italian Folkways* is not flawless. One major problem is the fieldwork, which evidently was done almost exclusively in New Haven, Connecticut, and the immediate vicinity. That in itself is not problematic except that Williams provides no details, save the most general, about how the interviews were conducted. What questions were asked? Was a questionnaire used? What interview methodology was employed? Did all interviewers follow the same interviewing techniques? Were all informants asked the same questions? How were the informants chosen? Was it because they had special insights into their cultural lore? Or was it because they had exceptionally large folklore repertoires? Or was it simply because they were willing to talk about such matters? What were the circumstances of the individual recording sessions? It would be useful to know the answers to all of these questions, but Williams reveals nothing about the interviewers and, except for a few names cited in the preface, nothing about the informants themselves.

From a purely comparative viewpoint, another problem is that the Old World folklore and the New World traditions were collected during different periods. While the Italian-American material was up to date as of 1938, the data dealing with Italians in Italy was, in some instances, more than sixty-five years old. This problem would have been lessened if the Italian folklore had been collected from the same regional groups from which Williams garnered her Italian-American materials. Unfortunately, this was not the case; rather, the American traditions were elicited from groups that had little in common with Pitre's informants beyond their Italian ancestry. This situation, and most other problems that modern folklorists have with the book, result from the simple fact that Williams was not a folklorist and had other primary concerns than those of folklorists.

Broad-ranging as *South Italian Folkways* is, it does slight some aspects of the folk culture it discusses. For example, it contains no lengthy consideration of folk speech or material culture, although it does touch on these topics in several chapters. Yet, whatever its flaws, *South Italian Folkways in Europe and America* is a noteworthy study of the tenacity of Old World folkways in the New World and how one immigrant group responded to life in America. It was almost four decades before a similar book appeared.

Williams's important work was immediately followed by a sizeable number of short articles on various aspects of folklore. It is hardly necessary to add that these were of varying quality. Some excellent work was done on festival days by Charles Speroni, whose "The Development of the Columbus Day Pageant of San Francisco" is an important historical examination of a specific celebration.[13] Worthwhile papers also appeared on songs, proverbs, and folktales. Some, such as Elvira Francello's "An Italian Version of the 'Maid Freed from the Gallows,'" presented Italian versions of songs well known in Anglo-American tradition.[14] Others, such as Manuel D. Ramirez's "Italian Folklore from Tampa, Florida," presented songs transcribed in dialect.[15] Unfortunately, in this instance, the transcriptions were poorly done. By contrast, Ramirez's collection of more than one hundred Sicilian proverbs recorded in Tampa is an exemplary early paremiological work that gives sayings both in Sicilian and in useful English translations.[16] Louis C. Jones, a specialist in ghostlore, produced a brief article on "Italian Werewolves" in which he noted that "among the great variety of people living in New York State to whom the werewolf is a folkloristic commonplace in their native lands, it is only with the French Canadians and Italians that the material seems to survive in this country in any profusion; it should also be observed that...the Italians tell the stories as having happened only in the Old World."[17] This comment was one of the early pronouncements by a folklorist about the changes in supernatural traditions when transported from the Old World to the New.

Richard M. Dorson supplied a noteworthy article to the 1948 issue of the *Journal of American Folklore* with his "Dialect Stories of the Upper Peninsula: A New Form of American Folklore."[18] This form of folk narrative had many antecedents, including the vaudeville stage, minstrel shows, and Yankee yarns of the mid-nineteenth century press. Although, strictly speaking, it was not new, it certainly had not previously received much attention from folklorists. Dorson found that "in their geographic concentration, wide dispersion, multiplicity, and extreme oral popularity, the Upper Peninsula dialect tales represent a novel folklore phenomenon."[19] He provided eighty-four examples of the tradition taken from French, Finnish, Cornish, Swedish and Italian informants and outlined some of the characteristics of these narratives.[20] Generally, much of the humor derives from the use of native grammar and alphabet structure applied to American English forms; syntactical malformations also often function "independently as choice comic morsels."[21] The rhythmic cadences in which the stories are told also are an essential part of their delivery. In these tales each ethnic and cultural group has certain distinctive speech patterns, so Italian dialect stories would not be given in the same cadence as, for example, a Finnish dialect story. Despite Dorson's lead, relatively few folklorists have followed in examining this aspect of twentieth-century American folklore.

Interestingly, the largest collection of Italian-American folklore published during the 1940s was, like Phyllis Williams's 1938 volume, compiled by a non-folklorist. Jerre Mangione, who eventually became a professor of English at the University of Pennsylvania, was an author of several fiction and nonfiction works. He is mentioned here because of his *Mount Allegro* (1942), a nearly three-hundred-page book reprinted several times in the past fifty years. This view of a large Italian immigrant family in Rochester, New York, was originally passed off as a novel but in recent years has been more accurately categorized as a memoir. In subsequent years Mangione followed it with two other volumes of memoirs, *Reunion in Sicily* (1950) and *An Ethnic at Large* (1978), but *Mount Allegro* remains for those interested in Italian-American folklore the most significant of the three.

As sociologist Herbert Gans notes in his introduction to a 1981 reissue, the "heart" of *Mount Allegro* is the narratives told by family members almost nightly at their gatherings.[22] These range from widely known folktales to more obscure yarns, but they are not presented as lifeless texts without accompanying data. Instead, they are given in the contexts in which they were commonly related. Moreover, much information is provided about the individuals who told these narratives. Several other types of folklore also are included—for example, customs and folk beliefs. One of the more interesting chapters is a lengthy discussion of evil eye beliefs.

In the 1950s and 1960s a handful of articles relevant to the folklorist concerned with Italian-American culture appeared. Among the better of these is the essay "Italian Immigrant Life in Northampton County, Pennsylvania, 1890-1915" by Clement Valletta, who grew up in the settlements he discusses. Valletta uses written records and the recollections of a number of informants in an attempt to reconstruct some of the life patterns of these people.[23] Mildred Urick's "The San Rocco Festival at Aliquippa, Pennsylvania: A Transplanted Tradition" provides a detailed description of the festival, several illustrations, and historical data, making it a fine contribution in the tradition of Charles Speroni's 1940s essays. [24] There were also several sociologically and historically oriented books of some value to the folklorist, like Laurence Pisani's *The Italian in America* (1957). But it was not until the 1970s that a folklorist undertook a book-length study of Italian-American lore. The seeds of this work were planted in 1966 when Carla Bianco spent one day doing fieldwork in Roseto, Pennsylvania; eight years later, she published *The Two Rosetos* (1974).

By the time Bianco visited Roseto, the town had gained a degree of international prominence for a reason that seemed to have little, if any, connection with folklore. In 1963 an American cardiologist examined Roseto's eating habits and noticed that the death rate from heart disease was much lower than in surrounding communities even though caloric intake was high and there was widespread obesity.[25] This publicity may have made Roseto more appealing as a place in which to do fieldwork than it might otherwise have been and probably made one aim of her fieldwork, albeit one that was never explicitly stated, to determine if anything in the town's folklife explained the relatively low instance of heart disease deaths.

Unlike *South Italian Folkways in Europe and America, The Two Rosetos* is based on original fieldwork in Italy and America. Twelve months were spent doing fieldwork in both countries, the result being almost 150 hours of interviews, including songs, tales, proverbs, beliefs, superstitions, traditional habits, and life histories. Bianco's goal was to record a "fully representative sampling of the Rosetan tradition and to use this sampling as a basis for the study of the process of adaptation of this rural group to American conditions."[26] In short, here was a study of culture change based on folklore.

Bianco's fieldwork revealed instances of change in folklore texts of the sort surmised, but not proven, by other researchers dealing with Old World-New World cultural groups. For example, she noted that folklore texts which "are only vaguely recalled in the parent community or are remembered only in a fragmentary form, have survived in the United States in older and completer versions."[27] This is essentially the idea that Cecil Sharp had in mind when beginning his collecting of English folksongs in southern Appalachia in the early twentieth century.[28] Bianco found that narratives changed more dramatically than other forms of oral tradition, mainly because they have a freer structure—allowing the narrator much more latitude for personal interpretation and manipulation—than most other forms of folklore. Songs, on the other hand, changed more slowly because of the close relationship between their metrical and musical structure. There were, however, new songs created in response to the American experience that entered folk tradition.

An important consideration in examining change is determining why second- and third-generation immigrants retained their Old World traditions "even when they no longer need to or understand why."[29] The answer Bianco found in the attitudes of the Italian immigrants. Many came with the idea of eventually returning to Italy; and, even though in some cases their plans never materialized, their intentions reinforced their desire to hold on to their traditional behavior patterns, a tenacity that was then passed on to their descendants. There were, however, immigrants who had no plans for returning to Italy and who intended to integrate fully into American society. This fact, and divisive historical conditions in Italy, led to a multitude of cultural patterns and divisions in Italian-American society that ultimately prevented Roseto, Pennsylvania, from becoming a mere duplicate of Roseto Valfortore.

The Two Rosetos is divided into two parts, the first five chapters presenting a description of the two towns and a discussion of their traditional life with ample quotations from the numerous informants. The second part contains three chapters giving abundant examples of folktales and folksongs as well as excerpts from several interviews. Bianco reveals that the New World folklore is as rich and varied as the traditions left behind in Italy. Although never exactly saying so, Bianco seems to suggest that the relatively low incidence of cardiac problems is a result of the successful manner in which most Rosetans adapted to life in Pennsylvania, a transition that enabled them to enjoy the best of both worlds.[30] This matter aside, Bianco's study is still one of the most important works on Italian-American folklore and acculturation. Furthermore, nearly two decades after it appeared in 1974, it remains the only lengthy comparative investigation of two Italian communities done by a folklorist.

Indeed, after the publication of *The Two Rosetos* only one major work in Italian-American folklore has appeared, but it had an even longer gestation period than Bianco's book. This project really began in 1941 when Bruna Todesco took a folklore course at Wayne State University in Detroit. For her class project, Bruna collected

Märchen, legends, and religious tales from her mother Clementina, an immigrant from Faller, a village in the Veneto region of northeast Italy. Bruna translated the texts from her mother's Italian dialect into English and, apparently, planned to publish them someday. Unfortunately, she died at age thirty-nine in 1961, and her texts lay forgotten in the Wayne State Folklore Archive. Then, in 1974, John Gutowski, director of the archive at the time, discovered the collection and realized its importance. Two scholars, Elizabeth Mathias and Richard Raspa, were invited to work on Bruna's manuscript because of their long-term interest in Italian culture and folklore. Both had extensive fieldwork experience in northern and southern Italy, had taught at Italian universities, and lived in the Dolomite region, where Clementina Todesco was born. Moreover, both had done fieldwork in Italian-American communities in the United States. Their collaboration resulted in *Italian Folktales in America: The Verbal Art of an Immigrant Woman* (1985).

The Mathias-Raspa volume deals with memory culture but is far superior to most works of this type. Rather than just reprinting texts with reference notes citing other examples, Mathias and Raspa found Clementina Todesco and interviewed her about life in Faller and the circumstances under which she learned the narratives. In short, they tried to determine when the stories were typically told and why, as well as the meaning of specific characters and incidents. The stepmother, who appears in many of the *Märchen* and personal narratives as a very unlikable character, had real meaning for Mrs. Todesco. For many years she had a poor relationship with her own stepmother, the ill will between the two ending in 1950 when Mrs. Todesco returned to Faller for a visit.

It will perhaps be surprising to some readers to learn that in Faller the stories were usually told in the stable. This surprise disappears when one realizes the importance of the stable in Faller, and probably other Italian communities. There, the stable was the major place to socialize, serving as "a comfortable family room, where guests were greeted cordially and invited to pass the long winter evenings in the coziness of human companionship." It served as a communication and medical center for villagers as well as a parlor, folk school, community hall, dining room, and dance hall.

The stable was a free zone that "functioned to mediate the intimate gestures of home life with the formal rituals of public interaction."[31] So, what more appropriate place could there be for storytelling?

Most of Mrs. Todesco's narratives have Old World settings, the personal-experience tales being the only ones set in America. Interestingly, one of Clementina Todesco's favorite places to tell stories in New York was Central Park, a setting most American readers would probably consider an unlikely place to hear folktales. The ten personal narratives touch on a variety of beliefs in Italy and the United States and reveal the cultural factors making it possible for Mrs. Todesco and her family to survive war, poverty, and the untimely death of her daughter, Bruna. Taken together, the book's various chapters provide a history of an individual storyteller and the development of her art over both time and space. Not only is this feat rarely accomplished, it is rarely attempted; and, to date, no one has done this better than Mathias and Raspa. In other words, this is a model folklore study.

One hopes that *Italian-American Folklore* also will come to be regarded as an exemplary collection. It attempts to show the breadth and depth of the subject and departs from most previous publications in that it deals with the lore of all Italian Americans, not just those whose ancestors came from a single town or region in Italy. Moreover, the book is not just the result of raiding some folklore archives, but also includes material the authors gathered from their own fieldwork especially for this volume. Like Italian-American culture itself, it blends both old and new elements.

—*W.K. McNeil*
The Ozark Folk Center
Mountain View, Arkansas

NOTES

1. See Carla Bianco, *The Two Rosetos* (Bloomington: Indiana Univ. Press, 1974), 143.

2. This essay by A. Morgan appeared in *Popular Science Monthly* 38 (December 1890): 172-79.

3. The note is titled "Calling on the Devil to Cure Disease" and appears in the *Journal of American Folklore* 5 (1892): 238.

4. Irwin's topic and approach are accurately described in the title "Where the Players are Marionettes and the Age of Chivalry is Born Again in a Little Italy Theatre in Mulberry Street." This essay appeared in *Craftsman* 12 (1907): 667-69.

5. All of these articles appeared in *American Speech*. Vaughan's first piece appeared in 1, no. 7 (1926): 431-35; the second in 2, no. 1 (1927): 13-18. Zallio's article appeared in 2, no. 2 (1927): 501-5.

6. Speroni's article appeared in *Southern Folklore Quarterly* 4 (1940): 135-39.

7. Spicer's article appeared in *Hygeia* 4 (May 1926): 266-69.

8. See Carla Bianco, *Italian and Italian-American Folklore: A Working Bibliography*, Folklore Forum Bibliographic and Special Series no. 5 (Bloomington, Ind., 1970), 32.

9. Phyllis Williams, *South Italian Folkways in Europe and America* (1938; reprint, New York: Russell & Russell, 1969), xvi.

10. The Italian word for "witch," which did not necessarily mean one who worked evil.

11. Williams, 154.

12. See, for example, the prefatory remarks to the reprint of Dorson's *Bloodstoppers and Bearwalkers* (1952; reprint, Cambridge: Harvard Univ. Press, 1972).

13. This article appeared in *Western Folklore* 7 (1948): 325-35.

14. This piece of collectanea appeared in *New York Folklore Quarterly* 2, no. 1 (1946): 139.

15. This collection appeared in *Southern Folklore Quarterly* 5 (1941): 101-6.

16. This article appeared in *Southern Folklore Quarterly* 13 (1949): 121-31.

17. Originally published in *New York Folklore Quarterly* 6, no. 3 (1950): 133-38, it is quoted here from Louis C. Jones, *Three Eyes on the Past: Exploring New York Folk Life* (Syracuse: Syracuse Univ. Press, 1982), 77.

18. Originally published in *Journal of American Folklore* 61 (1948): 113-50, the article was reprinted in Richard M. Dorson, *Folklore and Fakelore: Essays Toward a Discipline of Folk Studies* (Cambridge: Harvard Univ. Press, 1976), 223-66.

19. Dorson, *Folklore and Fakelore*, 227.

20. Only five of Dorson's examples, numbers 17 and 60-63, are Italian, meaning that they were either from Italian-American informants or attributed by informants to that ethnic group.

21. Dorson, *Folklore and Fakelore*, 227.

22. Jerre Mangione, *Mount Allegro: A Memoir of Italian-American Life* (1942; reprint, New York: Columbia Univ. Press, 1981), xii.

23. Valletta's article appeared in two parts in *Pennsylvania Folklife*, the first section in 14, no. 1 (Autumn 1965): 35-45; the second in 14, no. 2 (Winter 1966): 39-48.

24. Urick's essay appeared in *Pennsylvania Folklife* 18, no. 1 (Autumn 1969): 14-22.

25. One of the early, and more official, reports about the long-lived Rosetans is in Stewart Wolf, "Mortality from Myocardial Infarction in Roseto," *Journal of the American Medical Association* 195 (1966): 142; but news of the phenomenon also appeared in more popular publications, such as the *Washington Post*. The research team that conducted the study was headed by Dr. John G. Bruhn, a medical sociologist at the Galveston branch of the University of Texas medical

school. The team discovered that not a single Rosetan under forty-seven had ever suffered a recorded heart attack, and that residents of the Pennsylvania town seemed to live ten and twenty years longer than most Americans.

26. Bianco, *The Two Rosetos*, xi.

27. Ibid., xii.

28. See the comments about Sharp's collecting in Dorson, *Folklore and Fakelore*, 43.

29. Bianco, *The Two Rosetos*, xii.

30. This is explicitly stated in John G. Bruhn and Stewart Wolf, *The Roseto Story: An Anatomy of Health* (Norman: Univ. of Oklahoma Press, 1974), particularly in the chapter titled "Myocardial Infarction in Sociological Perspective," 118-34. Also see Bianco's chapter 5, "The Community and the World," 122-42.

31. Elizabeth Mathias and Richard Raspa, *Italian Folktales in America: The Verbal Art of an Immigrant Woman* (Detroit: Wayne State Univ. Press, 1985), 38-39.

Vincenzo Ferraro and Lucia Matera Ferraro. Photographs courtesy of Lucia Peek.

Setting the Scene

EARLY IN THE SECOND DECADE of this century Lucia Peek's grandparents, Vincenzo and Lucia Ferraro, migrated from their home in a Campanian village near Naples to Peace Dale, Rhode Island, to work in the textile mills. Sara Vittone's father came in 1904 from his southern Italian *paese* (village) to mine for coal near Boomer, West Virginia. Rocco Capello, a native of the Italian Piedmont, settled nine years later at Rillton, Pennsylvania, also to work in the coal mines. His wife and two children followed him in 1920. Mamie Jo DiMarco Chauvin's parents emigrated from Palermo, Sicily, to southern Louisiana, where her father—though trained as a physician—found employment on the Godchaux sugar plantation.[1]

More than five million other Italians have left their homes in Europe for a new life in the United States, and they and their descendants number over twelve million, according to the 1980 federal census.[2] Though a significant Italian presence in the New World dates from the eighteenth century, this massive population movement—"modern history's greatest and most sustained movement of population from a single country"[3]—actually began about 1880, less than twenty years after the politically and culturally disparate provinces that now comprise the nation of Italy had been unified. The earliest wave of immigrants came from such northern regions as Liguria, the Piedmont, Lombardy, and Veneto, where even though conditions were relatively prosperous, economic opportunities were more limited than those promised by life in the New World. Many of these northern Italians made their way across the Atlantic and then across the continent to settle in California, where some became prominent merchants, farmers, and vintners.

The bulk of Italian immigrants, though, came from the south. Campania, Apulia, Calabria, and Sicily contributed six times as many immigrants as did northern Italy.[4] A multitude of reasons accounts for this overwhelming number of immigrants from southern Italy (1,911,933 in the century's first decade):

> the pressure of population on the land; the miserable wages, amounting to only a few cents for twelve or more hours of work a day; infertility of the soil, combined with little or no risk capital and with primitive agricultural methods; poor health conditions in general and a terrible cholera epidemic in 1887 in particular; industrial backwardness or actual stagnation; a stubbornly lingering feudalism providing a jarring contradiction in a modern era; a system of heavy indirect taxation combined with an excessively high cost of living; an inexperienced, inept, incapacitated, and distant national government; corruption in local government; the secular exploitation by a privileged upper class.... [and] the cruel social and psychological punishment of the peasant by the master class and its satellites, to the point where to be a peasant, a *contadino*, in southern Italy was to be a stupid and despicable earthworm, an image accepted even by the peasant himself.[5]

Despite their peasant roots in the Italian soil, most of these southern Italian immigrants settled in large cities in the northeastern United States, where they established still identifiable "colonies" of Italian culture.

Like other immigrants to the New World, Italians from both north and south transported a rich cultural heritage, much of which had developed and was maintained without the support of official institutions of church or state. The folkways of the regions of Italy relied for their dissemination and survival upon oral tradition, conservatism, and other factors within the communities themselves. Members of those communities brought their folkways with them, preserved features that were useful in their new lives, adapted other features to New World contexts, and discarded those features that were no longer useful or adaptable.

As Italian immigrants and their children became more and more a part of American society, their ever-dynamic traditional culture went through other changes. The immigrants (or first generation) found that their children and grandchildren preserved

Italian identity in some ways that seemed very familiar, but also in ways that were strikingly new and different. Some forms of folklore completely disappeared with the immigrants themselves; others have persisted relatively unchanged even through the third and fourth generations; still others have been adjusted to American ways; additional traditions have been borrowed from other nationality groups in the New World; and, finally, new folklore has developed.

These generalizations can apply to the folklore of any immigrant group in the United States. But the distinctive circumstances of Italian life in the Old World, the process of Italian immigration, and the transformation of Italians into Italian Americans have contributed to some special emphases and themes in Italian-American folklore.

The most important factor in Italian culture and Italian-American folklore has been regionalism. In a very broad sense, there were two Italys at the time of unification and for many generations thereafter. They were divided traditionally by a line running from the Abruzzi coast on the Adriatic Sea to central Latium south of Rome on the Tyrrhenian Sea.[6]

Northern Italy included the provinces of Tuscany, Liguria, Piedmont, Lombardy, Veneto, Emilia-Romagna, Umbria, and the Marches; while southern Italy encompassed Abruzzi, Molise, Apulia, Basilicata, Calabria, Campania, parts of Latium, and the island of Sicily. The north, source of the Italian Renaissance and more recently of the movement to unify Italy in the 1860s, reflected the influence of central Europe. Economically shaped by agricultural lands along the Po River and its tributaries and by industrial cities such as Turin and Milan, northern Italy was relatively wealthy, its citizens enjoying opportunities for economic and educational growth.

The experience of southern Italians was considerably different. Economic conditions in their region were far from prosperous, and the influence of the Mediterranean cultures of the Near East and northern Africa had helped to create cultural forms that differed markedly from the beliefs and practices in the north. Geography,

*Though unified politically in the late nineteenth century, Italy remains a nation of regions. During the peak years of immigration most Italians identified more with a particular region or even community **(paese)** than with Italy as a whole. That **campanilismo** has continued to affect the nature of Italian-American folklore. Map drawn by Carl Lindquist.*

culture, and standard of living contributed to the separation between northern "high" Italians and southern "low" Italians.[7]

Actually, the situation in Italy was much more complex even than this; for not only was there a distinction between north and south, but within the two regions, provinces often had little in common. In fact, cultural differences, extending into almost every facet of life, might characterize each village, or *paese*. It was with the level of *paese* that the average Italian identified most closely. For many people, "Italy meant only their native town or province."[8] As a Campanian immigrant to the United States said, "[F]or me, as for the others, Italy is the little village where I was raised."[9]

This exclusive loyalty to the *paese* is what is meant by the picturesque term *campanilismo*, defined as "a view of the world that includes reluctance to extend social, cultural, and economic contacts beyond points from which the parish or village bell could still be heard." Stemming from the isolating topography of much of Italy, lack of mobility, and linguistic and cultural diversity, *campanilismo* represents "a marked tendency... to move and act in very narrow social circles."[10] It also results in a sense of closeness with fellow villagers (*paesani*) and an abiding distrust of anyone else (*forestieri, stranieri*), even those from the village just five miles away, but especially those who might speak a completely different dialect. Rosa Cavilleri, who immigrated from Lombardy, expressed this sentiment unreservedly:

> The people from *Toscana* [Tuscany] they're not good like the people from *Lombardia*. But they're not bad like the people from *Sicilia*—I should say not! The people from *Piemonte* [the Piedmont] are a little more bad than the people from *Lombardia*, but they come next. *Lombardia* is the last in the world to do wrong things. The Italian government made that investigation and they said so.[11]

Cavilleri, who had worked in several different northern Italian communities, had broadened her views beyond *campanilismo* in the strictest sense of identifying only with her *paese*, but the regionalism that infused the Italian consciousness is clear from her remarks.

Since the political unification of the *paesi*, provinces, and regions of Italy had not had much time to affect the person who was

likely to emigrate, most Italians who came to the United States in
the peak years of 1880 through 1910 left not Italy, "a nation which
did not exist for them before their emigration from it,"[12] but villages
like Monteu da Po (the Piedmont), Roseto Valfortore (Apulia), or
Corleone (Sicily). Their tendency upon arrival in the New World
was to seek out *paesani*. Consequently, most Italian colonies were
actually groupings of immigrants from the same region or village.
As a religious writer noted in 1918, "In the heart of the nearest city
one can find in the Italian colony a Sicilian, a Calabrian, a
Neapolitan, an Abruzzian village, all within a few blocks, and each
with its peculiar traditions, manner of living, and dialect."[13]

In New York City during the 1890s, people from specific
regions tended to settle in specific neighborhoods: Neapolitans in
Mulberry Bend, Genoese on Baxter Street near Five Points, and
Sicilians between Houston and Spring streets.[14] A generation later,
a similar phenomenon was noted in Greenwich Village, where
immigrants from the same town tended to move into the same
tenement and those from the same province inhabited the same
block.[15] Other American cities exhibited regionally identifiable
Italian communities. People from Abruzzi dominated Pittsburgh's
Panther Hollow district, and Sicilians from just four villages (Santo
Stefano Quisquina, Alessandria della Rocca, Cianciana, and Con-
tessa Entellina) comprised the Italian-American community in
Tampa, Florida.[16]

Small cities, towns, and rural communities in the United States
also attracted immigrants from a single province or community.
Roseto, Pennsylvania, for example, was settled almost entirely by
people who had come from Roseto Valfortore, in Apulia. Rillton,
also in Pennsylvania, attracted a substantial number of immigrants
from the Piedmontese village of Monteu de Po. And the Italian-
American fishing community in Galveston, Texas, was composed
almost completely of people tracing their ancestry to a village near
Catania, Sicily.[17] Even when representatives of more than one
Italian region came to a small American town, they maintained their
distinctiveness by means of residential segregation. In the mining
town of Krebs, Oklahoma, for instance, the northern Italians who

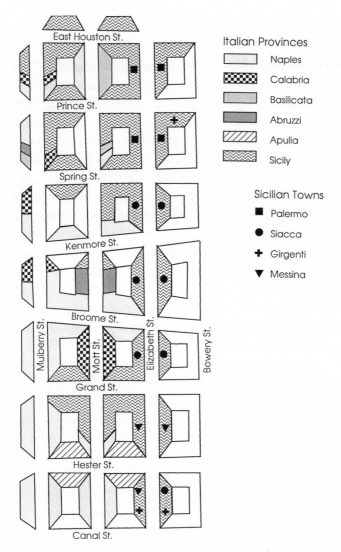

Italian Provinces

	Naples
	Calabria
	Basilicata
	Abruzzi
	Apulia
	Sicily

Sicilian Towns

■ Palermo
● Siacca
✚ Girgenti
▼ Messina

*Identification with a particular region or **paese** found expression in settlement patterns of Italian "colonies" in American cities. Immigrants who settled in New York City's Bowery maintained distinct ties with the communities from which they had come. Diagram drawn by Carl Lindquist. Based on Robert E. Park and Herbert A. Miller, **Old World Traits Transplanted** (New York: Harper, 1921), facing 146.*

first came to the community carefully isolated themselves in a part of town away from the later southern immigrants.[18]

Several factors allowed and encouraged Italian immigrants to cluster in regional and village enclaves when they came to America. Many Italian men who made the Atlantic crossing did so with the intention that their stay in the New World would be temporary. Called "birds of passage," they planned to remain only long enough to earn money to purchase land back home. Or following a longstanding practice, particularly in the Italian north, they might work for a season or so in the United States, return to their villages for a few years, and then come back to the United States again when they needed more cash.[19]

Such seasonal migrants often traveled with their *paesani*. Villagers in groups of two or more might arrive at Ellis Island or another port of entry and, relying on recommendations from the folks back home, go directly to living quarters where only their *paesani* dwelt. Their jobs, sometimes arranged through *padroni* (labor brokers) before they left Italy, might also involve only co-workers from their own villages or provinces. They made little or no attempt to interact with *forestieri*, even fellow Italians from other regions, and many of them—perhaps as many as sixty percent of Italian immigrants— repatriated successfully.

An institution that particularly encouraged the maintenance of *campanilismo* in the New World was the boarding house. Often a more-or-less permanent immigrant and his family would open their house to boarders, almost invariably men from their own *paese* who were in America temporarily and thus were not accompanied by their families. Boarding houses allowed the maintenance of regional ties since all the boarders came from the same part of Italy. They also encouraged the survival of traditional culture. Even the foods prepared by the womenfolk approximated—so far as ingredients accessible in America would allow—the cuisine to which boarders were accustomed at home.[20]

Another force that contributed to the endurance of regional and village ties was "chain migration," the process by which one individual or family from a *paese* would establish residence in an American community and then encourage family members and *paesani* to join them. A sociologist describes the process thus: "[T]he first to leave from a particular village became a nucleus of attraction abroad. Those who migrated after them from the same village tended to gravitate toward the places where the first to leave had settled." The reasons contributing to chain migration included "the need to be near someone who had to some extent solved the mystery of transculturation and would...help the newcomers adapt to the strange new life." Persons established in America would often provide financial and moral encouragement for their *paesani* to follow them.[21] Often the colony from the home village served only as a temporary locus of adjustment for immigrants, who would leave it for independent lives after finding suitable jobs and adapting to the American way of life. Many "Little Italys" served several generations of immigrants in this way.[22]

The sort of interregional rivalry and hostility expressed by Rosa Cavilleri characterized the lives of Italian Americans, in some cases even after the first generation. A general antagonism between northern and southern Italians was clearly evident. As early as 1881, an observer of Italian life in New York City noted that Ligurians (from the north) "repudiate indignantly all kinship with the Neapolitans and Calabrians [from the south], whom they refuse to recognize as Italians, thereby showing how little the sectional sentiment of Italy has been affected by the union of its parts under one ruler."[23] Northerners assumed a sense of superiority over southerners, a feeling due perhaps to their having come to the New World a generation or so earlier, their generally higher level of education, and their more ready acceptance by American society.[24]

Interaction between Italians from the two regions was seldom amicable. An Italian-American novelist has noted that northerners regarded southerners as "practically enemy aliens."[25] Getting them to work together required "a strong, tactful, experienced authority," according to a commentator in 1920.[26] In Centreville, Iowa, the first Italians to settle were from the Piedmont. They were followed soon by a group of Sicilians with the result that "Not a half-dozen years passed before all the Piedmontesi left the city and went to live ... away from the Sicilians."[27]

As far as more intimate social relations were concerned, northerners had very strong feelings about southerners. As a Piedmontese who grew up in southwestern Pennsylvania during the 1930s remembered,

> There was a nice young Sicilian boy from Masontown—very nice. I wanted to go out with him. My father wouldn't let me because he was Sicilian. And I said, "But, Daddy, he's so nice." My dad always said, "Better see your daughter buried in a casket than married to a Sicilian." ... When it came to dating, I was allowed to go out with a Slovak; I was allowed to go out with a Polack. I mean I dated a Polish boy through high school, you know, and it was fine. But don't bring a Sicilian in the house.[28]

Southern Italians responded to northern prejudice with defensiveness. Jerre Mangione, who grew up in Rochester, New York, recalls a running feud throughout his childhood with a northern bully who called him a "lousy *Siciliano*."[29] Jerry Della Femina, a Neapolitan American from Brooklyn, recalls his childhood response to northern prejudice:

> We had no northern Italians in our neighborhood. The Milanese simply stayed the hell home: arrogant, smug, holier-than-thou. What did they need with the United States? I'm quite sure that if a Milanese [from Lombardy] would deign to take a trip to the New World to see how the southern Italian immigrants were doing, he would return with, "Jesus, they're living like dogs."[30]

Christopher Hodgkins, three generations removed from Calabria, still recognized the prejudice directed toward immigrants from his ancestors' part of Italy. Identity as a Calabrese elicited "a kind of mix of embarrassment and cockiness," he explained:

> It meant that you were really a bumpkin. I mean, there are Italians, and then there are Italians. There's Italianos, and there's Wops. And the Wops—they're from Palermo in Sicily and ... from Castagna in Calabria. So you're Calabrese—it means on one hand your ancestors—your father, your mother, whatever, had the good sense to get out of that place before they starved to death or got shot by the mafiosi or something. On the other hand, it meant that you were close to the earth, that you knew which way was up, that you believed in the little guy.[31]

Regional antagonism was not just a northerner-southerner phenomenon. Even people from nearby provinces expressed some hostility toward one another. In Boston's North End, William Foote Whyte found that a young man of Sicilian background had to disguise his origins to placate his future father-in-law, an immigrant from Abruzzi, who was "dead set against Sicilians."[32] A similar hostility between people from Abruzzi and those from Sicily colored life in Philadelphia's Italian community well into the 1960s: "Most of us down here are originally Abruzzesi or Siciliani and we don't get along. Up until ten or fifteen years ago there was trouble if kids tried to marry across the line."[33]

Joseph Napoli, who grew up in an Ohio community, recalled his Sicilian mother's intense dislike of Neapolitans. Upon seeing a Neapolitan in the distance, she would direct the *mano di cornuto* (the fist with the index and little fingers extended that is a shield against *malocchio*, the evil eye) at the person. She would cross the street to avoid meeting Neapolitans or passing by their houses. Union with a Neapolitan, she averred, was like "going to bed with a woman who has small pox."[34]

A repatriated Sicilian recalled his uncle's reaction to the people from various regions whom he encountered in America: "My uncle said that all Calabresi have hard heads. The people of Sardinia are treacherous, the Romans rude, and the Neapolitans are a bunch of beggars."[35] A proverb which seems to have been current in various Italian communities succinctly expresses interregional rivalry: "*Campobassiani, mangia patani, cide pidocchi e suona campane*" ("People from Campobasso eat potatoes, kill lice, and ring bells"). For "*Campobassiani*" one could substitute the regional identity that he or she wished to insult: *Piemontesi, Siciliani, Calabresi,* or whatever.[36]

Despite these regional loyalties and hostilities, the American experience gradually forged an *Italian* identity for some immigrants and their children. Sicilians, Calabrians, Campanians, and even Piedmontese met and interacted with one another on the job, in church, and sometimes in their homes. They also began to recognize their shared identity in distinction from the other ethnic groups they might encounter, especially the Irish. This resulted in their beginning "to think and talk of themselves as Italians, a considerable expansion of provincial horizons."[37]

Other factors contributed to the emergence of a homogeneous Italian-American identity. Particularly important were the formation of interregional organizations such as the Order of the Sons of Italy in 1905; the creation by the Roman Catholic Church of "national parishes" catering specifically to Italian immigrants; and, in the 1920s, a drop in the number of immigrants from Italy who might rekindle regional feeling in increasingly Americanized communities.[38]

By the 1910s a sense of Italian ethnicity found expression in the United States in the erection of monuments to the national hero Garibaldi, the movement to establish Columbus Day as an American national holiday, extensions of charity for victims of devastating earthquakes in Abruzzi and Sicily, and support for the Italian cause in World War I.[39] Still, the movement away from regional identities to Italian identity was much more pronounced in urban areas, where Italians from different *paesi* often were forced into contact with one another, than in small towns and rural areas where regional homogeneity endured.[40]

The implications of Italian regionalism and Italian-American identity for folklore have been profound. On one level, Italian-American folklore should be seen as a conglomerate of regional folklores. This is particularly true of traditions tied to the Old Country or those such as proverbs and folksongs that depend upon specific language (in the Italian case, a regional dialect) for their communication. But it is also true of customs such as the southern Italian observance of Saint Joseph's Day, which has remained largely Sicilian in this country except in some urban areas such as New Orleans where it has even spread to non-Italian groups such as African Americans.[41] Moreover, regional differences in supernatural belief such as that in *malocchio*, associated more with Italian Americans from the south than from the north, remain evident.

On another level, a more general Italian-American folklore may be detected both in traditions that originated in this country (such as festivities on Columbus Day) and in those that had general currency throughout Italy or were adopted by various Italian regional groups in the United States (such as the game of *bocce* and traditional cuisine like pasta).

The first level of Italian-American folklore, the regionally based, survives in many communities but flourishes with most vitality away from urban concentrations of Americans of Italian ancestry. It is also stronger among Italians of the first generation, even recent arrivals in the New World; for even though regional distinctions in Italy have been challenged by such forces as the mass media, they remain a factor in Italian folk culture.

The family (*la famiglia*) continues to provide an important context for the enactment of Italian-American folklore, and the nature of the Italian family, though subject to some regional variation, generally colors Italian-American folk culture. Loyalty to family and suspicion of outsiders have been a central principle of Italian childrearing practices, "the first warning taught to any Italian child."[42] A Sicilian-American writer has noted the following hierarchy of distinctions among people, based upon the degree of loyalty one should feel: family members (*sangu du mi sangu*, "blood of my blood"); intimate friends of the family, including but not limited to godparents (*compari* and *commari*); people whose social status demanded respect (*amici di cappello*, "those to whom one tipped his hat"); and everyone else, including even those such as shopkeepers with whom one might interact every day (*stranieri*).[43]

For children, loyalty to family meant strict obedience to an institution dominated, especially in the first generation, by the father. To do otherwise meant, according to a Sicilian expression, that one would "die like a dog" (*fa la morte di un cane*).[44] A person who rejected family was said to "live like a hibernated bear."[45] The profoundest curse that a parent could direct at a child was *"Si possa perrdere il nome mio in casa tua"* ("May my name be lost in your home").[46]

L'ordine della famiglia, the traditional organization of family life, has been described as it survived among Sicilians who settled in southeastern Texas:

> The father was the head of the family; and no one in his household would make a major decision without his permission. The mother was the center of the family; and her authority was also greatly

respected. She often took charge of her husband's earnings and those of her unmarried children. Daughters-in-law were generally obedient and submissive to their mother-in-law. Also, the mother made most of the decisions in the everyday affairs of the family. Marital discord was never discussed with neighbors, as husbands and wives would tolerate no interference with their personal relationships. Family loyalty was a cardinal virtue for the Sicilian *contadini.*[47]

The pithy characterization of Italian-American family life by Michelena Gaetano Profeta represents the usual situation: "My husband was the boss of the family. He had the money."[48] While granted more freedom than their sisters, male children lived under the control of their parents, sometimes even after they themselves married. Ideally, they would live at home after going to work and contribute their entire paychecks to the household, receiving some of it back for their own spending money. Though often the process of Americanization of Italian family life modified her circumstances, the typical girl, especially in a southern family, lived an extremely circumscribed existence. Joanne Dorio recalled the limitations placed upon her while a child:

> I never was allowed to work, and I wanted to work in the worst way. I remember at the academy [the high school she attended], they asked the girls to serve as volunteer ushers at the Syria Mosque [concert hall]. I wanted to do that because I loved the opera and I loved the symphony, and I thought this was a good way to see it for nothing. But I was not permitted to take that job, because no daughter of his was going to work![49]

Dorio was also not permitted to participate in such social activities as ice skating, nor was she allowed to go to her class prom. Girls who tried to expand their limited horizons might be contemptuously dismissed as *"americanizata."*[50]

While the restrictive family life created some tensions as younger members observed the relative independence enjoyed by their peers from other ethnic groups, it also encouraged the loyalty to family that has continued to characterize Italian-American life. Folklore reflects that loyalty: traditional foodways endure partly because of their associations with the familial experience; bits of folk speech that may be the only vestiges of dialect to survive are used because one's grandmother (*nonna*) had used them; and among the most precious times in an Italian American's life are those traditional celebrations of birth, marriage, and even death that bring the entire family together.

Campanilismo and *la famiglia* dominate this sampling of Italian-American folklore. In part, it is a highly personal document. Frances Malpezzi grew up in a Piedmontese-American household with representatives of first and second generations. Other family members lived in the small town in southwestern Pennsylvania where she lived, and she participated actively in Piedmontese traditions that were brought from northern Italy and adapted to the New World as well as in the more generalized Italian-American folklore that the American experience had generated.

Relying only upon her memories, though, would provide an extremely restricted view of Italian-American folklore, which is marked by extreme heterogeneity. The Piedmontese among whom Frances Malpezzi grew up knew the evil eye only by reputation, knew nothing of Saint Joseph's altars, and viewed *polenta* (cornmeal) rather than pasta as the traditional staple in their cuisine. Moreover, her experience was small town and rural; she did not experience the flavor of an urban Little Italy or of suburban *Italianata*. And her forebears had come to this country relatively late, her Piedmontese grandfather immigrating in 1913 and his wife following seven years later. Also, her firsthand knowledge of Italian-American folk culture represents a specific time, when she was growing up in the 1950s and thereafter. To provide a broader (though far from complete) picture of Italian-American folklore, we have had to supplement Frances Malpezzi's participatory knowledge with a variety of data.

One important source of information has been interviews. We have attempted to talk with as many Americans of Italian ancestry as possible, especially those whose families came from regions of Italy other than the Piedmont. We are grateful for the cooperation and assistance of the following interviewees: Joanne Terranella Burleson (Sicilian, third generation); Frances Gueri Byrd (southern Italian, third generation); Joseph Capello (Piedmontese, first generation); Mamie Jo DiMarco Chauvin (Sicilian, second generation); Ray

Ferraro (Campanian, second generation [interviewed by Lucia Peek]); Sam Gennuso (Sicilian, second generation); Etta Ferraro Goodwin (Campanian, second generation [interviewed by Lucia Peek]); Christopher Hodgkins (Calabrian, third generation); Augustina Lovoi (Sicilian, second generation); Albina Malpezzi (Piedmontese, second generation); Guido Malpezzi (Tuscan, second generation); Pearl Malpezzi (Piedmontese, first generation); Marie Marchese (Sicilian, second generation); Salvatore Marchese (Sicilian, second generation); Lucia Peek (Campanian, third generation); and Sara Rao Vittone (southern Italian, second generation).

We recognize both the strengths and weaknesses of folklore materials gathered through interviews. A positive feature of the interview is that it affords an opportunity to record folklore texts accurately, but reliance on interviews does not allow contact with folklore in its natural context. Furthermore, interviews may encourage the collection of folklore as "memory culture"—what *was* done instead of what is being done now. While documenting the folklore of earlier times is an important undertaking, researchers should note as far as possible when their findings represent the past. Although virtually everything in this volume may still be encountered in Italian-American life, much of what we have included is primarily the folklore of earlier in the century. We have tried to identify it as such by dating it or by using the past tense in our commentary.

We have also relied heavily upon previously published materials of four major types. The first is the body of literature on Italian-American traditional culture published by folklorists. Numbering only slightly more than a hundred books and periodical articles,[51] this is of varying quality, though all of it has some value—especially in providing us with a more balanced view of the heterogeneity of our subject than personal experience allows.

Our second category of published source material is scholarly literature on the Italian-American experience produced in disciplines other than folklore studies, especially sociology, history, and linguistics. Here folklore data occur as a secondary emphasis to the principal concerns of the authors, but literature in this category has been especially valuable for corroborating the significance of some of the folklore items we found elsewhere.

Our third category of published sources, one of the most valuable, has been memoirs written or narrated by Italian immigrants and their descendants. Such works have been published since early in the century and frequently include folklore and—of special importance—its *contexts*. We also place within this category life stories collected and published by oral historians.

Finally, we have drawn to some extent upon belletristic writings, especially fiction, by Italian Americans. Novels of Italian-American life often use folklore to help create realistic settings and to embody the themes developed in the works.[52]

Even with all these supplementary sources, we recognize that the subject of Italian-American folklore is too complex to be treated in a survey format without serious drawbacks. Certainly regional differences and the problem of distinguishing memory culture from contemporary practice complicate matters. But also such factors as how many generations families or individuals may be removed from the actual immigration experience, what part of the United States they live in, and what sort of community (for example, metropolitan Little Italy or small town) they have chosen affect the nature of Italian-American folklore. At times, then, we have undoubtedly omitted traditions that some Italian Americans may find central to their lives, and have emphasized others with which some may be totally unfamiliar.

Even so, we think we have given a satisfactory overview that will provide the general reader with a picture of the distinctive folk culture of this important ethnic group in American society. For the reader with specialized interests, we hope we have suggested some directions that more in-depth research might take.

Our organization for this overview is generic. While there are drawbacks to such a plan (primarily that it may result in separating materials that often occur together in the natural contexts of folklore enactment), it offers the handiest way for presenting a vast amount of disparate material.

Believing that folklore is a means of communication, we have begun with those genres in which little distinction exists between the person who produces the folklore and his or her audience. We follow these conversational genres with five chapters emphasizing customs in which virtually anyone can participate in some way: the traditions of the life and annual cycles, supernaturalism, medical practices, and games and other recreation. Then come two chapters on what might be termed "performance genres," folklore forms that require pronounced artistic ability and often involve some separation between performer and audience. Our final chapter treats foodways, one of the most important continuing vehicles for the articulation of Italian-American identity.[53]

Pietro Di Donato, one of the most successful Italian-American novelists, once wrote that to his people the non-Italian population of the United States consisted of "gasoline drinkers without culture, who spoke with a vocabulary limited to repetitive four-lettered words, listened to caterwauling, imbecilic music, and all looked more or less alike." But, he added, "there was no confusing one paesano for another and no two resembled each other in any respect."[54] This diversity among Italian Americans is evident in a vital folklore which continues to relect *campanilismo* and to emphasize the centrality of *la famiglia,* even while forging an emergent pan-Italian consciousness that identifies and unites those whose ancestors immigrated from culturally distinct *paesi.*

CHAPTER TWO

Conversation

IMMIGRANTS FROM TUSCANY and their descendants who live on Chicago's Lower West Side love to gossip. Their talk focuses on personality types who in some way transgress what is considered normative behavior: misers, spendthrifts, liars, virgins, and even inveterate gossips.[1] Men and women exchange anecdotes about individuals who fit into these and similar categories and offer opinions about how they might behave more appropriately. Sometimes gossip will occur during lengthy sessions of conversation, and at other times it may be communicated in passing, as friends and acquaintances meet one another on the street or encounter each other while shopping. Though commonplace and everyday, the gossip of these Tuscan Americans represents the most fundamental level of their folk expression. Not only are the values and attitudes they articulate traditional, but the speakers also voice them in verbal forms reflecting a distinctive folk group identity.

Folklore permeates the normal conversations of everyone. The language we choose—its grammar, pronunciation, and vocabulary—derives in part from the traditions of the folk groups to which we belong. We are also likely to enliven our discourse with traditional formulas we have heard others use in similar contexts— proverbs pithily summing up the situation we're talking about, for example. The conversational genres of folklore are those that occur in daily interactions with other people. All of us use them, and they require no special talents or skills beyond the ability to engage in conversation. While they may not be as esthetically rich as folktales and folksongs nor as exotic as arcane superstitions, folk speech, proverbs, and other folklore genres which we—and Tuscan Americans from Chicago—use when we simply talk to one another provide the most fundamental opportunities to express cultural identity.

Folk Speech

In 1879, according to one estimate, 97.5 percent of Italians spoke only the language of their *paesi*, regional dialects that might be incomprehensible to people from other regions.[2] The official language of their newly unified country, which was based on the fourteenth-century Tuscan dialect used by Boccaccio and Petrarch and codified at the beginning of the sixteenth century,[3] was known only to the educated elite, many of whom used it solely as a medium of written communication. While *paesani* who seldom, if ever, got beyond the sound of their village bells could rely on a regional dialect as their chief mode of communication without great inconvenience, the immigration experience forced them to consider linguistic alternatives.

Language certainly contributed to establishing and maintaining regional enclaves in the Italian sections of large American cities and to the congregating of immigrants from one region in small towns. But especially in the cities, the proximity of Italians from other regions highlighted the need for developing a common language. Official Italian might fulfill this function, or an amalgam of grammar and lexicon from Italian, various dialects, and English could emerge as a lingua franca.[4]

The latter alternative, the development of a shared language based upon influences from a variety of sources, produced what has been called "Italglish," defined as "an idiom, simply constructed and quickly learned by any greenhorn [newly arrived immigrant] within a few weeks, that proved to be an effective and practical medium of communication among Italians and between Italians and Americans."[5] Largely a first-generation phenomenon, Italglish began with the basic structures of Italian or a dialect, incorporated some English vocabulary, and transformed the sounds of those English words to correspond with the speakers' native pronunciation habits. As speakers became more accustomed to American life, English syntactical patterns gradually replaced those from Italian.[6] For example, in 1910 people in the Panther Hollow district of

Pittsburgh were using a language based on the Abruzzese dialect with vocabulary from other southern Italian dialects. Within half a century this had been replaced by a predominantly English grammar and an Italian lexicon.[7] Similarly, by the early 1970s the "Italian" spoken in Boston's North End had become a conglomeration of various southern Italian dialects and English words.[8]

The English words that became a part of the Italian-American language early in the century fell into three categories: those representing concepts unknown in Italy, words that were phonetically simpler than their Italian counterparts, and terms whose equivalents in official Italian might be unfamiliar to the largely peasant population that had come to the New World.[9] When these words became a part of Italian-American speech, they often assumed forms that conformed to Italian or dialect morphological patterns. Examples of words that were adapted from English because they represented concepts unknown in Italy included:

ais crima—ice cream
baccausa—toilet (for "backhouse")
campo—lumber camp
ghenga—gang
gliarda—yard
pichinicco—picnic
rancio—ranch
sanguiccio—sandwich
sonamagogna—son of a gun
visco—whiskey.[10]

A partial list of English words that were phonetically simpler than Italian words includes these:

boya—boy
bucco—book
carro—car
cotto—coat
denso—dance
faiti—fight
gambolo—gambler
loncio—lunch
storo—store

stritto—street
tomate—tomato.[11]

Immigrants who did not know the relevant Italian words might use English-derived terms such as *morgico* (or *morgheggio*) for "mortgage," *lista* for "list," *bosso* for "boss," and *bisinisso* for "business."[12]

Occasionally words and usages in the Italglish vocabulary represented a blending of Italian and English lexicons. Single words such as *canabuldogga* for "bulldog" and *mezzo-barbiere* for "part-time barber" as well as phrases such as *fare scecchenze* for to shake hands are examples. One of the most colorful such constructions is a euphemism for "to die": *andare a flabussce* (or *brucculi*), meaning "to go to Flatbush" (or "to Brooklyn") since a cemetery where many New York Italians were buried is located there.[13]

The ways in which Italian Americans have adapted English words to Italian morphological and phonological patterns have provided a component in the group's popular culture stereotype. They have also figured in some family and personal narratives. For example, Sam Gennuso, whose father had been born in Sicily, related a story illustrating the older man's characteristic use of English. Gennuso had just recalled how his father would rely on pictures on food products when he went grocery shopping because he could not read the English labels.

> He was asking my mother one day where his khaki pants were. You know, he had some khaki pants, and he said he wanted to know where the "kak pans" were. "Where're my 'kak pans'?" And my mother would say, "The cake pans?" She knew what he was talking about, but she would tease him, you know.[14]

Pascal D'Angelo, an immigrant from Abruzzi, recorded a story with a similar theme about his own linguistic difficulties. The foreman of a work crew sent the young D'Angelo to a village store to buy a dozen eggs. Over and over he repeated what sounded like "aches" to D'Angelo so that he could remember what he was supposed to purchase. By the time he arrived at the store, though, he had changed the word to "axe," and the grocer tried to sell him a dozen axes.

D'Angelo finally made his order clear by cackling like a hen and making an oval with his fingers.[15]

The Reverend Enrico C. Sartorio, an Anglican clergyman who was active in social and religious work among his fellow Italians in the United States, related another anecdote illustrative of the linguistic adjustments that immigrant speakers of English made:

> An Italian tried to explain to me the meaning of Thanksgiving Day. "You see," he said, "the word explains itself, 'Tacchinsgiving Day'"; "tacchin" meaning turkey in Italian, it was, according to this man, the day on which Americans gave away turkeys.[16]

The retention of pronunciation patterns as well as other dialect usages may often have been intentional. Language had an integrative effect for immigrant families who needed something to counteract the disruption produced by their relocation in a strange country. In fact, entire communities such as the regionally homogeneous Roseto, Pennsylvania, retained a distinctive dialect because "it stood for a successful and independent group of people."[17] Among Italian-American schoolchildren in Pittsburgh, language served as a means to distinguish themselves from members of other ethnic groups. Non-Italian peers knew that they had been accepted as friends when an Italian-American child taught them dialect terms.[18]

Even when dialects ceased to be a normal mode of discourse within the family or in the company of *paesani*, distinctive usages survived. Examples include terms of opprobrium. Gennuso noted several used in his Sicilian-American family: *son de diavolo* ("I was the son of the devil"); *Qui chi pra la piedo* ("It meant that I was a crazy, mixed-up kid. I was born backwards with my feet first: '*la piedo.*' A baby born with the feet first"); *faccia la cane* ("dogface"); and *faccia la robillarda* ("face like dirty clothes").[19] More widely known than these expressions among Sicilian Americans is *caffone*, which, though literally meaning "simpleton," has much broader connotations: "a man ... who has the least possible association with any group, has no regard for opinion, wears, for example, the same clothes during his whole stay in America, ignores his surroundings, and accumulates the sum of money he has in mind [before returning to Sicily] as rapidly as possible."[20]

Other regional dialects have produced similar expressions of disapproval still used among Italian Americans: Neapolitans may refer to an enemy as *sfaccim'*, or "sperm of the devil";[21] Piedmontese call someone who is stubborn and intractable a *testa dura* and characterize a lazy person as a *plundruna*.[22] Other Piedmontese insults that survive in folk speech in the United States include several terms that refer to someone deemed to be foolish: *panada* (literally, a soup consisting of nothing but bits of bread crumbled into broth), *pachoc* (related to the *pachuco* character type in Mexican-American popular culture), and *terremot* (an earthquake and, by extension, someone who makes a mess of everything). A chronic whiner may be called a *piansnon,* and someone who does not participate in conversations is a *marmonton.* A consummate villain is a *bestia gramma* (literally, "an evil beast"). A Piedmontese American may offer insult by telling someone that he or she is *bella me na quel de padella* ("beautiful like the back end of a frying pan") or offer the ultimate dismissal by angrily demanding, *Pia se porta e va* ("Take the door and go").

Not all such dialect retentions express negative sentiments. Terms of endearment, especially those used for and by children, also frequently occur. Examples include *pac e sonne* ("peace and sleep"), said when a young child yawns, and *Crisce sante!* ("Grow holy!"), uttered when a child sneezes. Both these come from the Abruzzese-Neapolitan dialect spoken in Pittsburgh's Panther Hollow.[23]

Children may themselves be encouraged to address grandparents by the Italian forms *Nonna* and *Nonno.* Piedmontese-American children may refer to an uncle as *barba* instead of the standard *zio* and an aunt as *magna* instead of *zia.*[24] *Compare* and *comare,* originally "godfather" and "godmother," have come to be loosely applied to any close family friend and may in some cases be used very casually to designate even slight acquaintances.[25] The Piedmontese equivalents are *marenga* and *peringu.* Terms such as *chicking* ("dear one", masculine), *chickinga* ("dear one," feminine), and *chita chickinga* ("little dear one," feminine) may be used among Piedmontese family members. Sometimes personal and group nicknames remain in dialect. For example, the phrase *bruccia la terra* ("burn the earth") has been used for Sicilians because of their swift, intense way of working.[26] Albina Malpezzi recalled that her Piedmontese grandfather had been called *Troon* ("Thunder"), which explained her habit of saying "Troon is playing *bocce*" whenever it thundered.[27]

Italian Americans have also developed interlingual puns in which English and Italian homonyms and near homonyms merge to create striking phonological and semantic effects. A forceful example is the term *merigan,* which in the folk speech of Italian Americans in Pittsburgh's Panther Hollow refers to someone who is unimaginative and lacking in feeling. It blends "American" with the Abruzzese word *merdagan,* meaning dog excrement. Other varieties of Italglish utilize the same pun: *americane* or *merichen* suggests "American dog," and *merdacane* connotes "dog excrement."[28] Another example is the laughter occasioned among Piedmontese Americans by the American term "barbecue," which sounds very much like *Barba Culo*—dialect for "Uncle Buttocks." The term *pizzapaia* had multiple meanings in Italglish: a pizza pie, a piece of pie, or a man of "questionable masculinity."[29]

Because language retention—even if it only occurs in terms of opprobrium and endearment or in puns—signals ethnic identity, many Italian-American families, bent on becoming Americanized, have consciously tried to suppress use of dialects and of official Italian. For example, according to his grandson, Louis DeFazio, a second-generation Calabrian American, "would not allow Italian to be spoken in his own house by any of his children or by his wife. He insisted on his children being a hundred percent American."[30]

Similarly, Frances Gueri Byrd remembered that her father, who entered this country as an infant through Ellis Island around the turn of the century, "never spoke Italian." She quoted his philosophy of childrearing: "'No, my children would be Americans.'"[31] Joseph Capello reared his own children with careful attention to the language they were learning: "We never talked Italian when we got married. Our kids—we never talked to them in Italian. We talked to my mother, but they had to practice English, you know. That's the only way you learn it."[32]

People who did persist in maintaining ties with the old country by speaking their ethnic language might be called "greasers" or "greaseballs." Both terms have been used for recent Italian immigrants or for those "who still cling to old world practices."[33] They might also denote someone who was ostentatious, parsimonious, oriented only toward work, and generally ignorant of American ways of doing things.[34] People so designated might respond by using the term "American" to refer pejoratively to the habits of those who overvalued assimilation. As a modifier, "American" can denote inferior quality or bad manners: "For example, to leave a gathering quickly without saying good-bye is called to leave 'American style.' A well-mannered Italian will not leave even his neighborhood food store without taking care to greet the shopkeeper as he leaves."[35]

Clearly, most Italian Americans have had a range of language choices available to them. A recent survey of Italians who had immigrated to New York City since the late 1940s revealed four general usages: the regional dialect (often in a form that would be considered archaic back in Italy), official Italian, Italglish, and English.[36] Speakers carefully based their choice of which usage to employ upon context. For example, one might use the dialect when conversing with parents and grandparents, the dialect or English with other family members, official Italian with unrelated Italian-American friends and acquaintances, and English at work. The dialect may also be used for expressing strong sentiment and for thinking.[37] Even among members of the second and later generations who cannot converse in a dialect or official Italian, some Italian usages survive especially "in joking expressions, insults and terms relating to Italian food-ways."[38]

Names also served to reflect an individual's or family's degree of involvement in Italian ethnicity. Officials at Ellis Island and other ports of entry may have contributed to anglicizing and simplifying Italian surnames, but the process probably arose more from the assimilation efforts of Italians themselves. Several typical processes characterized name changes.

Sometimes letters would be removed from the middle of a name to reflect Americanized pronunciation. In such a case, Cuomo might become Como and Bernardo would change into Bardo. Often the last part of a surname would completely disappear: Bartolo may be short for Bartolomeo, and Presto may derive from Prestogiacomo.

Similarly, the first part of a name could be dropped, especially if it were an article. In this way, Teodoro would yield Doro, and Angelo might replace D'Angelo. Sometimes names could be easily anglicized by simply dropping a final vowel: Ross from Rossi, Gilbert from Gilberti. Or a name might be translated into English: Chiesa becomes Church, Piccolo is transformed into Little, and Barbieri might turn into Barber.[39]

Sometimes the only change would be in spelling. For example, Lydia Pofi's father changed the family name Iorio to Yorio because he wanted it spelled "the American way."[40] Yet most immigrants retained the spellings and pronunciations of their surnames. Sometimes attempts to Americanize names actually produced family disagreements. Sara Vittone emphasized her father's devotion to the family name, Rao, despite his brother's family's interest in changing it:

> You know, he had a brother, the one I told you that he got killed in the explosion. They had three boys. He had three boys and three girls—my dad's brother. But my dad had all the girls. So when they wanted to Americanize their name, they spelled it then R-A-W-E, you know. And then we'd tell people they were our cousin. "How could they be your first cousin? You're R-A-O, and they're R-A-W-E." I said, "Well, they Americanized it. They—they're ashamed of the name." I said, "Not my father." He'd get so mad at them all the time for changing their names. But we always spelled it R-A-O, yeah.[41]

The old-country custom of nicknaming persisted in some Italian-American communities. Nicknames were usually assigned on the basis of appearance, occupation, or behavioral characteristics. Usually unflattering, these might be synonymous with *ingiurie*, the Sicilian dialect term for "insults."[42] Richard Gambino recalled a woman in his Brooklyn neighborhood known only as *La Sporca* ("The Dirty One") because of her unkempt appearance. In sixteen years of living on the same street, the young Gambino never learned her real name.[43] More lighthearted and also illustrating the merging of dialect and English was *capo de nuts* ("peanut head"), the nickname Lucia Peek remembers being assigned to her brother by family members,[44] or *tuturuga* ("little turtle"), which Rocco Capello used for his infant granddaughter because of the turtle-like stance she assumed when crawling. Other nicknaming patterns involved attaching a regional designation to one's name (as in Maria Marchesciana, "Maria from the Marches").[45]

Everyday language use of this sort represents one of the clearest badges of group identity. For Italian Americans, retention of dialects, either as primary means of communication or only in occasional words, has reflected the continuing importance of *campanilismo*, regional identity, at least on a symbolic level. Learning official Italian suggests a sense of broader ethnicity, a cultural loyalty to the political entity Italy. Rejecting either dialect or Italian and insisting on using English in every verbal interaction indicates unmitigated commitment to the values of assimilation. The investigation of Italian-American traditional culture, the folklore that survived the Atlantic crossing and that which Italian Americans developed and adapted to their New World situation, must begin with folk speech.

Proverbs

Jerre Mangione's Uncle Nino believed that proverbs incorporated all the philosophy and ethics one needed to know. He told his nephew, "If you knew all the Sicilian proverbs, ... you could act wisely in any situation that presented itself."[46] Italian Americans, like members of other ethnic communities, have often encapsulated traditional wisdom, particularly of the practical sort, in terse, witty, often poetic sayings. The natural context for proverbs is conversation. One uses them to comment on someone else's behavior or to defend one's own action and attitudes. Because they are traditional and thus suggest that generations of experience lie behind them, proverbs may be accepted more readily than if the same idea were expressed in one's own words. When used to criticize, proverbs act as a shield since they imply that the negative comment comes not from the individual speaker but from the whole society whose values have been expressed in the proverbs perhaps for generations.

Because they are poetic, usually relying on metaphor as their primary artistic device, proverbs may be subject to varying interpretations. Their meaning depends on the precise conversational situation in which they arise. For example, a proverb collected from an Italian American in southern Illinois indicates the range of meanings that metaphor may allow a proverb to suggest. *"Bandiera vecchia onore di capitale"* literally means "An old flag is an honor to the capital."[47] The proverb could be applied in conversational situations to any person, place, or object that is valued for its age—which, in turn, can connote wisdom, experience, tradition, and other positive features associated with the past. A similar proverb, using a slightly different metaphor, holds, *"Gallina vecchia fa buon brodo"* ("An old chicken makes good broth") and has equally broad applications.[48]

Another example of the "social use of metaphor" which characterizes the deployment of proverbs is reported from a Tuscan American living in the state of Washington. At a meeting where there was much talk but little action, someone said, *"Ragazzi, questa vigna non favva,"* literally, "[t]his vineyard produces no grapes," a figure of speech that could apply to a variety of specific situations where little of substance was being accomplished.[49] The same metaphor informs a Sicilian proverb: *"In questa vita si fa uva"* ("In this life one produces grapes"), meaning that one should be fruitful and industrious.[50]

Sometimes proverbs may become self-contradictory when employed in different situations. For example, Constantine Panunzio, who ventured from his home in Molfetta on the Apulian coast for the life of a sailor early in this century and arrived in the United States in 1904, recalled a proverb from his homeland: *"Chi lascia il vecchio e prendo il nuovo, sa che lascia ma no se che trova,"* which translates, "He who leaves the old and takes the new knows what he leaves, but does not know what he hath in view."[51] In most contexts, this might be taken as an encouragement to be cautious, not to risk the unknown by giving up the familiar. In some situations, though—particularly when the known is unpleasant—one could use it to justify expanding one's horizons in search of a better way of life. Panunzio's proverb also illustrates some of the poetic sound devices that this conversational genre of folklore may employ—especially parallelism and rhyme.

Because of their reliance on such devices, proverbs learned in *paesi* in Italy often did not survive the process of amalgamation and Americanization. They might rhyme in the regional dialect, for instance, and not do so in official Italian or English. Yet because of their formulaic nature, proverbs sometimes have outlasted other dialect usages. Even people who do not speak their ancestral dialect may remember the traditionally worded proverb. Moreover, proverbs—as Uncle Nino believed—do represent folk philosophy. This should be claimed with some qualification, especially since proverbs are subject to varying interpretations, may survive because of their esthetic qualities as much as for the wisdom they embody, and may in fact contradict one another. Still, the general values and attitudes of a culture can sometimes be derived from investigating its proverbial lore.

In the 1940s Manuel D. Ramirez compiled more than a hundred proverbs from Sicilians living in Tampa, Florida.[52] While many of these proverbs have analogues in other Italian regions and in English, as a group they represent the largest single body of proverb material published from one regional Italian-American community. Categorizing some of these proverbs in terms of the values they seem to stress emphasizes how this folklore genre can reflect a group's ethos.

For instance, a trait of the southern Italian world view that many commentators have emphasized is fatalism,[53] and the Sicilian proverbs from Tampa suggest that attitude:

> *Chi nasci di gatta surci piglia.*
> (One born a cat will run after mice.)

> *Chistu munnu è fattu a scala; cu lu scinni e cu l'acchiana.*
> (The world is like a staircase; some go up and some go down.)

> *Curri quannu vo', che ca t'aspettu.*
> (Run whenever you will, for I shall await you here.)

> *I pesci grossi mángiano i piccini;* or
> *Lu pisci grossu si mangia lu nicu.*
> (The big fish eat the little fish.)

> *Oggi tu, e dumani iu.*
> (Your turn today, mine tomorrow.)

Tu ridi oje che jeu rido dumani.
(You laugh today, for tomorrow it is my turn to laugh.)

Pessimism also emerges as a recurrent attitude in these Sicilian-American proverbs:

Li disgrazie nun vennu mai suli.
(Misfortunes never come singly.)

Nun c'è rose senza spini; or
Ogni rosa ha la so'spina.
(There's no rose without a thorn.)

Ogni focu forte torna cinere.
(Every great fire turns to ashes.)

Some Sicilian proverbs collected in Tampa also emphasize the importance of caution and circumspection, imply that one should be satisfied with the status quo, and warn of the dangers of taking risks:

Anche le muri hannu oricchi.
(Walls have ears.)

Avvanta lu munti e téniti a u chianu.
(Praise the mountain and keep to the plain.)

Chi vo pianu, va sanu e va luntanu.
(Who goes softly, goes safely and goes far.)[54]

Cu cancia la via vecchia pi la nova guai trova.
(One who leaves the old road to take the new finds trouble.)[55]

È megliu un' ovu oyi che una gaddina dumani.
(An egg today is better than a hen tomorrow.)

Megliu lu malu conosciùtu ca lu bonu a canuscisi; or
Megliu lu vecchiu canusciùtu ca lu novu a canusciri.
(Better the evil you know than the evil you don't know.)

Megliu un oceddu manu che cento volando.
(A bird in the hand is worth two in the bush.)

Mezzu pani è megliu di nenti.
(Half a loaf is better than none.)

Nenti dire ca nenti si sapi.
(Say nothing when you know nothing.)

Nun sputari in celu, / Ca mucca te torna.
(Do not spit against heaven less it falls in your face.)

Pianu pianu se va luntanu.
(Little by little one goes very far.)

But the dangers of making one-to-one correlations between prover-bial lore and cultural values is demonstrated by aphorisms such as *"Cu arrisca, rusica"* ("Nothing ventured, nothing gained") and *"Cu guarda pi dumani, guarda pi li cani"* ("He who saves saves for dogs")—also from the Sicilian material collected in Tampa—which seem to contradict directly the conservative emphasis that charac-terizes most of the sayings.

Some of the proverbs focus on friendship and the values of family and *paese:*

A ogni aceddu lu so nido è beddu.
(Every bird thinks its own nest beautiful.)[56]

Ama l'amico to cu lu so' diffetu.
(Love your friend with all his faults.)

Amico e vino vògliono essiri vecchi.
(Friends and wine should be old.)

Li veri amici sunnu comu li muschi bianchi.
(True friends are as rare as white flies.)

Un bon amicu val cchiù ca un tisoru.
(A good friend is worth more than treasure.)

Vali cchiù averi amici in piazza che dinari nella cassa.
(It is worth more to have friends in the marketplace than money in the bank.)

Finally, industry and the importance of work receive attention from several Sicilian-American proverbs:

Batti lu ferru quannu è cajdu.
(Strike while the iron is hot.)

Chi fa pi iddu, fa pi tri.
(He who helps himself helps three.)

Cu paga alla sira è franco nella matina.
(He who pays in the evening is privileged in the morning.)

Cu s'aiuta, Diu l'aiuta.
(God helps those who help themselves.)

Quilie chi dormi non piglia pisci.
(He who sleeps catches no fish.)

Lu surci ci dici all' nuci, "Dunami tempu che ti spertusso."
(The mouse says to the nut, "Give me time and I'll open you.")[57]

These examples do not exhaust Sicilian-American proverbial lore, but they do suggest the ways in which a body of proverbs can reflect in very general terms the values of a group. But these proverbs take their richest depths of meaning in the context of actual usage when someone recognizes their applicability to a particular situation.

The last example represents a fairly common device in southern Italian proverbs. The presentation of proverbial wisdom as a quotation attributed to a specific individual has been called a Wellerism in reference to a character in Charles Dickens' novel *The Pickwick Papers*. For example, someone who finds himself criticized for offending another person might respond, *"Come disse il riccio alla lepre: 'Chi non ci vuole stare, se ne vada.'"*[58] This translates, "As the hedgehog said to the rabbit, 'If you don't like it here, go somewhere else.'" In fact, Italian Americans apparently tend to add *"come disse quello"* ("as one said") to almost every proverb, thus creating the effect of Wellerisms.

The art of proverb use lies not so much in the sort of verbal agility that makes for true folklore performance. Instead, it stems from the ability to select the appropriate traditional idea for the specific occasion. In every case, proverbs represent the force of a community opinion that has been honed by generations of experience. Using and heeding Italian-American proverbs allows one to follow the advice of another saying from the Sicilian heritage: *"Impara a spesa d'altri"* or "Learn at the expense of others."[59]

CHAPTER THREE

Customs: The Life Cycle

AMONG ITALIAN AMERICANS, traditional beliefs and practices have clustered around transitional events in the individual's life. Called "rites of passage" by anthropologist Arnold Van Gennep, experiences such as birth, coming of age, marriage, and death amount to changes in personal identity. Van Gennep believed that these changes were universally regarded as perilous because, as one moves from one state of being to another, he or she may be especially vulnerable to supernatural attack. Thus, for those transitions which recur from generation to generation, people have developed practices to insure that the passage from one identity to the next is safe.[1]

Another feature of these key transitional events is that they may erase social distinctions derived from wealth or education. According to Victor Turner, also an anthropologist, rites of passage remind people of their common humanity, their shared participation in a cycle of life that must be experienced regardless of the riches or status they may have acquired.[2]

In addition to these generally recognized transitions, many Italian Americans also stress the importance of such sacramental rites as baptism and christening, first communion, and confirmation. These three events—defined and carried out according to the directives of the Roman Catholic Church—have not produced an array of folk customs; however, birth, marriage, and death *do* provide settings for traditional beliefs and practices to coexist with the rituals and conventions prescribed by official religion, civil authority, and modern medicine.

Birth

Traditions may begin to affect the Italian-American child even before birth. Beliefs about conception, pregnancy, and childbirth

have influenced his or her parents' behavior and contribute to
matters directly affecting the child such as his or her birth date,
number of siblings, and relationships with father and mother. Folk
eugenics among Sicilians and some of their descendants in the New
World suggest that the child inherits only the father's "blood." The
mother's role during pregnancy is only as vessel for the father's seed,
which is the sole contributor to the child's genetic identity.[3] However, since the mother's "blood" was supposed to be mixed with the
milk her child suckled, a woman could contribute to the child's
inherent composition through the way in which she cared for it. In
fact, the woman who nursed a child—whether its biological mother
or a wet nurse—was supposed to have so close a relationship with
it that she experienced every pain it felt. Some went so far as to aver
that when a baby was bottle fed, it would assume bovine qualities
and that the cow would feel all its pains.[4]

Like many agricultural peoples, Italians counted children as a
valued resource, and that attitude persisted among Italian immigrants, who ensured fecundity by carefully sustaining fertility-in-
ducing practices at marriage. Though it certainly represents a point
of view that most Italian Americans could now accept only with
modification, the characterization of a commentator writing in 1928
does capture the viewpoint of many immigrant women: "To be
childless is a terrible humiliation to an Italian woman. Children are
the highest aspiration of her life; she would rather die than not have
them."[5] Traditional ways to avoid childlessness included throwing
confetti (candy-covered almonds) at weddings, having the mothers
of the bride and groom prepare the bed for the wedding night, having
a new bride avoid contact with salt, or—in seeming contradiction—
sprinkling the bridal bed with salt.[6] Tradition also encouraged large
families by warning about the dangers of sexual abstinence—uterine
tumors for women and tuberculosis for men, according to southern
Italian belief. A woman's use of any contraceptive agents was
thought to cause her husband to become ill.[7]

But since certain days were especially inauspicious for birth,
other days, scrupulously avoided by married couples, were regarded
as dangerous for conception. For example, abstinence traditionally
characterized the Feast of the Annunciation (25 March) when the

Holy Spirit was supposed to have impregnated the Virgin Mary. Christmas falls nine months from that date, and a child born at the same hour as Jesus (midnight on Christmas Eve) was doomed to dire consequences. If a girl, she would likely become a *strega* (witch), while infant boys would become werewolves. An alternative fear held that children born on Christmas would inevitably be deformed.[8] Conversely, some Italian Americans have believed that one born on Christmas Eve has healing powers, especially the ability to cure the effects of *malocchio.*[9] Couples had to make more complicated calendrical computations to avoid having a child born on the day of a quarter moon, which was regarded as unlucky.[10]

Some dates were regarded as especially favorable for birth. A child born at any time during the month of January may be immune from the effects of being "overlooked" (that is, becoming a victim of *malocchio)* and may have power over snakes, so a couple might pace themselves accordingly the preceding April. A child born on a Tuesday would always live under the protection of Saint Anthony, and one born on the thirteenth of any month would become the special ward of that saint and also of Saint Lucy.[11] A couple might also try to time conception according to the lunar cycle, since a child conceived during the full moon would be a girl and one conceived during a quarter moon would be a boy. A boy would also result from conception on Sunday.[12]

Even though tradition may deny the mother's genetic contribution, what she does while pregnant can decidedly affect the child. A strong belief in prenatal marking has characterized Italian-American pregnancy lore. Usually this belief has manifested itself in careful attention to the food cravings of pregnant women. While she is carrying a child, a woman's dietary whims should be completely and immediately gratified. If they are not, the child will either bear a birthmark shaped like the desired food or be more generally disfigured. At the very least, throughout its life the child will crave the food (frequently strawberries) its mother did not get.[13] Accounts which validate the postnatal effects of unrequited prenatal craving abound in Italian-American folklore. For example, a Calabrian-born woman who migrated to the United States at the age of twenty-one recalled a telling incident:

> This woman went three door next to where she livin'. She was all swell with baby. She smell fish fryin' in the pan, but the owner of the fish, she have no sense enough to offer the fish to the pregnant lady. My mother tell me, this pregnant woman, she good friend of my mother.
>
> She ... say, "My God, I want the fish the lady fry so bad." She say she feel funny all over, she crave so bad and the baby want too. The lady rubbed her face and arms with her hands....
>
> When the baby was born, the skin was all scales like a fish skin.... My mama say from now on when you meet a pregnant lady, if it be bread or cherries from the country, whatever, you offer.[14]

As in this account, a frequent component of prenatal marking is the woman's touching some part of her body when she comes into contact with the food she craves. The baby may be marked on its body at the spot where its mother had touched herself. A similar fate had befallen the storyteller herself while she was pregnant. She recalled,

> Myself, I went to grocery store and I no have enough money to buy everything I want. It was Depression. So, I say I buy what I need is important first. I see black olives o[n] shelf. I keep look but I have no money for. I was pretty big with my Frankie.... So, I keep lookin'! ... My back hurt, so I put my fingers on my back. When Frankie born, he had five olives on his back.[15]

The necessity of gratifying the cravings of pregnant women inspired the taunt heard among Italian Americans in Greenwich Village during the 1920s and directed against the self-indulgent: "You're like a pregnant woman."[16]

While prenatal marking caused by unrequited craving might be avoided, that which resulted from the expectant mother's being frightened often lay outside human control. The woman's only recourse was to lead as sheltered an existence as possible, remembering admonitory stories such as that which Rose's mother offers in Jo Pagano's *Golden Wedding,* a novel about Campanian immigrants: "Remember Annie Masto I told you about in Denver? She was frightened by a cat while she was carrying her first boy, and when he was born he had a red mark just like a cat on his forehead."[17]

Specific kinds of frights could yield specific results. A pregnant woman's being frightened by a hare might produce a child with a harelip, and her seeing an automobile accident resulted in an infant with serious physical deformities.[18] Sicilian American Richard Gambino wrote of his grandmother's fury when she learned that her daughter had gone to see a horror movie while pregnant with Richard.[19] A woman, though, could protect her unborn child from prenatal markings from any source by eating a broiled kingfish "marked with cabalistic signs."[20] Once a child had been marked, the blemish was difficult to remove, though rubbing some afterbirth over the mark was sometimes thought to effect a remedy.[21]

Other proscriptions have applied to Italian-American women and their husbands during pregnancy. For example, it has been considered dangerous for either one of them to work on Saint Aniello's Day (14 December). The consequences of violating this taboo may be a deformed child.[22] A pregnant woman should avoid lifting heavy weights since doing so will result in a premature birth, and her gazing into a fire will prove fatal to her child.[23] At the same time, it is important that special preparations be made for an expected baby, since not to do so would make it seem unappreciated. Social worker Dorothy Gladys Spicer discovered that some of her Italian-American clients during the 1920s would often go to great expense to provide, for example, a new crib for a child when they had receptacles such as clothes baskets already available that would serve the same purpose.[24]

Although now virtually all births take place in hospitals under the care of physicians, traditional practice once designated a midwife as the principal attendant during a woman's labor. The midwife figures prominently in the remembered lore about birth among Italian Americans earlier in the century, and women such as the fictional Dame Katarina, characterized as "high priestess of ceremonials from cradle to grave" in Pietro Di Donato's novel *Christ in Concrete,* were held in high esteem.[25] Letitia Serpe, an immigrant from the Apulian city of Bari, described how a midwife officiated at the birth of her first child:

> I got my midwife through my mother-in-law. The midwife and I got acquainted a month before I delivered. When it was time, my mother-in-law, the midwife, my aunt, and I were all together

in the bedroom. The midwife was lovely—clean—she was like a she-doctor today—that's what she was.

I had a beautiful nine-pound baby and the midwife wrapped her in swaddling so her legs would grow long and straight.[26]

Midwives often practiced general folk medicine in addition to their role at births and might complement their mundane knowledge with magical practices such as placing salt at the four corners of the bed to ward off evil.[27] Di Donato's Dame Katarina began the birthing process by anointing the pregnant woman's forehead and stomach with holy water and after the delivery "with spittle did benediction" upon the new mother's brow.[28]

A birth was heralded with celebration, at least by members of the immediate family. Spicer reported in the 1920s that Italian Americans saluted the birth of a boy by drinking three glasses of wine and of a girl by drinking two glasses, the lesser amount due to her being "born to suffering."[29] The celebration would be intensified if the baby had been born with a caul, for then he or she could look forward to being brilliant, talented, generous, healthy, lucky, and famous.[30] In some families custom dictated that relatives who had come to visit a newborn be entertained with sweet drinks such as anisette and other cordials.[31] After a woman had given birth, she was allowed forty days of rest, during which time she remained inside the house, was exempt from housework, and ate only chicken broth and soup.[32]

More general festivities accompanied christening and baptism, which occurred soon after a child's birth. It was a particular honor to serve as a child's godparent, and persons chosen for this role "were really kind of like the guest of honor other than the baby" at the baptism ceremony and subsequent reception.[33] The relationship between *compare* and *comare* with the child and with its parents has been one of the most important in Italian-American life. As Jerre Mangione describes it,

A *compare* occupies a special place in the hierarchy of Sicilian friends. No firmer relationship can exist between two men who are not related by blood than that of *compare*. Sometimes a relative would choose another relative to be his *compare* [that is, godfather to one of his children], but more often the honor was reserved for unrelated friends. It was a simple way of making them almost related.[34]

Becoming a godparent was taken very seriously and might be subject to traditional taboos. A pregnant woman, for instance, could be discouraged from becoming a godmother, since doing so might cause bad luck for both her godchild and her unborn infant. To refuse a request to become a godparent amounted to a grave insult.[35] Though the official role of godparents emphasized their participation in a child's spiritual development, folk custom dictated that especially the godmother should involve herself in all phases of the child's rearing. For example, she was supposed to be the first to cut a child's hair and nails.[36]

Folk beliefs and practices governed the ways in which the mother and father attended to their offspring throughout infancy. For instance, babies often had pierced ears so that they could wear gold earrings, since gold near the eyes was supposed to be beneficial to eyesight.[37] This custom might result in intergenerational disagreements, as Etta Ferraro Goodwin recalled:

> And there was another thing I remember my mother relating to me as I grew older.... It was something that she never forgave my grandmother for. It was the custom in Italy that little girls when they were several days old—babies—have their ears pierced. They would have good eyesight for the rest of their lives. Well, in this country my mother learned that it was not a custom, and she didn't want her girls to have pierced ears. Because none of the other little American girls had pierced ears. And she wasn't going to have this.
>
> Well, my grandmother wasn't going to have my mother have her way. So one day (I wasn't more than two weeks old), my mother relates to me she had gone to the neighborhood butcher and left me with my grandmother babysitting me. And she had warned my grandmother. Every time my mother would say— relating to me—"Etta, I hated to leave you with Nonna because I was afraid she was going to pierce your ears. Well, I thought, well, she knew I didn't want it. She wouldn't do it. She hadn't done it in the two weeks. She probably wasn't going to do it. However, when I was walking up the path, I could hear this screaming, and you were screaming. I knew then. Nonna had pierced your ears. Lo and behold! I came in, and there you were in that little bed that she had for you especially, for all the little grandchildren when she babysat.

There were little threads in your ears where she had pierced your
ears. There was very little I could do. I could scream; I could holler.
But you had done all the screaming for me. And I didn't win that
round."

Until this day, not because my mother didn't want me to have
earrings, I don't wear earrings, and everybody else is wearing.[38]

Some Italian Americans also believed that one should not
weigh or measure a baby, since doing so would retard its growth.[39]
If a baby was not growing as rapidly as traditional authority thought
proper, its weight could be increased magically by cutting its clothes
into twelve pieces and burning them at midnight at a crossroads.[40]
Special baths and rubs might also be used on an ailing child or simply
as a general health measure. Albina Malpezzi attributed the strength
in her infant daughter's legs, which had been deformed at birth, to
her Piedmontese-born mother's scrupulously massaging them with
warm olive oil three times each day. Joseph Napoli described his
Sicilian-American mother's weekly anointing of him with olive oil,
and bathing a baby in wine has been supposed to give it strength.[41]

Specific ailments in young children might yield to specific
remedies in the folk pharmacopeia, but magical practices could
supplement these. An example, reported from Ligurian miners in
California, required that a sick infant be rubbed with warm oil to
which scorched bits of its father's clothing, especially the shirttail,
had been added. As one passed a silver coin down the baby's back,
one recited the following three times:

Monkey's blight,
She-goat's bane,
Halt thy ravage,
Cease thy pain,
Wither away
Like the pomegranate spray,
Holy Trinity,
Release this child
From its infirmity.

The whole procedure should be repeated on three consecutive
days.[42]

Lullabies provided a less dramatic way of quieting a fretful
child. An example in the Piedmontese dialect has been used to

comfort children, grandchildren, and great-grandchildren in the United States:

> *Din-da-lon, Lucia,*
> *Cioppa cul passarot.*
> *Se tua mamma at cria*
> *Disii cha lal Pinot.*
>
> (Rock-a-bye, Lucia,
> Catch a little bird.
> And if your mother scolds,
> Blame it on Joe.)[43]

Another brief lullaby stanza comes from Sicilian tradition. Several second-generation members of the Gennuso family recall its use among their elders:

> *La pechalita mia,*
> *Se brusha care;*
> *Yo vogya par besada,*
> *Su mama more.*
>
> (My darling little baby,
> My heart is breaking;
> And when I want to kiss her,
> Her mama will scold me.)[44]

Italian-American customs and beliefs associated with childbirth certainly suggest that people recognized the importance and perils of this event for both the child and its parents. While protecting from supernatural and natural threats and reminding us of the universality of much associated with this fundamental human experience, Italian-American birthlore has also emphasized the involvement of the group (especially the family and its extensions) in ensuring a safe passage for the newborn baby and the new mother and father.

Weddings

Memories of growing up in Italian-American households frequently emphasize the circumscribed existence of girls, whose principal life goal was in almost every case to be married as soon and as auspiciously as possible. A middle-aged Italian's description of the ideal behavior of the Italian girl growing up in Greenwich Village during the 1920s represents what was common especially in families which had come from southern Italy: "Prior to her marriage she should not be permitted to go out unchaperoned even with other girls or to entertain men at her house."[45] A Sicilian-American woman reared in New Orleans during the thirties and forties confirmed that this remained the ideal: "My father and mother were very, very strict with me. I could not go out without a chaperone.... I could not date. My husband was my first date." Even when she was named Miss New Orleans in the late forties, her protective mother insisted on accompanying her to all the festivities associated with that office.[46]

While restrictions on girls and young women lessened with time and assimilation, as late as the 1960s a sociologist could write of Italian-American family life in New York City, "Norms attached to their [Italian-American women's] family role discourage extra-familial activities."[47] That the adjustment to the relative freedom accorded to American women was particularly difficult forms a theme for a Sicilian-American woman's recollections:

> The most common problem of family adjustments that caused great trouble was the freedom given to females in the United States. Even coeducation was terrifying to the first immigrants. I personally have case histories of how girls were not allowed to attend English and/or citizenship classes. This problem was especially true among Sicilian families whose conduct was subject to many taboos. Rules of courtship, marrying of people from other parts of Italy or from other nationality groups, from other religions, or from the lower social strata, all were (and still are) problems.[48]

To ensure that daughters were not exposed to unapproved influences, they might not be "introduced" into extrafamilial society until the age of sixteen or seventeen and then only under the auspices of an organization such as an Italian social club.[49] A proverb summarized the situation: *"Una ragazza per bene non lascia il petto paterno prima che si sposi"* ("A good girl does not leave the parental nest before she is married").[50]

An ostensible motive for the sheltering of girls was to guarantee their suitability for marriage, an event that families hoped would occur before their daughters had become very old. Proverbial wisdom prescribed the ideal ages for bride and groom: *"L'uomo di venotto; la donna diciotto"* ("The man at twenty-eight; the woman at eighteen").[51] While the pressures of Americanization especially challenged traditions regarding this important rite of passage, many Italian-American families tried to maintain practices that characterized marriage in Italy. The most notorious of these—and the one most directly opposed to conventional American custom—was marriage by family arrangement.

The custom may have been perpetuated in the New World, in part, because of the large number of single Italian men who had crossed the Atlantic and, having decided to remain in America, wanted Italian wives. They could obtain these only through arrangement with their families back in Italy since single Italian women were scarce in the United States. In Newark, New Jersey, for instance, the practice of a matchmaker's delivering a *masciata*, a message to the family of a prospective bride, persisted among single Italian immigrant men who wanted to marry someone from Italy.[52] The parents of Michelema Gaetano, only fifteen years old at the time, received such a message on behalf of her future husband, Vincent Profeta, who sent tickets for her and her father to come to America from Italy.[53] But the practice of arranged marriage sometimes occurred even when all parties were living in the United States. This had been the case with the parents of Joanne Terranella Burleson.

> They married in 1929, and years before that they started thinking about Raymond Terranella for Josephine Genaro. And he came from such a good family—hard-working and everything. And he was so intelligent. Look at all the things he's done. So one person from the Terranellas came over to the Genaros' house and talked to them—talked to my grandfather Lawrence about marrying Mother. They never could go out together. They never had dates, and if they did, it was chaperoned.[54]

Josephine Fastuca was able to go out on dates with her intended husband, but always with a chaperone. Their initial contact occurred through arrangement:

> When I got married, the way it came about was that my husband's brother went to my father's brother to tell him about his brother's intentions. And then my father's brother came to my father and told him that my husband would like to ask for my hand in marriage because he had seen me.[55]

To guarantee good luck in arranging a marriage, matchmakers might place a sheaf of wheat tied with pieces of jewelry as a centerpiece for the table where they were conducting their business.[56]

Even when such arrangements did not occur directly, families might exert subtle pressure on their offspring to select specific spouses or people from specific groups. Some Sicilians favored what anthropologists call "cross-cousin marriage"—that is, a young woman's marrying the son of her mother's brother.[57] Italian Americans from various regions generally encouraged marriage between *paesani* or at least people from the same region. As a Sicilian put it, "Like takes like—chickpeas with chickpeas and broad beans with broad beans, to have a good crop."[58] Josephine Fastuca's husband believed it to be very important that their children "marry the same." He was bothered if their ancestors came from different *paesi*, if they were not of the same social class, or if their economic status differed. The prospective bride's and groom's families "had to match."[59]

In a case reported from Buffalo, New York, a woman's Sicilian-born parents had approved their daughter's marriage to a non-Sicilian, but on the eve of the wedding her protective brother wounded the prospective groom. Even though the parents had sanctioned the marriage, the brother could not bring himself to do so.[60] After *compaesani*, next in order of preferred spouses were other Italians from different regions, though some northern Italians might assert a preference for non-Italians over despised Sicilians. Intermarriage outside the ethnic group and especially outside Roman Catholicism was informally, but decidedly, proscribed.

Despite restrictions that might seem to deprive marriage of the romance with which American custom invests it, Italian-American girls devoted considerable attention to their marital prospects. Like girls from other traditions, they developed methods for predicting the identity of their future husbands. One procedure required that at midnight when the moon was full, a young girl sit alone in a room with a front door. The door should be locked, her eyes should be closed, and her mind should be blank. The door will suddenly jerk open to reveal a vision of her future husband.[61]

Another method required that on Saint John's Eve (23 June), a girl should put an egg white into a bottle of water. If this were left outdoors, the next morning the bottle would contain an image of her husband. Or two young women could bake an egg on Halloween. Each should eat half the yolk, then fill the empty cavity with salt, and eat all of that. If they walked backwards to bed, they would dream of their future spouses bringing them glasses of water. Another method of prophesying marital prospects required that a girl make a bouquet of artichoke leaves, being sure to burn their tips. If the bouquet were still upright the next morning, she could expect to have a happy marriage; but if the leaves were wilted, her marriage would prove a failure.[62] There were also methods for ascertaining the nature of a hoped-for lover's intentions. If a girl's left eye itched, she could trust in his honor, but an itching right eye indicated infidelity.[63]

Anticipation of a possible wedding might affect not just the couple and their families. Once rumor had suggested that an engagement was in the planning stages, the couple might be subjected to not-so-subtle pressure to expedite the process. For instance, dinners at which both were present might feature the pasta *mezzo-zittu*, which signaled that they were "half-engaged" and that a formal announcement of their intentions was in order. Once that announcement had been made, dinners for the couple would feature *zittu*, a pasta that symbolized their public declaration of marriage plans.[64]

Preparations for a wedding involved the prospective bride's assembling a trousseau, which might include not only household items and her own clothing, but clothing for her future husband as well. The custom of a family's providing each daughter with a dowry persisted from the old country, three or four hundred dollars being the amount specified among Sicilians in Columbus, Ohio, around the turn of the century.[65] Even after the dowry had ceased to exist formally, it remained the bride's responsibility to contribute the mattress to the newly married couple's domestic economy.[66]

While the actual marriage ceremony was shaped primarily by the dictates of the priest or civil authority who officiated, folk belief figured in such practices as the groom's carrying a piece of iron in his pocket to ward off the evil eye, a special threat at this time since his happy situation might provoke envy, and this ritual of transition might invite supernatural danger. According to some Italian Americans, the bride's wearing a veil was done for the same reason. Some brides considered it good luck to tear their wedding veil.[67] Church tradition forbade marriage during Lent and, until recently, Advent; but folklore also suggested that the month of May, reserved for veneration of the Virgin Mary, was unpropitious for marriages. Marrying in August invited sickness.[68] It was also considered bad luck for a wedding ring ever to be removed. Once it had been put on during the ceremony, it should remain on the finger even after death.[69]

The celebrations associated with weddings remain highly anticipated events in Italian-American life. Characterized as "the highest-level feast" and "the most celebrated and memorable" occasion in the life cycle,[70] the typical Italian wedding has provided the context for significant displays of festivity. The tone for such events is suggested by a description of the first Italian wedding observed in Newark, New Jersey, in 1877. The occasion was "celebrated with exceptional pomp and gaiety. Everybody was there." A local farmer

> supplied the homeland delicacies of broccoli and pot-cheese which were spread lavishly on the tables. Alfonso Ilaria's tavern was emptied to furnish the endless bottles of wine which inspired the guests to dance to his sad mazzuccas and gay tarantella[s], in which he was accompanied on the guitar by Alfonso Cervone, a baker.[71]

Around the turn of the century in Thurber, Texas, a similar outpouring of celebratory expression characterized wedding observances:

Usually a band provided music the first day, and an accordion player was retained for the remainder of the observance. A special rice dish called *rizzotto* was served to wedding guests. For many Thurber weddings, the rice was cooked in a large washtub, into which were poured gallons of chicken broth, chicken giblets, tomato sauce, and grated cheese. Along with *rizzotto* was served a salad, a variety of meats, and barrels of wine.[72]

The emphasis on food in this account reflects a common theme at Italian-American weddings. Symbolic foods prepared for weddings included candy-covered almonds (*confetti,* jordan almonds, Italian wedding candy), which were deemed essential for the good fortune of the newly married couple. These were tied up in mesh bags and distributed to the guests, who might toss them at the newly married couple. Frances Gueri Byrd remembered trays heaped with bags of *confetti* at the weddings she attended as a child.[73] Preparing these bags of candy required considerable work, as did other foods especially associated with weddings such as *wanda,* or bow ties. Lucia Peek recalled that preparations for an aunt's wedding required several women to spend a day making these treats from strips of dough that were folded, fried, and then powdered with sugar. The result was "bushel baskets" full.[74]

The sheer amount of food available at weddings marked them as particularly special events. Long tables at a church hall or Italian social club would be "loaded" with food.[75] An especially elaborate wedding feast appears in Pietro DiDonato's *Christ in Concrete.* This novel, treating the lives of immigrants from Abruzzi, describes a multi-course meal that climaxes the nuptial festivities. Drinks appeared before the food was served: sweet liqueurs for the ladies and stronger alcoholic beverages for the men. The *antipasto* consisted of olives, pickled whiting and *calamari* (squid), salami, mortadella, pickled eggplant, and peppers. The soup course was chicken broth flavored with eggs, fennel, artichoke, and parmesan cheese. Broiled eels garnished with garlic and parsley were followed by fried squabs with mushrooms. An escarole salad dressed with wine vinegar and olive oil preceded the main course: a suckling pig on a bed of truffles and potatoes. Next came platters of snails and bread and then dandelion salad and boiled lobsters and clams. Dessert consisted of pastries, spumoni, gelati, and tortoni.[76]

Most Italian-American families, of course, could not afford to entertain their wedding guests so lavishly, but food—special dishes as well as large quantities of familiar fare—defined the consummately festive nature of the wedding celebration. Moreover, many Italian-American communities maintained the custom of *buste* to help a family defray wedding expenses. The bride would carry a satin bag called *la borsa* into which guests, recognizing that their hosts would reciprocate when another wedding occurred in the community, placed envelopes containing money.[77]

Before the bride and groom retired for the night, they often broke a vase or glass. The number of pieces into which it shattered represented how many years of happy marriage they might expect.[78] Their bed, prepared in advance by their mothers, might have a pair of scissors in the springs and be sprinkled with salt to ward off evil. Custom required that the groom's mother accompany them to their chambers and be the last to leave, extinguishing the lights as she departed.[79]

Death

Characterizations of southern Italian life often emphasize the importance of customs and beliefs associated with death: omens foreshadowing its occurrence, funeral and burial practices, and prescriptions and proscriptions regarding mourning. The culture's concern with such deathlore has been attributed to anxiety about the soul's reluctance to forsake its earthly abode for life in the afterworld. Death rituals encourage the soul to begin its journey into the afterlife and protect survivors from its return, thus effecting a safe transition for all.[80]

While immigrants from southern Italy certainly brought such concepts with them, they modified their funeral observances in the New World. Improved economic conditions may have inspired former peasants to emulate the customs of the Old World elite. Elaborate floral decorations, funeral bands, and paid mourners used by Italian Americans early in the twentieth century paralleled practices of the *signori* (gentry) which peasants could not afford.[81] Other influences, especially a general trend toward adopting mainstream American ways and the regulations of the Church, have also contributed toward the evolution of Italian-American traditions regarding death.

The inevitability of death and the uncertainty of when it will happen have prompted Italian Americans—like people from most cultures—to develop ways of forecasting its occurrence. Traditional death omens include natural happenings such as howling dogs, chirping "death watch" crickets, and hooting owls as well as domestic accidents. Among the latter are breaking a mirror, spilling olive oil, or allowing a religious statue to fall. If one violates a customary taboo such as carrying out ashes on New Year's Day, that may mean that a death in the family will take place before the year is over. Dreams are regarded as having special prognosticative significance. A friend or family member will die soon if one dreams of raw meat, a priest, a dead person (particularly if that person seems to touch the dreamer), losing a tooth or having one pulled, or getting married. Mysterious, unexplained knocking or hearing footsteps when no one is there may mean that a death is imminent.[82]

When a death occurred earlier in this century, the funeral Mass took place only after the body of the deceased had been waked for a period of at least forty-eight hours.[83] Ideally, this would have taken place at home where the coffin was surrounded by palms, floral wreaths, and religious artifacts. A description of a "laying out" in the 1920s noted a silver cross on the wall above the body and pairs of candles in silver candlesticks at its head and feet.[84] Shades were drawn, mirrors were covered, and clocks were stopped at the time of death. Friends would visit to pay their respects and console the extended family, all of whom were expected to be in attendance and remain with the body around the clock.[85] The deceased would be dressed in his or her communion garb if a child, while a woman might be laid out in her wedding dress.

Italian-American wakes lacked the festive spirit associated with similar occasions in other ethnic groups, but plenty of food (especially meatless dishes) was on hand. Minestrone soup might be provided to replace fluids lost in weeping. This was offered by friends and neighbors so that family members could devote them-

selves entirely to mourning. Visitors would first express their con-
dolences to the bereaved, then offer prayers for the dead, and
conclude their visit by sitting, gossiping, and enjoying some of the
available food. In some cases, a "dinner of consolement," featuring
veal to symbolize new life, would be prepared for the mourners.[86]

People often anticipated the expenses of a wake and funeral by
joining a burial society, but in some cases the custom of *poste*, or
"burial debt," provided financial aid. Accordingly, the bereaved
family "would set up a table," and those attending the wake would
assist them with monetary contributions. Someone scrupulously
recorded names and amounts, since the family viewed it as a point
of honor to reciprocate when a donor needed funds for a similar
purpose.[87] In Greenwich Village in the early 1950s an Italian-
American family maintained a ledger listing those who paid their
respects to their deceased father: 117 gave Mass cards, 33 made
financial contributions, 26 sent flowers, and 19 extended sympathy
messages. They kept this record "so that obligations could be
properly discharged."[88] Ray Ferraro, a second-generation Campanian American, characterized the way in which this custom has
evolved:

> A lot of families instead of giving flowers—they would have
> what they called a "place," or *busta*. And a member of the family,
> one of the older members would sit—most of these funerals were
> held at home. And it was an all-night deal. And a member of the
> family would be present there—greeted people as they came in.
> And the families would come in, and they would leave money. And
> this money was recorded in a little book .... Their names and how
> much was donated. And all that helped to defray the expenses of
> the funeral. Plus they brought food. Everyone always chipped in.
> There was always something to eat because you had to feed all these
> people that came from out of town. They weren't small families.
> They were all big families. So that was a big experience for us.
>
> Now with this book with all the names I remember—I don't
> know whether it was my brother or my sister or my mother would
> say that would be our Bible because the first thing we did whenever
> we got the paper is look at the obituary notices to see who passed
> away. Or someone would call us. And we'd go to the book, and
> we'd look and see if they came to pay respects to us. If they did,

we had to reciprocate. And that's how this tradition helped everyone.

Now today in this time and age it's done, but done in a different way. We do it now where we're trying to break off that tie. And if anyone that we know that had contributed to our family, we put it in memory of our parents. And in this way here, that ends part of that tradition.[89]

Although funeral homes might be regarded as places too cold and impersonal to leave a dead relative's body, their use could be mitigated as long as a family member remained with the body at all times. Also, funeral homes frequently had a distinctly regional identity. For example, in the North End section of Boston, Italian Americans generally had "an undertaker of 'their own kind,' a man from the same part of Italy." In the 1930s this neighborhood boasted at least one undertaker for each region from which its residents had emigrated, and he maintained a highly influential profile among his *paesani*.[90] Even in communities where regional identities had given way to a more generalized Italian ethnicity, funeral homes catered to the traditional customs associated with death. In New Orleans, for instance, Italian-owned funeral homes remained open all night to allow mourners to stay with the body and provided doughnuts, other pastries, and coffee either around the clock or at designated times day and night.[91]

Floral arrangements in traditional designs remain an important decorative feature at a funeral home during a wake. Among the most popular have been a chair suggesting the throne awaiting the deceased in heaven, a pillar symbolizing the deceased's role as family support, and a clock with its hands stopped at the time of death.[92] It was once customary to place objects of special significance to the deceased in his or her casket, a practice that continues in modified form today. A reminiscence of a funeral held early in the century focused on what accompanied the body into the grave:

I recall that when grandfather died in 1915 at the age of eighty-eight, his wake was held in the home and the funeral begun there. He looked dignified in the vested suit which he made in the years when he had fashioned then-Governor Woodrow Wilson's clothes. Small change was placed in his pocket, as well as other mementos of the Knights of Columbus, Fourth Degree, the Sons of Italy and other fraternal societies of which he had been a member.[93]

Typically, jewelry, some change, and favorite articles of clothing would be interred with the body. Less common items left in caskets included *confetti* covering the body of a dead child and a *bocce* ball.[94] Some Italian Americans still believe that any articles of clothing or jewelry placed with a body must be buried with it.[95] Quite recently at the funeral of a Piedmontese immigrant, a bottle of beer and a sprig of dried edelweis, a native northern Italian flower, were placed with the body.

The fear that death had a contaminating effect caused southern Italians to avoid a direct route home after attending a wake or funeral. One should stop on the way home at a public place. Some believed that a purchase should be made before returning home, and if that proved impossible, "you must walk around outdoors for a while before going to your home."[96]

Visiting someone when returning from a funeral or wake might cause a person in that household to sicken. A young Italian American reported an incident from the 1950s demonstrating the persistence of this belief:

> A few years ago, I had taken my grandmother to the funeral home to pay respects to a deceased friend. After leaving the funeral home, she said that she would like to visit another friend while we were in that section of town. I started for the residence of this person, but didn't get half way before she told me to stop. She said that she would like to go into the A and P and get something she needed. I waited outside while she went in to make the purchase. Five minutes later, she came out, but had nothing in her hands. She said that they didn't have the article she wanted. It was not until later that I discovered why she went into the A and P store. She knew that she could not go directly to a friend's house and had to make a stop somewhere else first.[97]

In the home mirrors remained turned to the wall and covered with black for perhaps a week after a funeral. No cleaning was supposed to be done for the same period, and salt might be sprinkled as a prophylactic against the infection of death.[98] The emphasis on a lengthy period of mourning during which only black could be

Until fairly recently, many Italian-American families honored their dead by attaching porcelain photographic portraits to their tombstones.

worn has virtually disappeared, as has the necessity for families to attend personally to the maintenance of most gravesites.

Imposing grave markers are still in use, but the practice of affixing a porcelain portrait of the deceased no longer occurs to any significant extent. On older tombstones, though, one notices the effect described by novelist Tina DeRosa: "Set into the stone are the small framed pictures of the dead; their faces are set so that they always look directly into the eyes of anyone who looks into theirs."[99] Yet Italian-American graves still can be recognized on Palm Sunday and for several weeks thereafter: they may be decorated with palms woven into fancy shapes or stapled to cardboard hearts and crosses.[100]

Traditions literally accompany Italian Americans from before the cradle until after burial. Constantly evolving—a process accelerated by immigration, acculturation, and assimilation—folk beliefs and practices associated with birth, marriage, and death may no longer be interpreted in terms of Van Gennep's classic description of the purpose of a rite of passage. But they do continue to provide the assurances of support from a community that exists in both past and present during some of the most significant events in an individual's life.

CHAPTER FOUR

Customs: The Traditional Calendar

SUNDAYS SEEM TO HAVE BEEN special occasions in many Italian-American families and among *paesani* from various regions of Italy. Consider the DiMarcos of New Orleans:

> In my Italian family the whole family got together every Sunday. I don't know whether it was just Italians. I know that every Sunday the whole family just got together and met at one house. I mean all—the whole clan.... And I think really there was never any doubt that we would do this on Sunday afternoon. I mean we would do this on Sunday. We would go to church, and then we went over to my Aunt Camilla's house. This was just something that we were going to do.[1]

Earlier in the century when Italian laborers worked long hours six days a week, Sunday provided their only opportunity for socializing: "It was a time for gorging, a time for catching up on the week's gossip, a time for the continuation of old arguments and the invention of new ones, a time for venting frustration."[2] Sunday was a time for wearing your best clothing, according to Ray Ferraro: "You had to be dressed up on Sunday. God forbid you get dirty. Because Aunt So-and-so was coming, or Uncle So-and-so was coming."[3] His sister Etta Ferraro Goodwin remembered: "They would stay until one o'clock in the morning. The men would play cards. All the kids would be out in the yard. And then the women would be in the parlor talking."[4]

But even in descriptions of customary Sunday gatherings that show the totality of the experience, eating stands out. A Sicilian American who grew up in New York City could not avoid stressing food when he spoke of Sundays:

> It would be a total day, a day filled with eating, drinking, women preparing meals, talking, political arguing, storytelling—some of

the older people were great storytellers. Of course there were the traditional card games, when the men would break away from the women and play pinocle or poker, while the women would confide in one another about their husbands and their children. The meals seemed never to stop: First the *pranzo*, later the pastry and coffee, an hour after that sandwiches, then you start the supper—one meal leading to another, without end.[5]

A typical Sunday meal for Italians who settled in southeast Texas might consist of *minestrone alla milanese* (soup), *stracotto* (pot roast), *polenta e osei* (cornmeal with small birds), *risotto* (rice), and *zabaglione* (custard).[6] Even more lavish were the meals Richard Gambino enjoyed on Sundays while growing up. Starting at midafternoon and lasting into the evening, Sunday *pranzo* began with an *antipasto* consisting of cheese, fishes, salamis, capacola, mortadella, and melons if in season. A pasta dish, probably baked lasagna or rigatoni, preceded one or more main dishes of meat, fish, or poultry and several vegetable side dishes. Traditional households served only fruit and nuts for dessert, but sweets were offered in the more Americanized ones. Black coffee, sweetened perhaps with anisette, completed the meal. Wine was the favored beverage with all courses.[7]

In one Providence, Rhode Island, family, an uncle regularly provided an especially large dining table each Sunday so that the whole family could feast on traditional foods.[8] Another Rhode Island family, the Ferraros of Peace Dale, began with food in the early afternoon and ended only after a supper at ten or eleven o'clock.[9] For families whose means limited their diet during the week, Sundays were anticipated as the weekly "meat day," when they might have "a big leg of lamb or a big veal leg."[10]

Events such as these Sunday gatherings that Italian Americans observed on a regular weekly basis constitute the most fundamental of calendar customs, traditional practices and associated beliefs which occur according to the various time cycles that a culture recognizes. Usually thought of in terms of the annual cycle of the seasons, calendar customs can include recurrent behaviors that take place more frequently and help to segment the passage of time on even a weekly basis. More community-oriented than rites of passage, calendar customs often involve a reaffirmation of group identity—the family, as has usually been the case with Italian-American Sunday observances; the *paese,* as in many traditional saints' festivals; the local Italian community regardless of regional affiliations, as in Italian market fairs; or Italian Americans in general, as in Columbus Day parades. Calendar customs also offer opportunities to transcend the everyday; to do things that are not normally done, whether it be following the statue of a patron saint in procession, dancing *tarantellas* in the streets, or—as in the case of Italian Sundays—eating to repletion.

The basic pattern of the Italian-American customary calendar follows the liturgical cycle of the Roman Catholic Church. However, folk tradition has supplemented and reinterpreted official Church practice by attaching beliefs and behaviors that reflect the community's needs for expressions of group identity and for escape from routine existence. Moreover, the customary calendar has added a few occasions that derive more directly from secular than from religious sources.

Christmas

The Church begins its new year with the season of Advent, the preparatory period for Christmas, the most important event in the Italian-American traditional calendar. For immigrants from Limotola who inhabit a section of a northwestern Massachusetts town called "the hill" in Rocco Fumento's novel *Tree of Dark Reflection,* Christmas is more than a holiday or even a holy day. It is both climax and beginning of the annual round of celebrations, the festivity at which—even if at no other time during the year—the family "was once again a family."[11] For Italian Americans elsewhere and from other regions, Christmas has had much the same significance. Even though it might be less consciously an ethnic occasion than Saint Joseph's Day or a saint's *festa,* observed for the most part only by Italians, Christmas has remained a time for carrying out regional and family traditions.

Not as elaborate or as oriented toward display as the foods cooked for a Saint Joseph's altar, the baked goods which Sicilian-American women prepare for Christmas still reflect a consciousness of the holiday's importance. In some instances, the preparation process has become a part of the seasonal tradition. For example, according to Joanne Terranella Burleson, the preparation of *cuccidate*, cookies filled with a variety of dried fruit and spices, was a festive occasion. Under the supervision of her mother, Josephine Terranella, several family members might participate. A few days before the holiday, the cookie dough was rolled out on the kitchen table and cut into long two-inch strips. Various fillings could be used. Terranella preferred a mixture mostly of figs, nuts, and honey. Other ingredients might be raisins, citrus peel, and even chocolate. "All the Italian houses" made *cuccidate*, Burleson noted, "and it was kind of neat to compare the inside filling with your mother's." Once the dough was laid out and cut, the cookie-makers could begin spreading the filling onto the strips, which were then sealed by folding the excess pastry over the top. Households might complete the process by adding distinctive decorative touches:

> Then my mother always used a pair of scissors to decorate. And she would decorate with little snips of scissors on top, and then cut the cookies about two inches long all the way down the strip.... And then a lot of the Italian women roll those in confectioner's sugar, which is real good, or some of them get real fancy and put confectioner's sugar and a little bit of water glaze on top.

After leaving home, Burleson continued to associate *cuccidate* with the Christmas season: "The first thing I used to do when I walked in the house when we came home for Christmas is to go to the cookie tins and to see what cookies were made."[12]

Other special Sicilian-American treats for the Christmas season included *fati*, chocolate cookies complemented by the flavors of cloves and cinnamon, and *pignolatte*, fried bits of dough that also appear often on Saint Joseph's altars. For Christmas, *pignolatte* may be shaped into a wreath from which portions may be broken off as desired.[13]

Christmas may also be the time for a more basic cookie recipe, that for *biscotti*. According to Terranella family tradition, *biscotti* are made from flour, sugar, baking powder, butter, eggs, and vanilla. Balls of the resulting dough are pinched off and rolled between the hands to produce a thin rope of dough which may be twisted to form a Christmas wreath. Colored confectioner's sugar provides a decorative garnish. Some cooks create other designs besides wreaths—rings, strips, and letters being among the favored. Often cooks have preferred particular shapes, and their cookies can be easily identified. For example, Joanne Burleson says of the *biscotti* made by family friend Sara Oddo: "I can always tell when Mrs. Oddo's cookies have been brought to Mother's because they're in S's and then sprinkled with sesame seeds." The shaped, decorated *biscotti* are baked until golden.[14]

Regional differences in Christmas confections emerge clearly in the ways southern Italians and northern Italians approach *biscotti*. What the Capello family, whose ancestors came from the Piedmont, know as *biscotti* differs markedly from what the Terranellas mean by the term. One makes a cake from a batter of eggs, flour, and anise seed. After baking, this is sliced, toasted, and possibly dipped in wine when eaten. For *pizelle*, another treat often prepared by Piedmontese Americans at Christmas, traditional bakers press a batter of eggs, butter, flour, sugar, and anise oil or another flavoring such as almond in a special iron which creates intricately designed cookies.

Sara Rao Vittone has a reputation in her extended family for the wine cookies that she prepares for the Christmas season. She mixes a batter of flour, oil, yeast, and red wine: "And don't make it too soft, and don't make it too hard. And then after you work it, you see that it's nice and if it needs more wine." After she is satisfied with the batter's consistency, she lets it stand to rise "like bread dough." The risen dough is cut into small balls, which are fried in hot oil until they are brown. Then Vittone dips each fried pastry ball briefly into boiling honey: "That's my mother's recipe."[15]

Another treat enjoyed during the Christmas season by Italian-American families has been *frittole*, "little fruit cakes" made with yeast and fried.[16] Christmas also provided an opportunity for making *cannoli*, round shells of pastry filled with ricotta cheese into which honey or sugar, chocolate, and candied fruit have been mixed.[17] Homemade treats would be supplemented with items purchased only for the Christmas holiday such as *torrone* (Italian nougat candy), hard Italian macaroons flavored with anise or al-

Pizzelle, cookies flavored with almond or anise, may appear on some Italian-American tables at Christmas and other holidays. Noted for their elaborately decorated surfaces, these cookies may now be baked in electric irons. Formerly, though, cooks had to hold heavy, cast-iron devices over their stoves to achieve the desired effect. A niece's husband made this pizzelle iron for Pearl Malpezzi.

mond, and *panettone* (a festive cake). Families would also set out large bowls of nuts which they and their guests could shell and eat.

In addition to special baked goods, other foods have figured in Italian-American Christmas customs—especially on Christmas Eve, the traditional meatless vigil before the holy day itself. Relatively strict abstention shaped what was to be eaten on Christmas Eve after Mass. In the Marchese household, for example, custom dictates a meal of nine different kinds of vegetables: "Cabbage, turnips, asparagus.... Different kinds of vegetables. Anise, stuffed artichokes. Just nine different vegetables."[18] Other families also emphasize the importance of having seven, nine, or thirteen meatless dishes for Christmas Eve, while a variant practice specifies only that the number of dishes be odd.[19] Menus might include fish: spaghetti *algio olio* (with a garlic and oil sauce) or *vongole* (with mussels and oil), *baccala* (dried codfish), *sarde* (smelts), *anguilla* (eels), and *zeppole* (fried and sugared dough).[20]

Or a Christmas Eve repast could resemble that described in Fumento's novel: fried and baked squid, pickled eel, salted codfish, smelts, and spaghetti with a sauce consisting of anchovies, oil, garlic, and hot red peppers.[21] At midnight Richard Gambino's Sicilian-American grandparents always served octopus, which was offered hot or cold with lemon juice, olive oil, garlic, and other spices. Other sea creatures on the Gambino Christmas Eve menu included sea urchins. A special treat was roasted chestnuts, and in the early morning hours of Christmas Day the family might have soft-boiled eggs sucked directly from the shell.[22]

Italian Americans especially favored eel on Christmas Eve, some believing that eating it ensured them a year of happiness.[23] Other foods that might appear on Christmas Eve tables have been *lupini* beans[24] and a Sicilian pizza called *faccia la vecchia,* or "old lady's face." According to Sam Gennuso, who grew up eating it in Lake Charles, Louisiana, "It was like a cake really stuffed with things. You know, they'd stuff the cheese and the sardines and the onions and all the stuff in the dough and then bake it and then pour a little tomato over it." Joanne Terranella Burleson added, "Whoever makes it gets their finger and indents the dough real heavily about three times and just about an inch apart. And they insert little pieces of cheese in that and little pieces of anchovy in that and on top of that. And then they sprinkle it with oregano and a little olive oil." Because of its irregular surface, "it does look like an old lady's face."[25]

Eating a slice of orange as the first course on Christmas Eve also was thought to bring good luck.[26] But no matter what was served, many Italian Americans were careful not to eat everything. The dining table was left at least partially set with candles and a few treats in case the Christ Child should visit during the night.[27] Some of the foods prepared for Christmas were thought to have special properties. Broth made for the holiday was used to water carnations to ensure multi-colored blossoms, and the first slice of some Christmas cakes, which were thought to be immune to mold, was set aside to make poultice to cure infections during the year.[28]

Italian-American Christmas customs have not focused entirely on food. The Eve was also an occasion for playing special games such as *tombola* and *noccioli,* which resemble bingo.[29] Residents of Roseto, Pennsylvania, might make a *fagghia* for the occasion. A huge torch fashioned from a tree branch soaked in grease and oil, the *fagghia* provided festive illumination as people made their way to midnight Mass.[30]

For Italian Americans, as for other ethnic groups in the United States, Christmas has been a time for encouraging good behavior on the part of children by providing them with special rewards. Many Italian-American homes display a *presepio,* or creche, during the holiday. One way of encouraging children to be good allows them to add an item to the manger scene each time they behave. Since the creche must be completed by Christmas Day, it is important that children deserve rewards often enough so that no part of the scene is left out. Tradition holds that the *presepio* originated with Saint Francis of Assisi, who used it to vivify his narration of the Christmas story. In Italy children made a *presipio* each year, often including figures from their contemporary environment. In the United States, Italian families have come to rely on commercially produced Nativity sets which include only traditional figures and which children place under a decorated tree or in the front window.[31]

Parents can also influence children's behavior by referring to *La Befana,* who traditionally came on 6 January, the Feast of the Epiphany at the end of the Christmas season, but who has sometimes been conflated with the Americanized Santa Claus. *La Befana,* also called *La Vecchia di Natale,* rewards virtuous children by filling their stockings with candy and fruit but punishes the naughty by leaving them only lumps of coal. One explanation for this figure holds that she "came from the East in quest of the wisemen and continues her search every year."[32]

The scope of an Italian-American Christmas is suggested by the memoir of Bruna Pieracci, whose family left their native Modena to settle in the Iowa coal camps early in this century:

> My father would go to the city for Christmas shopping, but his pay did not allow him to buy very much. The night before Christmas, he would hang up for us, brightly colored knitted stockings, made by our grandmother and brought to America by another villager. On Christmas morning ... the *Befana* had left each of us a ten cent toy, an orange, a Hershey almond bar, and a pair of stockings or some much needed garment. Sometimes there would be chestnuts to roast or boil. The bread man usually brought every family a coffee bread called *panettone.* This was a great treat because it was sweet and had raisins in it.... For Christmas dinner we would have a big pot of soup with *ditalini,* sprinkled with Parmesan cheese.[33]

Lent, Good Friday, and Easter

The forty days preceding Easter begin after Shrove Tuesday, best known in the United States for French-American celebrations of *Mardi Gras.* While Italian-American observances of Carnival have not been as intense, communal recognition of the impending days of penance and abstinence is an Italian-American tradition. In Thurber, Texas, for example, Italian Americans who had come to mine for coal observed Shrove Tuesday by having masked and costumed men go from house to house entertaining children. Each housewife was expected to provide these jesters with wine and *crostoli,* a special pastry made from strips of brandy-flavored dough which were tied into bows, fried, and dipped in confectioner's sugar.[34] The Italo-American Citizens Club of Masontown, Pennsylvania, once held an annual Mardi Gras dance, to which families would come in costumes.

Families at home might observe Carnival on a less elaborate scale. For example, on the Sunday or Tuesday before the beginning of Lent, the Lovoi family, Sicilian Americans who lived in Fort Smith, Arkansas, played *settamenta*, a traditional card game, while they waited for the *sfinghi*, deep-fried balls of airy dough coated with sugar or honey, which their mother prepared only at this time of the year.[35] As might be expected, some families have observed the eve of Lent by eating heartily of meat dishes that in earlier days would have been forbidden to them in the weeks to come. An example is *braciola*, rolled beefsteak seasoned with garlic, parsley, and other spices and served with "gravy," either a conventional tomato-based sauce or a special sauce made from cinnamon, nutmeg, and cloves.[36]

During Lent itself, traditional meatless dishes were added to the usual cuisine. *Baccala, stoccofisso* (salted dried codfish), or hard-boiled eggs might replace meat in sauces or might serve as the major ingredient in stews.[37] Some Italian Americans preserved the Old World custom of personifying Lent as an old woman represented by a doll made from a potato decorated with feathers and cloth. Each week the children of the household would remove a feather from the doll until by the time Easter came it was totally denuded. Then the doll was burned.[38]

The climax of the Lenten season and Passion week on Good Friday begins a three-day period, ending on Easter Sunday, which condenses the previous seven weeks of spiritual concentration. Good Friday itself has been marked by religious processions, the most thoroughly documented being that of Maria Addolorata (the Virgin of Sorrows) in Brooklyn. Many residents of the parish of the Church of the Sacred Heart and Saint Stephen trace their ancestry to Bari in Apulia, where the tradition of the procession originated.[39] They gather in the church in the early morning on Good Friday to await the priest and several formally attired young men, who will carry the statue of the Virgin on a platform through the streets. Accompanied by various parish organizations, the church band (playing funereal music), and any parishioners who care to join, the statue makes its way through the neighborhood, pausing frequently to permit devotees to pay their respects. As the procession passes their houses, people kneel to receive a blessing or join the marchers. Many have put up special decorations of flowers and lights.

Shortly after the procession of the Virgin leaves from the front of the church, another group sets out from the rear. Bearing a glass coffin with a life-size statue of the crucified Jesus, several men set out through the streets on a route that will bring them into contact with the Virgin's procession when it ends at the church door. The meeting of the two processions *(la giunta)* climaxes the event, which is supposed to depict the mother's mournful search for her lost, now-dead son.[40]

Italian Americans in Brooklyn also process on Good Friday in reenactments of the Stations of the Cross, marked by black crosses at sites through the neighborhood. At each, the procession of parish organizations bearing their identifying banners pauses while a priest narrates the events depicted there, and some are enacted by costumed children.[41]

Such Good Friday customs serve as commemorative reminders of the events in sacred history which charter the fundamentals of Christian doctrine. They also allow participants a sense of imaginative identification with the happenings in the Passion of Jesus and the sorrows of his mother. The following day's activities offer opportunities for a final cleansing and purgation before the celebration of Easter. Purification on Holy Saturday may be domestic, as in the Sicilian-American custom of using the day to cleanse one's house of the devil,[42] or it may be personal. According to Ligurian tradition reported in California, after bathing the face on Holy Saturday, one should recite, "Flowing Water / Quench this ardent fire that courses through my veins."[43]

Easter itself may call for public festivals. An Italian-American novel set in Cleveland, Ohio, depicts an Easter *festa* with food vendors, carnival rides, a papier mâché chapel with a painting of Jesus rising from his tomb inside, strings of colored lights, balloons with the Madonna on them, a marionette show, and roulette wheels. Among the festive foods available were sausages made from pork and *finocchio* (fennel), *lupini,* and candies shaped like Jesus or the Virgin Mary.[44]

More often, Italian Americans have observed Easter in the context of the family, a special meal with foods appropriate for the season being the focus of the celebration. Lamb was the favored meat dish, though some families might prefer a goat or pig. Special pasta dishes such as ravioli or tortellini might supplement the meat.[45] Meat pies could provide a major ingredient for an Easter dinner. *Pizza chiena* (full or "money" pie) was filled with *salametti* (a hard sausage resembling pepperoni), *prosciutto* (ham), sliced boiled eggs, and several varieties of cheese. Some families followed the tradition of spelling their surname with strips of dough on the tops of Easter pies.[46] A special treat might be *pizza di grano,* a pie made from ricotta cheese, eggs, wheat, and candied fruit. In some cases, palms blessed on Palm Sunday might be inserted into the filling. A New World variation for this traditional Easter delicacy substitutes rice for the wheat.[47] One of the most popular special foods for this holiday among Italian Americans has been Easter bread, braided into a wreath into which colored hard-boiled eggs have been inserted.[48] Some of the same pastries and sweets that were prepared for Christmas, especially *cannoli* and *biscotti,* might be offered at Easter as well.

Even when the Easter feast involved only the family, the festive season and its delicacies might extend to Italian-American friends and acquaintances. Ray Ferraro remembered how his mother observed Easter:

> And all the Italian pastries: the *wanda,* the *biscotta.* So that was a festive time. And all this was made—you didn't make one or two—by the dozen because everyone that came to visit would either get a loaf of *panettone* or a rice pie, a farina pie, something to take home. And in exchange they would bring one of theirs. The only problem was that we liked my mother's better. And we'd say, "Oh, Ma, do you have to give them all away?"[49]

Like other calendar customs, then, Easter served to heighten its participants' sense of community: the family through the shared meal, friends and acquaintances through the distribution of special baked goods, and the entire ethnic-religious group through participation in processions and other overtly sacred behavior.

Saint Joseph's Day

The feast of Saint Joseph, foster-father of Jesus and patron of the family, orphans, and the poor, has traditionally fallen during Lent on 19 March. Among Sicilian Americans and other immigrants from the south, the feast day has provided a context for customs that emphasize the elements of society singled out for the saint's patronage. The central feature of Saint Joseph's Day has been a family's presentation of an altar to the saint in gratitude for a special blessing that he has granted or which they hope he will grant.[50]

Typical petitions made to Saint Joseph include requests for help in curing an illness, overcoming financial problems, assisting a loved one through a dangerous situation such as a war, or giving birth to a healthy child. A Sicilian-American woman in southern California told Charles Speroni how doctors had almost given up on her young son, ill with pneumonia, when she presented her case to Saint Joseph. She promised to set up an altar on his feast day should her child recover, and when the saint answered her prayer, she faithfully carried out her side of the bargain.[51] Augustina Lovoi had given an altar in the 1940s for an uncle who was suffering from Lou Gehrig's disease.[52] Petitions to Saint Joseph, though, need not be life-and-death matters. Marie Marchese related a miracle story involving the saint and his day which she had first encountered in a pamphlet published by the Saint Joseph Guild in New Orleans:

> Like this lady here saw a statue of the Blessed Mother in the window as she was going to work. And everyday she passed by this window to see the Blessed Mother there. And she said she was going to buy it whenever she gets enough money. So one day she passed by there, and the statue was gone. She went in and asked the man—said, "Where's the statue?" She said, "I was going to buy it, but now it's gone." And the man said, "Well, someone bought it." And she said, "Now, I would like to have it. I would like to buy it from this party that bought it." And he said, "Well, I don't know anything about that." So she left. She went on and on, and when she got home, the statue was at her door. It was a statue of the Blessed Mother. And she said, "Oh," she said, "the Good Lord has

Cannoli—special treats prepared for Christmas and other holidays by Italian Americans. These crepes of pastry contain a filling made with ricotta cheese, chocolate chips, and candied fruit.

In 1943 the Lovoi family of Fort Smith, Arkansas, "gave" this Saint Joseph's Altar in behalf of an uncle who was seriously ill. Before its treats could be shared, the altar was blessed by Father McLauglin, assistant pastor of Immaculate Conception Church. Photograph courtesy of Augustina Lovoi.

blessed me." Because she'd prayed so long to have this statue. And she said, "If you will let me have it—if I can keep it, I'll have an altar." So no one has asked for the statue from her, so she made an altar by this Blessed Mother—by promising.[53]

Bargains struck with Saint Joseph in this manner constitute sacred obligations that may involve more than the single petitioner, extending to his or her entire family and often to their friends. However, they frequently are not fulfilled until the lapse of several years allows enough money to be set aside to complete what may become an expensive undertaking. In some communities, a family may seek donations to help them finance a Saint Joseph's Day altar.

Construction of an altar begins sometime before 19 March. According to Marie Marchese, three or four weeks' worth of baking precedes the actual feast day. Among the baked goods that Italian-American women are likely to prepare for the occasion are *cuccidate* similar to those made at Christmas; *zeppoli,* puffed pastries filled with cream; and sheet cakes with "Saint Joseph" written in frosting.[54] Saint Joseph's bread, made from a dough stiffer than that used for usual bread and sometimes glazed with egg white, is molded into traditional shapes for the occasion. These include chalices, canes, Saint Joseph's beard, his sandals, baskets, and stars. Another frequent contribution to a Saint Joseph's altar is *pignolatte,* sometimes called "Italian peanuts." These are "real hard cookies. It's made with just flour and eggs, and you fry these. And you get them to put in the shape of a cone. You make up this sugar water like, and you put them together in the shape of a cone."[55]

While these baked goods can be prepared in advance, other foods for the altar require cooks' attention immediately before the feast day. Fresh and preserved fruits, vegetables such as stuffed artichokes, fish dishes, and candies may contribute to displays on altars which, according to an altar-giver in New Orleans, number as many as "five hundred kinds."[56] Although the family in whose home the altar appears bears most of the responsibility for preparing the array of food, members of the extended family and friends may contribute to the massive display.

Other items that appear on the altar (which is often three-tiered to represent the Trinity and covered with a lace tablecloth made by a female ancestor) include a picture of the Holy Family (Jesus, Mary, and Joseph), a statue of Saint Joseph, and possibly statues of other saints the family wishes to honor. There may also be a bowl of *fava beans*, which are considered to be lucky. Carrying one in a pocket is supposed to offer protection against becoming penniless, so people often pick up one or two when they come to visit an altar.[57] The colors red, white, and green may be featured, since those appear on the Italian flag.

A few days before Saint Joseph's Day, the family giving the altar will begin inviting as many people as possible to visit their offering to the saint. In New Orleans, blanket invitations are extended through the *Times–Picayune* newspaper. Formerly these appeared in the "Personals" column, but recently a special section in the classified advertising section has been assigned to "St. Joseph Altars" for a day or two before the feast days. Examples from the 18 March 1972 issue include the following:

> St. Joseph Altar given by Mr. and Mrs. Leo J. Baracco, 3110 Music St. open to the public for viewing on March 18th, 6 to 12 midnight. March 19th, 9 to 11 a. m. Closed from 11 to 2 p. m. Open again 2 to 10 p.m.

> St. Joseph Altar given by Mr. and Mrs. Albert Cucinella for safe return of all men overseas. Open to public Mar. 18, 3 p. m., 1204 Desire St. Cookies, Lucky Beans, and Bread.

> Public invited, St. Joseph Altar, March 18 & 19, given for health of daughters. 3126 Marais St. Given by Mrs. Mary Salvage & daughters.

> Mr. & Mrs. Edward Garey Jr., 4713 Iberville. Public invited to St. Joseph Altar for favor granted. Mar. 18, 6 p. m.; Mar. 19 after 1 p. m.

> A. Brocato Ice Cream Parlor, 617 Ursuline St. St. Joseph Altar will be displayed March 17, 18, 19.[58]

On the evening of 18 March or early the following morning, a priest visits the household to bless the altar, after which none of the food should be eaten until the actual Saint Joseph's Day dinner. Before that can occur, a dramatization involving persons—usually children—portraying the three members of the Holy Family must take place. They approach a house near the one giving the altar and request its hospitality, often using a traditional rhymed formula. By prearrangement the householder refuses them. This interchange is repeated at several other houses until the Holy Family arrive at the proper place, where they receive an enthusiastic welcome.[59] Marie Marchese described this process:

> They play the role of Saint Joseph, the Blessed Mother, and Jesus.... Before they start to go eating, they go knock, knock on three doors. And the first door they knock and say they were hungry and they want sleep because Mary was tired. They've been traveling a long way. They say, "Sorry, we don't have room. We have no food." The second door they do the same thing. But the third door, they knock and say, "This is Mary and Joseph. We are hungry, and we need food, and we need a place to rest." And so, "Oh come in! Come in!"[60]

Sometimes children portraying angels will join the Holy Family on their quest for hospitality.[61] An alternate custom has the Holy Family knock only at the altar giver's door, where they are refused twice before being invited inside.[62]

Once inside the house, the Holy Family have quite a spread laid before them. Not only the delicacies displayed on the table, but also mounds of pasta provide feasters with evidence of the family's hospitality. Since Saint Joseph's Day occurs during Lent, sauces for the pasta are traditionally meatless. Hardboiled eggs, sardines, or other fish may be a principal sauce ingredient. Breadcrumbs representing the sawdust from Saint Joseph's carpentry business may be sprinkled atop the pasta and sauce.[63] The Holy Family eat before anyone else and sample as many of the altar treats as possible. Then the doors of the house are literally thrown open so that families, neighbors, friends, people who have responded to blanket newspaper invitations, and even casual passersby can eat all they want. Sometimes a traditional hymn is sung before the meal:

> *Evviva la Croce,*
> *La Croce sempre evviva*
> *Evviva la Croce*
> *E chi la porto.*

(Long live the Cross,
May the Cross live forever,
Long live the Cross
And he who bears it.)[64]

In some communities it is traditional for the master of the house to bathe the feet of his guests.[65]

Domestic Saint Joseph's Day customs such as these emphasize the saint's role as patron of the family, since that unit, rather than the Church or a society, is responsible for carrying them out. The saint's patronage of the orphaned and the poor is evident in the family's making the feast available to anyone who wishes to participate and in the disposition of leftovers, which are donated to charity. Occasionally, though, a bit of the specially prepared food will be saved for protective purposes. One can break off a piece of Saint Joseph's Day pastry and toss it outside to prevent storms during threatening weather.[66] A bit of Saint Joseph's bread kept in the house throughout the year will also ensure that none of the occupants will starve.[67]

The charitable emphasis carries over into public ceremonies honoring Saint Joseph. In some communities parish organizations or Italian-American citizens groups have taken over the custom of dedicating an altar of food to the saint on 19 March. With many Italian-American kitchens contributing special foods, the table at such displays features a variety and abundance even beyond that available at a family observance. A list of some of the items at a New Jersey church suggests the extent:

> pizza *piena,* pizza *rustica, pasticcio* of spinach and meat, *baccala,* finnochio, onion torta, *ceci* beans [roasted chickpeas or garbanzos], *cuccidate,* oranges, marmalades, *zeppole, biscotti, cannoli,* rice fritters, ricotta and wheat pie, and, of course, the finest wines and the traditional blessed breads of Saint Joseph.[68]

After a public viewing of the altar, the individual foods are sold at auction, the proceeds going to charities such as the Hope Haven orphanage, which benefits from public Saint Joseph observances in New Orleans. The public observances involve not only Sicilians and southern Italians, but also Italians from other regional backgrounds who may not know the custom from their own traditional cultures.[69]

In New Orleans, Saint Joseph altars are constructed as well in African American Spiritual churches.[70]

Some communities such as New Orleans hold Saint Joseph's Day parades combining features of Mardi Gras and the traditional saint's procession. Through the city streets young men carry a statue of Saint Joseph surrounded by baked goods that will eventually go to charitable organizations. The 1972 parade in New Orleans, organized by the Italian American Marching Club, honored the recently deceased Vince Lombardi. Five bands, decorated carriages and pony carts, and floats resembling gondolas accompanied Saint Joseph's statue. An atmosphere of Carnival, undoubtedly a pleasant interruption from the relative austerity of Lent, developed as men wandered through the crowds tossing lucky *fava* beans and "doubloons"—coins similar to those distributed from Mardi Gras parade floats—bearing Lombardi's likeness.[71]

Feste

In an essay published in 1899, the chronicler of New York City immigrant life Jacob A. Riis wrote of a *festa* he had observed in the city's Mulberry Bend district:

> San Donato's feast-day is one of very many such days that are celebrated in New York in the summer months. By what magic the calendar of Italian saints was arranged so as to bring so many birthdays within the season of American sunshine I do not know. But it is well. The religious fervor of our Italians is not to be pent up within brick walls, and sunshine and flowers belong naturally to it. "Religious" perhaps hardly describes it, yet in its outward garb it is nearly always that.[72]

Riis exemplified his generalizations with an account not only of the celebration honoring Saint Donato, but also of the *feste* of Saint Rocco, Saint Anthony of Padua, and Our Lady of Mount Carmel. A couple of years later, an unsigned article in *Charities* added the Festival of the Crucifixion and that of Saint Michael the Archangel to the catalog of annual calendar celebrations among Italians in New York each summer and early autumn.[73]

The populous Italian-American community in New York City has not been alone in sustaining and reviving elaborate celebrations of saints' days. As Phyllis Williams wrote in 1938, "Practically any American town with an Italian community of any size and wealth observes one or more occasions of this nature."[74] Frequently, the saints whose days receive honor have reflected the regional loyalties of the specific communities. In New York City in the 1930s, Neapolitans honored Saint Gennaro, Saint Rossilia's Day was celebrated by Sicilians from Palermo, and immigrants from the east coast of Sicily observed the feast day of Saint Agatha. During that decade, it was noted,

> [H]ardly a day passes without some sort of *festa* in one or more of the half hundred churches of the city's several Little Italys. Most are purely local, given in honor of the patron saint of some city in Sicily, Calabria, or Campania (Naples), from which most of the worshipers originally came. These local celebrations are on a small scale and far from elaborate. In fact, one may see similar celebrations in almost any small city in the United States that has an Italian colony.[75]

The erosion of rigid *campanilismo* among later generations of Italian Americans has generated more broadly based *feste,* which attract not just *paesani* but reach out to Italian Americans in general (and often to other ethnic groups). But examples of the *festa paesana* still occur in communities populated by recent immigrants. For example, since 1971 immigrants in Toronto from the town of Quasano in Apulia have been observing their distinctive *Festa di Maria Santissima degli Angeli di Quasani.*[76]

Though the roots of most New World *feste* lie in Europe and Italians on this side of the Atlantic have tried to replicate structures of such events in Italy, saints' festivals have undergone necessary modifications in the American setting. Often only loosely connected with the official Church (and once vigorously opposed by the non-Italian ecclesiastical hierarchy in the United States), *feste* have typically been organized by independent groups—sometimes a social or community club, sometimes an organization whose only function is staging the *festa* and maintaining the saint's statue between the yearly celebrations. *Feste* themselves have been described from various points of view, but a common theme has been to focus on their extravagance. For example, a Protestant clergyman writing in 1922 noted,

> On religious holidays, usually occurring in midsummer, the greatest and most extravagant celebrations take place. There is prodigal decoration, street illumination, and fireworks for the processions when the patron saint is honored with festivity. Thousands of persons are often in line, curious and sometimes vulgar expressions of religious emotion occur, and large offerings are frequently made to the saints.

The clergyman held out some hope for those whom he considered to be benighted idolators when he concluded, "But with the sloughing off of superstition, the tendency year by year is to reduce these celebrations to more limited proportions."[77]

More objective and more detailed is an account of *feste* as they occurred in Newark, New Jersey, during the 1930s:

> The streets of the Italian quarters ... were gaily decorated under a panoply of brilliant multicolored lights, banners and giant candles artistically arranged, becoming veritable replicas of the old village feasts. Statues of the revered Saints and Madonnas would be drawn along the streets, littered with bunting, corn-cobs and empty clamshells, on the brawny shoulders of sweating, happy and reverent workers dressed in their Sunday best, their coats or shirts burdened with religious medals, badges and buttons, and wreathed in red, white and green sashes with tinsel letters. They would be followed by throngs of pious wives, mothers, children and grandmothers, chanting prayers, often barefoot, dressed in somber brown or black dresses of peasant simplicity, covered by dark or polka-dotted aprons whose hems touched the cobble-stones.[78]

Though some of the extravagance has disappeared from *feste,* they remain one of the most important events in the traditional calendar in some Italian communities. Typically nowadays, a *festa* occurs on the weekend nearest the officially sanctioned saint's day. The center for activities will be the grounds of a parish church or a community park, where by Friday evening booths offering food ("traditional" Italian food such as pizza and sausage sandwiches as well as the popcorn, cotton candy, hot dogs, and funnel cakes that commonly constitute carnival cuisine), religious items, or games of chance (to recover some of the costs of the *festa* or to raise money for the church) have been set up. There also is a stage for musical entertainment, featuring Italian folk and popular music, polka bands, and even rock groups. Music and perhaps dancing provide Friday-night diversions.

The most important religious component of the *festa,* the procession, may take place on Saturday morning. The statue of the saint (which may be life-size or larger) is removed from its usual spot in church or in the headquarters of the organizing society, placed on a platform, and lifted onto the shoulders of six or eight strong men, who view their role in the procession as an honor. In some communities, the statue may be placed on a cart instead of lifted on a platform. Accompanied perhaps by the clergy and by delegations from parish religious groups, the statue makes its way through the streets to the *festa* site—either church or park. (If the statue normally remains in the parish church, the procession may involve walking it around several blocks and returning it to its point of origin.)

Frequent stops along the way allow onlookers to join the procession if they wish (formerly some walked barefoot), to decorate the statue with flowers, or (more frequently in the past than now) to pin cash offerings to its robes as inducements for the saint's intercessory efforts on their behalf. Some people may make such offerings in gratitude for past beneficence from the saint. In the past, they might have carried in procession a wax representation of some body part that had been healed through the saint's intercession.[79] Though joining in the procession may be a sacred obligation, it can also have more prosaic consequences. Proponents of the *festa* of San Gennaro in New York City claim that young women who participate in the saint's procession as queen have heightened marriage prospects.

At the conclusion of the procession, the parish priest (or in more affluent communities, a visiting cleric from Italy) offers Mass, often using Italian or the relevant regional dialect for parts of the service. His homily will usually be a synopsis of the life of the honored saint. Saturday afternoon marks a return to festive socializing. Organized activities may include a talent show, eating contests, and *bocce* and *morra* tournaments. The social climax of the festival occurs that evening with a community dance and perhaps a fireworks display, once a virtual necessity for such occasions but now often dispensed with because of safety concerns. After morning Mass the next day, the booths are likely to reopen for a final expression of festivity before the weekend concludes.[80]

Of course, this generalized account fails to convey the rich variety that may actually characterize *feste:* from the celebration of Saint Donato in the backyard of a saloon which Riis observed in 1899 to the "flight of angels" witnessed by Williams at a *festa* for Saint Gandolf (children dressed as angels and suspended from ropes strung between fire escapes who would recite appropriate verses when the processing saint paused beneath them).[81]

One of the most colorful specific enactments occurs during the festival of Saint Paulinus in Brooklyn, which originally fell on 22 June, but is now combined with the *festa* for Our Lady of Mount Carmel (16 July) into a two-and-a-half-week affair. In honor of the saint, descendants of immigrants from Nola—a village near Naples in Campania—have been reenacting part of his legend since the 1880s by "dancing the *giglio.*" Saint Paulinus' hagiography holds that as bishop of Nola during the fifth century, he voluntarily gave himself into slavery in place of a widow's son when pillaging Vandals invaded southern Italy. Soon gaining the confidence of his master, Paulinus prophesied the death of the Vandal king, who ordered the bishop and other enslaved Nolani to be freed and returned to their home. Upon their arrival, Paulinus was greeted by the people of the village, who carried lilies in his honor.

The *giglio* ("lily") that the Brooklyn Nolani "dance" is a sixty-foot, two-ton, steeple-shaped structure decorated with papier mâché and plastic representations of saints, angels, birds, vines and leaves, and flowers and resting on a platform carried a short distance by a squad of 128 lifters. During the course of the *giglio*'s procession, it is carried by several squads, each wearing a distinctive uniform of scarf, soft cap, and T-shirt. The Nolani also construct a representation of a ship on the same scale; this is also carried on the shoulders of 128 strong men. Both structures pass through the streets as the men beneath them, directed by a squad leader called a *capo,* move in time to sprightly music performed by players seated on the *giglio*'s platform. Ultimately *giglio* and ship meet in a massive

*A special feature of the **festa** honoring Saint Paulinus of Nola in Brooklyn is "dancing the **giglio**," a towering representation of the lilies with which, according to legend, the Nolani in Italy welcomed the saint when he returned from self-imposed captivity among the Vandals some fifteen hundred years ago. Photograph by Wayne Narey.*

reenactment of the fifth-century Nolani's welcome of their returning bishop—the small flowers they carried replaced by the towering structure of the *giglio*.[82]

Another distinctive saint's day observance occurs in Jessup, Pennsylvania. The majority of Italian Americans in this town in the north-central part of the state trace their ancestries to communities in Umbria, especially Gubbio, where the original of Jessup's *Festadei Ceri* took place. First staged in Jessup in 1909 and revived in 1976, the event happens on the weekend nearest 15 May, the feast day of Saint Ubaldo. Yet actually, the *festa* honors Saints George and Anthony in addition to the patron of Gubbio.

The unique feature of the *Festadei Ceri* is a race involving teams (called *famiglie*) representing the three saints. On Saturday evening, each team lifts a quarter-ton platform bearing the statue of its saint onto their shoulders for a two-mile "run" through the city streets, a race which requires two or three hours because of frequent, lengthy pauses to allow the runners to refresh themselves. Although considerable verbal dueling among the teams occurs before and during the race, actual competition is minimal since the order in which the *famiglie* run is predetermined: Saint Ubaldo followed by Saint George and then Saint Anthony. The race reaches its climax at the community athletic field where the teams finish their run with three laps around the track. Competition does occur as the teams rush to detach the statues from the platforms and elevate them for a final run around the field.[83]

Some *feste* involve special foods. An example is the *chiambelli*, doughnut-shaped bread baked especially for the festival of Saint Rocco (16 August). Made from a basic dough of flour, eggs, sugar, and oil, the *chiambelli* represent the bread which a friendly dog brought to the leprous saint while he was living as a recluse. The bread is stacked around the foot of the saint's statue during the procession.[84] For the feast of Saint Gennaro, patron of the city of Naples, *capozzelli*, sheep's head, may be especially prepared.[85]

Sometimes *feste* focus on particular segments of the Italian-American community and their special concerns, examples being fishermen's festivals which honor and invoke the blessings of saints for safety and success in an often treacherous enterprise. In San

Pedro, California, three days of prayer to Saint John of the Cross in August elicit his mediation. Statues of the saint are carried in boats. A similar event has occurred farther up the coast at the time of the September full moon. Italians of Sicilian descent in Monterey carry a statue of Saint Rosalia from San Carlos Cathedral to the marina, where the blessing of the fishing fleet occurs. Early in October the fleet at San Francisco is blessed after a procession honoring Maria Santissimi del Lune, patron of fishermen in Porticello, Sicily.[86] Meanwhile, Sicilian-American fishermen in Boston have traditionally feted Madonna del Soccorso to enlist her protection during their ventures into the North Atlantic.[87]

Although the *festa* tradition derives from Italy, it seems to have proliferated more in the New World than in the Old.[88] Reasons for this development include the structure of Catholicism in the United States, which at the time when the major waves of Italian immigration occurred was dominated by an Irish-American clergy whose emphases differed from what Italians—especially those from the south—had experienced at home. *Feste* allowed Italian immigrants to recapture some of the southern Italian Catholicism, oriented toward the saints and the cult of the Virgin, that received little support from the American Church. Consequently, *feste* served the ethnically based religious needs of the group, at the same time helping to define the group's sense of identity.

In the early twentieth century, when *feste* might be associated with the religious traditions of a particular village or region whose emigrants had settled in the same town or urban neighborhood, the occasion helped to reinforce ties with the *paese*.[89] Later, as saints' festivals began to appeal to entire Italian-American communities regardless of specific points of origin, they became ways of asserting a common ethnicity among people whose ancestors had not recognized their commonality. In fact, *feste* have often been times for homecoming, when former residents of an Italian neighborhood return to renew old friendships and acquaintances.[90] The procession has given particular expression to such sentiments since it serves as a public display of cooperative effort while defining the physical boundaries of the community as it moves through the streets and roadways.[91]

Columbus Day

Variously described as "the real national *festa* of all Italian immigrants" and "at once the most Italian and the most American of holidays,"[92] Columbus Day (12 October) has been observed among Italians in the United States since 1866. That year's celebration in New York was followed three years later by similar events in Boston, Philadelphia, Cincinnati, New Orleans, St. Louis, and San Francisco.[93] In 1909, Columbus Day became a legal holiday. New York Italian Americans staged three parades that year—two in Brooklyn and one in Manhattan, the latter characterized by the *New York Times* as "the most brilliant parade ever given by Italians in this city." Italian residents of the East Side also marked the occasion on a domestic level: "Not a window in the Italian districts but held an Italian or American flag. And in many a window was the picture of Columbus."[94]

Columbus Day celebrants in San Francisco have staged an especially elaborate ceremony which culminates in a reenactment of Christopher Columbus' landing in the New World. Scheduled for a weekend near 12 October, the California city's Columbus Day has usually begun on Saturday night with a Grand Ball where the young woman chosen to portray Queen Isabella in the next day's reenactment receives her crown. In 1947, a special Mass was celebrated in Saints Peter and Paul Church in the North Beach section of the city, a neighborhood with a considerable Italian-American population. At one o'clock a parade assembled at the Civic Center to begin its route to Aquatic Park. Led by a float bearing "Queen Isabella," five thousand marchers represented a variety of organizations: military bands, drill teams, horseback patrols, and ethnic societies including the Irish Freedom League and the Native Daughters of the Golden West as well as the Italian Catholic Federation.

Meanwhile, festivities had begun at Aquatic Park with such entertainments as a symphony concert and a firefighters' demonstration. These climaxed in patriotic displays upon the arrival of the parade. On the nearby beach, an "Indian" village and a platform for the queen had been set up to await the arrival of Columbus. Three boats donated by Italian-American fishermen and outfitted to resemble the *Pinta, Niña,* and *Santa Maria* sailed into the cove and lowered anchor. A local organizer of the event, assuming the role of Columbus, came ashore by rowboat, smoked a peace pipe with some people costumed as Indians, and concluded the day's activities by giving an account of his voyage to Queen Isabella.[95]

Observances such as this, which have remained a feature of the city's calendar for late September or early October into the 1990s, represent an elaborate extreme, in which Italian-American ethnicity may become secondary to generalized civic patriotism. In fact, some commentators have argued that most Columbus Day parades and other ceremonies represent a combination of American features such as the San Francisco pageant with traditional Italian ways of honoring admired individuals, particularly the saint's procession.[96] Moreover, as an expression of group identity, the secular Columbus Day has tended to obliterate the regional loyalties that have characterized many religious *feste* patterned on Old World models. For example, an account of the 1909 Columbus Day in Hurley, Wisconsin, emphasized that this "occasion for the display of both American patriotism and Italian pride" resulted from the cooperation of the town's six Italian clubs, most of which represented regional Italian identities:

> The parade will be one of the chief features of the celebration and will be participated in by all of the Italian societies of the [Gogebic Iron] Range in their regalia and several fraternal organizations. The Hurley and Norrie bands will furnish music all day. A large float has been constructed representing the *Santa Maria*, Columbus' flag ship.... [T]he parade will be through the principal streets of Hurley and Ironwood and on its return will go to the Hurley ball park where the representation of the landing of Columbus will be enacted.... [A]n elaborate dinner will be served at the Burton Hotel at one dollar per plate. In the evening the grand ball will be given at Bonino's Hall.[97]

Less grandiose recognitions of Columbus Day may involve special dinners at the local Italian club. For example, the traditional Columbus Day menu at the Masontown, Pennsylvania, Italo-American Citizens Club features *tripa* (beef tripe) with appropriate sauce and pasta and plenty of red wine. Other Italian-American communities might hold a dance to honor the anniversary of the

Ligurian explorer's landfall in the New World. As third- and fourth-generation Italians in America have lessened their ties to the *paesi* of their ancestors, Columbus Day has become the quintessential expression of their sense of ethnicity, even if the celebration seems to pale in comparison to those in San Francisco and New York City.

Other Calendar Customs

Christmas, the Lenten season interrupted by Saint Joseph's Day and culminating in Easter, summer saints' *feste,* and Columbus Day represent the most visible events in the Italian-American traditional calendar. Several other seasonal customs should be noted because they contribute to community-building and provide welcome breaks in the routine of existence, just as their better-known counterparts do.

Beginning again with Advent, the start of the Church year, some Italian Americans observe the feast day of Saint Lucy *(Santa Lucia)* on 13 December. This Sicilian virgin martyr lived, according to her legend, during the reign of the emperor Diocletian. When her mother was cured of a serious illness, Lucy persuaded her to distribute all her wealth to the poor. The young man to whom Lucy was betrothed denounced her to the Roman officials, but they could not remove her to their dungeon. Miraculously affixed to the spot on which she stood, Lucy endured boiling oil and burning pitch until she was slain by a sword.

Tradition holds that Lucy was blind, and she is often depicted bearing her eyeballs on a platter. Saint Lucy, thus, became associated in folk religion with eyesight, and people with vision problems took their cases to her. Italian Americans might observe Saint Lucy's Day by abstaining from eating anything made with flour. According to Josephine Fastuca, "We wouldn't eat any noodles or anything made with flour. We would eat beans. We'd eat rice and meat and potatoes, but no bread that day."[98] Etta Ferraro Goodwin remembered a Campanian custom her grandmother, who had immigrated to Peace Dale, Rhode Island, at an advanced age, continued to practice on St. Lucy's Day:

> In the little neighborhood where we lived there were many other Italian families. And this was an Italian custom. She would be up

at five o'clock in the morning and with her pot of hot chocolate and with her dish or plate of these goodies that she had prepared the day before she would knock at the doors of her special friends and share with them this custom which she celebrated in Italy.[99]

Italian-American celebrations of the secular New Year's Day on 1 January and its Eve have drawn as much from contacts with other ethnic groups in the United States as from distinctive Italian heritages. Occasionally, recent immigrants will continue Old World customs for this holiday. One restaurateur, who first came to this country in 1960s, invites friends and employees to join him in breaking crockery on New Year's Eve, a rite of purgation from his native Tuscany.[100] Elsewhere Italian Americans have adopted and adapted customs from other ethnic groups for their New Year's observances. For example, a favored food for New Year's dinner is pork, which is supposed to bring good luck or wealth in the coming year. On the other hand, one should avoid fowl, especially chicken, since eating it will produce poverty. Some hold that eating fish at midnight on New Year's Eve will result in good luck.[101] Leaving a coin on the windowsill on New Year's Eve may generate wealth for the year to come.[102]

Coming near the summer solstice, Saint John's Day (24 June) has provided the setting for many folk customs in Europe and North America. Ligurians who settled in California believed that the dew on the morning of this day had beneficial effects and that people should walk out barefooted before it evaporated. They hung clothes out on the Eve of Saint John so that they might catch the morning dew. These clothes were then stored and used to wrap sore throats. Saint John's Day dew could also serve as a moth repellent. Moreover, if one cut the flowers of the elderberry before sunrise on Saint John's Day, when its healing power peaked, they could be steeped to make a tea efficacious for treating colds and sore eyes.[103]

On All Souls Day (1 November) some Italian Americans set food on the table for their dead relatives. They might also leave a light illuminated all through the night on All Souls Eve so that the dead might easily find their former dwelling places. Children who put clean, polished shoes outside their doors on All Souls Eve might find them filled with candy the next morning.[104]

The yearly round—which would include events like these and more family-oriented customs such as birthdays and wedding anniversaries—continues to provide Italian Americans with a sense of group identity. More than anything, calendar customs demonstrate that one belongs to a community composed of family members, *paesani,* or Italian Americans in general. In short, they help people know who they are.

CHAPTER FIVE

Folk Supernaturalism

IN AN ESSAY PUBLISHED IN 1928, Giuseppe Cautela described how, when a friend's son died, the local parish priest refused to bless the dead boy until after the regularly scheduled noon Mass was over. When he did say a few words to the grieving family, he spoke in "incorrect Italian," and the gist of his remarks was that everyone in attendance should buy a candle for twenty-five cents from the sacristan to hold during the blessing. The priest's behavior produced some strongly worded sentiments, especially from the male mourners, who directed a "terrible lashing" at the "tyranny of the church and the priests."[1]

This incident exemplifies the relationship between the Roman Catholic Church in the United States and Italian Americans during the peak years of immigration and for some time thereafter. Representatives of the Church bemoaned what they called the "Italian Problem," the sad fact that many of these ostensible Catholics did not attend or support the Church, preferring to devote themselves to what one observer called "a hideous web of superstition."[2] They particularly lamented the anti-clericalism of southern Italians, who tended to equate the Church with the oppressive forces which they had fled Italy to escape. Italian-American men were especially hostile to the clergy, whose authority might sometimes conflict with their own patriarchal control of the family. Joanne Dorio characterized her male ancestors' attitude toward the authority of the Church:

> It was almost a conflict of power between the Italian priests and the Italian families.... My grandfather was that way too. The men didn't believe in the priest's authority.... [T]hey did not want the priest to tell them how to raise us. I remember that just out of spite, my father did not have me baptized until I was twelve years old.[3]

Joseph Napoli's Sicilian-American father bluntly characterized priests as "crows."[4]

The Catholic hierarchy in America, largely Irish and German, emphasized the importance of respect for the clergy, financial support for the Church, and routine piety, all of which were foreign to the religious experience of most *contadini*.[5] Religion for southern Italians had reflected the spirit of *campanilismo,* more devotion sometimes being offered to the patron saints of specific communities than to the Trinity. Emotional identification with these saints and the Virgin Mary—much more approachable than God the Father—manifested itself in *feste* such as those described in chapter 4, in home and yard shrines, and in practices verging on magic. The Church, which traditionally received much more support from women than from men, figured in their lives only at rites of passage such as baptisms, weddings, and funerals.

When southern Italians came to the United States, they found the tone of Catholicism much different from what they had previously known. Legalistic and formal, the Church focused on a patriarchal deity and opposed many of the practices which the Italian immigrants believed to be central to religious devotion. Consequently, Italian immigrants found the American Church to be "a cold and almost puritanical organization" that failed to meet their religious needs and in some cases overtly opposed their devotional activities.[6]

The antagonism between American Catholicism and Italian-American folk piety can be exemplified by the situation in Providence, Rhode Island. In an attempt to win Italian loyalties, Bishop Matthew Harkins established an Italian "national parish," Holy Ghost, on Federal Hill in 1889. Not reckoning on *campanilismo,* though, he appointed a succession of northern Italian priests, who had as little sympathy for southern Italian vernacular religion as the Irish-American clergy. Particular conflict arose between the priests and the Italian mutual benefit societies which sponsored saints' *feste.* Tension peaked in 1907 when Father Anthony Bove halted the collection of funds for fireworks for the *festa* of Saint Rocco on 16 August. Several thousand Italian Americans gathered at his church with the intention of taking the keys from the sexton and closing the building to the priest.[7]

Most often poor relations with the Church assumed the form of indifference. As in the Old World, women continued to be more interested in religion than men, but even they utilized the Church only for the most necessary purposes. For example, a Sicilian-American woman recalled,

> The religious services available to us during our early years were adequate. We availed ourselves only of church attendance and priests' services for special religious holidays and what I term vital statistics. That is, we were baptized soon after birth, made our First Communion after proper instruction, took on an additional name for Confirmation, were married in the Church and buried with a High Mass and/or grave rites.[8]

On a day-to-day basis, Italian Americans continued to cultivate affective relationships with supernatural figures "who seem[ed] so human to them," entities such as the Virgin Mary, the patron saint of the *paese,* and other saints as needed. So in times of special concern, Italian Americans might appeal to Saints Biagio (for sore throat), Lucy (for eye problems), Rita (for gynecological ailments), Rocco (originally for plague, but by extension for other serious diseases), and Jude (for seemingly hopeless situations).[9]

Devotion to the Virgin and the saints could involve home altars with candles and votive lamps burning before holy pictures and statues, yard shrines (perhaps built in fulfillment of a vow) which displayed plaster statues often protected from the elements by carefully constructed shelters, special prayers and foods for the saint's feast day, medals and other amulets associated with the saint worn around the neck or pinned to clothing, vows fulfilled in return for the saint's positive response to petitions, and participation in the elaborate summer *feste* which honored the saint and during which vows might be kept by walking barefoot in procession behind the saint's statue.[10] A Protestant clergyman, though influenced by his own religious attitudes, characterized one way in which Italian Americans continued the relationships with patron saints that they had begun in their native *paesi:*

When the peasant leaves his native village, he will forget everything but his patron saint. So far well and good. The trouble is that he makes all kinds of bargains with him, ranging from offering to burn a candle before the image of the saint if the latter will help him to carry out a business transaction, to promising to bring a twenty dollar bill when the statue of the saint is to be carried through the streets if he can have the honour of being one of the bearers. A good lady said in reply to my question as to whether she had gone to church on Easter, "I go to church on St. Anthony's Day. He is my favorite saint and is more powerful than Christ, for he has performed more miracles than he. Besides, he is so handsome." The most amusing part of it all is that if the saint by misfortune does not grant the request of his follower, the latter does not hesitate to curse him as a good-for-nothing.[11]

The situation described by Josephine Fastucca was certainly not unusual: in return for a favor, an Italian-American woman might "promise some of her jewelry, like earrings or a pin. When that prayer was granted, she would go and pin this jewelry onto the saint's [statue's] robe."[12] In addition to its spiritual functions, devotion to the saints helped immigrants to maintain ties with their homes in Italy and, in some cases, may have been consciously emphasized to counteract the influence of the Irish- and German-dominated American Church.[13]

In addition to this saints' cult, Italian Americans have recognized a system of angelology and demonology that coexists alongside official Catholic supernaturalism. On one hand, guardian angels watch over each child. Characterized as "extremely partisan," they not only protect their charges, but hide "their heads under their wings" when a child engages in mischief.[14] More obvious than the work of these positive spirits for a people who had inherited a world view tinged with pessimism and fatalism have been the forces of evil. These may be the only moderately harmful *munaceddi*, who engage in simple mischief such as petty thefts and deceptions.[15] But evil finds particular and usually more serious expression in the complex of beliefs and practices known as *malocchio*.

Malocchio

Dorothy Gladys Spicer, a social worker whose clients during the 1920s included many Italian Americans, reported what she considered a curious incident:

> There was Mrs. Vitelli's baby, who was so plump that a neighbor said, "Oh, doesn't Tony look just like a cow?" Immediately ... the baby grew black and frothed at the mouth. To see if he was "overlooked," or afflicted by the dreaded Evil Eye, a drop of oil was put into a glass of water. Instead of spreading over the surface of the water, the oil stayed in one place and looked just like an eye, thus proving the nature of the baby's ailment.
>
> A cure was wrought by bringing in a woman who said an incantation learned on Christmas eve. Any one taught the incantation on the eve of Christ's birth has the power to cure "overlooked" persons; consequently, old wives knowing the charmed words are still much sought after, even in this country.[16]

Especially for southern Italian immigrants, cases such as that described by Spicer have represented folk supernaturalism in its most dramatic form: *malocchio,* belief in the evil eye—also called the "overlook." Connected with the deeply rooted fatalism of the southern Italian peasant world view, *malocchio* reflects a pessimism that perceives potential threats from almost anyone and assumes that good fortune cannot endure. To prosper, according to this world view, is to invite envy. And envy generates ill feelings that may result in harm befalling its target. *Malocchio* makes concrete the abstract envy that pervades a universe defined by only a limited amount of good.[17]

For many Italian Americans the move to the New World mitigated belief in the evil eye. In most cases, *malocchio* seems not to have endured much beyond the first generation of immigrants whose children—upwardly mobile in an economy that did not constrain their dreams of worldly success—accepted a world view in which good was virtually unlimited. For example, 144 questionnaires distributed to Italian Americans living in Greenwich Village in the late 1920s showed that thirty percent of the respondents who were over thirty-five years old believed in the evil eye, while only nineteen percent of the young people admitted such a belief.[18] Though some features of the evil eye belief complex have survived among third- and fourth-generation Italian Americans, they have shed much of their original import and have become associated with more generalized concepts of good and bad luck. For example, in the contemporary Italian-American youth subculture known as "Guido" or "Cugine," some of the amulets that have been traditional protectors from the evil eye have become merely symbols of ethnic identity.[19]

A person falls victim to *malocchio* from either an envious compliment or just an "overlook" by someone with the power to cast a harmful spell.[20] Though this power may have come from a conscious bid such as a diabolical pact, most often people are born with the power to cast *malocchio*. For example, one consequence if a pregnant woman or her husband works on 14 December, the Feast of San Aniello, is having a child born with *malocchio*. Or if a pregnant woman turned her back to the Host when it was elevated during Christmas Eve Mass, her child would be empowered to cast *malocchio*.[21]

Anyone is a potential threat, but Italian Americans have particularly feared a person with heavy eyebrows that grow together in one line. They are also suspicious of someone whose eyes are of different colors.[22] Some believe that a person with the power to cast the evil eye can be identified if people begin to yawn when he or she enters a room.[23] People who do not fit easily into conventional categories are also especially distrusted. For instance, Caroline Ware, who studied Greenwich Village Italian Americans during the 1920s, learned that people were performing traditional acts to ward off *malocchio* behind her back.[24] In practice, though, one has to be cautious around almost anyone.

Particularly susceptible to the evil eye are those who are already otherwise vulnerable, especially children and pregnant women, who may attempt to hide their condition as long as possible.[25] Albina Malpezzi recalled an elderly woman warning her to keep people away from her young daughter:

> In fact, she used to tell me I shouldn't take Francie out so much because Francie was a beautiful child. She had great big black eyes and real curly hair and just as cute. And she'd say, "Somebody's going to give her the evil eye and cause problems."[26]

Frances Gueri Byrd remembered how her mother administered a "mother's blessing" to protect her offspring from "overlooking" by someone they might happen to meet while outside: "There is evil in the world, and she was very careful to keep it away from her children."[27]

Some hold that those who have just recovered from illness should be particularly wary lest their weakened condition allow the gaze of someone with the evil eye to harm them.[28] Still another category of persons especially susceptible to the evil eye are recent immigrants, whose marginal status as expatriates not yet assimilated into the American way of life (not yet "become white") explains their vulnerability.[29]

People born on Tuesdays or Fridays have a natural immunity to being overlooked.[30] Those who are not so fortunate and fear *malocchio* can protect themselves, their loved ones, or their possessions in a variety of ways. When someone offers a compliment without using such ritual disclaimers as *"Benedica"* or "God bless you,"[31] or when in the presence of a person suspected of possessing the evil eye, the preventive response may be a gesture: the sign of the cross, the *mano di cornuto* (extending the index and little fingers from the clenched left fist to resemble a goat's horns), or the *mano in fica* (the "fig gesture" representing sexual intercourse in which the thumb is inserted between the first and second fingers).[32] Or one can keep his fingers or legs crossed while in the presence of a suspected possessor of *malocchio*. Some recommend spitting upon being complimented or immediately touching an object made from iron.[33] A more elaborate ritual has the recipient of a compliment say while scratching his or her buttocks: *"Fo sangue mio fratella / Sempre e buona una gratella"* ("Even if it is my brother, I will scratch myself anyway").[34]

Yet it may not always be convenient to respond immediately to specific threats of *malocchio*, and one cannot always be sure that every threat will even be detected. Consequently, Italian Americans may wear or carry amulets which offer more or less constant protection from the evil eye. Such objects can assume several forms, many of them with points perhaps to pierce the evil eye threat.

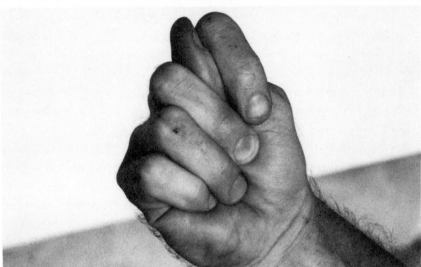

*Hand gestures can offer protection from the threat of **malocchio**. The **mano di cornuto**, representing a pair of horns, and the **mano in fica**, which has obscene connotations, are usually made furtively when in the presence of someone suspected of having the power to cast the evil eye. Amulets made in the shape of these gestures are also available.*

Particularly favored is the *corno,* which may take shape as the actual horns of an animal such as a goat, crab claws, pointed "horns" made of gold or red coral, or even pointed vegetables such as peppers (especially red chiles). In plastic versions, the *corno* appears as a merging of horn and chile and may be worn on key rings, around the neck, as a bracelet charm, or as a watch fob. Hung from the rearview mirror of an automobile, it has lost some of its specific significance as a shield against the evil eye and has come to mean general good luck.[35] Richard Gambino's Sicilian-American grandparents kept a pair of bull's horns painted bright red hanging over their front door to ward off evil. In Jerre Mangione's family, also from Sicily, a visitor "could not enter the house without passing underneath the locked horns over the doorway, thereby losing whatever evil he might be trying to smuggle in."[36]

Other amulets cast in coral, precious metal, or (most often) plastic represent the hand gestures *(mano di cornuto* and *mano in fica)* used to respond to immediate evil eye threats. Or one may ward off *malocchio* by wearing a charm in the form of *il gobbo,* a hunchback carved from mother of pearl, coral, or white plastic and often depicted clutching a *corno.* Horseshoes can also offer protection from evil eye—real ones nailed over the door of one's home, or plastic imitations dangled from the car mirror. The latter take on additional efficacy when a small plastic *corno* hangs from the arch.

Scissors also can "pierce" the evil eye and so may be used as an amulet. Leaving the imprint of scissors in freshly poured concrete protects a new building. Other objects with protective properties include a red ribbon tied on a newly purchased object such as a car, boat, or house, a pinch of salt kept in the pocket or tied in the corner of a handkerchief, a gold key, a clove of garlic, crossed straight pins, any metal worn next to the skin, a religious medal (one depicting Saint Christopher being particularly effective in automobiles), or blessed palms from Palm Sunday placed under the carpet with salt or incense. One may be able to prevent *malocchio* by the simple method of putting on the left stocking first each morning.[37]

Since the very young are especially vulnerable to evil eye, mothers take special precautions. For their protection babies once were swaddled from head to toe in cloth strips which could be removed only under the most guarded conditions. Or they might wear entire necklaces of red coral *corni*. A religious medal or piece of cowhorn may be pinned to a child's undershirt, and garlic placed in the crib. Alternatively, the child may be made to wear a bag filled with salt, bits of palm blessed on Palm Sunday, and pictures of saints.[38] Frances Gueri Byrd's mother was among the especially cautious:

> In New Jersey it was cold most of the time, and we wore under-shirts most of the year, you know, except summer—deep summer. And we always had—we either had a cross hanging on us, you know, a crucifix on a chain.... Or we had little—as little babies we'd have them pinned on: little medals, blessed medals, and the scapulars.[39]

Angelo Bertocci's mother maintained her vigilance even after he was fully grown. He went off for the first day of college with a string of rosary beads, color pictures of the Virgin Mary and Saints Cosimo and Damiano, and an amulet of garlic for protection against "the evil eye and all demons within and without."[40]

No matter how careful one is, though, *malocchio* does sometimes take effect. Typically one who has been "overlooked" or received a compliment from a person with evil eye will suddenly and unexplainedly become ill. Afflicted people may experience a "special kind of headache" with "pain so acute as to prevent them from continuing normal activity." The pain may be "centered around the forehead and eyes," producing a sense of having "heavy eyes." The general effect may be a "groggy" feeling: "It's like you're on dope and you've taken an overdose of sleeping pills and you get up, and you keep yawning and yawning. It's a tired, tired feeling." Other symptoms may include stomachache, nausea, nervousness, and fever.[41]

Since these symptoms may also arise from purely natural causes, traditional diagnostic procedures may be called upon to confirm that evil eye is indeed a factor in a person's illness. Sometimes called "making" *malocchio*, the most widely reported of these procedures requires someone, usually a matriarch who is regarded as *comare* to the community, to let three drops of olive oil fall into a bowl of water. If the drops remain intact, the victim's symptoms have resulted from natural forces; but if the drops coalesce and produce an amorphous slick on the water surface, evil eye is present.[42] That social worker Spicer reported just the opposite conclusions from the disposition of the oil upon the water may reflect traditional variation in the procedure or her own misunderstanding of the diagnosis.

Another diagnostic procedure requires that a saucer be half filled with water. Then a piece of olive leaf blessed on Palm Sunday is dropped in, and the saucer is briefly placed on the victim's head. While the victim holds the right index finger in the water, the diagnostician begins to add the olive oil. If the first drop disperses, then a man has overlooked the victim. If the second drop spreads, a woman is responsible. The diffusion of the third drop suggests that the source of the *malocchio* comes from beyond the grave.[43] One may be able to determine the gender of the person causing the evil eye by how the drops of oil hold together in the water. According to one theory, if they break apart, a woman is the source, but a man is indicated as perpetrator of *malocchio* if the drop coheres.[44] A variant method of diagnosis has one drop grains of wheat into a saucer of water. If they float, the presence of evil eye is indicated. The pattern they form can determine the remedy.[45]

Once the diagnosis of *malocchio* is confirmed, a curing procedure should immediately begin. If a victim of evil eye sleeps before being cured, the case will worsen. One point of view holds that *malocchio* must be removed by sundown on Friday, or it will persist throughout the victim's life.[46]

Italian Americans have utilized a wide variety of cures, most said to have been discovered by Saint Lucy. They have generally held that the healer must be a woman and that she can only learn the procedures for curing on Christmas Eve from a family member. She must also accept no money for performing these procedures.[47] Perhaps the most common cure is an extension of the oil-and-water diagnostic test. After confirming that *malocchio* is present, the curer disposes of the water where no one is likely to walk over it. Then she prepares another dish of water. The simplest procedure requires that she recite a prayer or charm while making the sign of the cross over the victim. Her words may be a familiar religious invocation

In order to diagnose and cure illness brought on by **malocchio,** many Italian Americans have used a procedure involving olive oil and water. If, after being dropped into the water, the oil disperses, the evil eye is indeed present. To counteract it, one may pierce the oil with scissors while reciting a charm learned on Christmas Eve.

such as the Hail Mary or the Our Father, or she may recite special, often esoteric healing formulas:

> *Occhi e contro occhi e perticelli agli occhi.*
> *Crepa la invidia e schiattono gli occhi.*
> (Eyes and against eyes and the little openings to the eyes.
> Envy splits [or dies] and eyes burst.) Sicilian.

> *Schiatta mal occhio*
> *E non piu avanti.*
> (Burst evil eye
> And go no further.) Sicilian.[48]

> *Santa Rosalia,*
> *l'acqua veniva.*
> *C'era una donna,*
> *mal'occhio teneva.*
> *Passò nostro Signore*
> *con palma d'oliva in mano.*
> *L'acqua fece seccare,*
> *L'erba fece malagnare,*
> *a quattro cantoni spumicava.*
> *Padre, Figlio e Spirito Santo.*
> (Saint Rosalie,
> The water came flowing.
> There was a woman,
> Who had the evil eye.
> Our Lord passed by
> With an olive palm in his hand.
> He made the water dry up,
> The grass he made to wither,
> Cast it to the four corners [of the earth].
> Father, Son and Holy Spirit.) Calabrian.

> *Corpus Domine e Passione di Cristo*
> *libera nos dal'occhio tristo.*
> (May the Body and Passion of Our Lord
> Save us from the Evil Eye.) Campanian.

> *Occhio morto, occhio tristo*
> *ti seguito coll'acqua, olio*
> *e Gesù Cristo.*
> (Eye of death, Evil Eye,
> I am following you with water,
> Oil and Jesus Christ.) Campanian.

Ciglia cigliamo,
coltello tagliamo,
menamelo a mare.
(We pare the eyelash,
We cut it with a knife,
Take it to the sea.) Campanian.

Ciglia di fronte
male che affronta.
(Eyelash of the face
Evil which insults.) Campanian.

Cristo, Cristiello!
Tu sei buono
Ma è più buono quello.
(Christ, little Christ!
Thou art good
But how much better is he [Satan].) Calabrian.[49]

Then the olive oil drop test is repeated. If the drops still disperse, the curer goes through the procedure again, repeating it up to a dozen times or until the drops retain their shape. Variations on this ritual suggest that the oil will form "eyes" when poured into the water. These should be cut with scissors. Others believe that the saucer filled with oil and water must be held over the victim's head while the charms are recited, that the oil and water should be poured onto the victim's head, or that the curing procedure must always involve three iron tools (usually scissors, screwdriver, and knife).[50]

An elaborate variation on this process has the curer dispose of the oil and water from the diagnostic ceremony by either dumping it in an out-of-the-way place, having the victim drink it, or adding salt and throwing it out the window. The last alternative has the curer saying,

Aqua e sali
Soco fanno limaari
Non chi pozza giovaro.
(Water and salt
I hope that whatever
The witches devise will fail.)

Then the victim should respond,

San Anna, San Anna sia
Cu ava fari mali a [own name]
Bene sini sia.
(Saint Anne, Saint Anne,
Whoever wish[es] harm to befall [own name]
I only wish you well.)[51]

Other ways of curing *malocchio* involve cutting through the oil slick on the surface of the diagnostic water with a knife or key three times. The knife or key may also be used to make the sign of the cross over the victim and to drop the olive oil into the water, or one can fashion a cross by inserting a needle through the eye of another needle. Then that should be floated in a saucer of water.[52]

Another set of beliefs recognizes gradations of severity in the illness caused by overlooking. For easy cases, the curer would simply dip her thumb in olive oil and make the sign of the cross on the victim's forehead; more serious cases require that the victim's entire body be anointed with olive oil; the most extreme cases call for the application of a mustard plaster to the afflicted person's chest.[53] Or evil eye sickness may be combatted by dropping a pair of scissors near the victim, hanging a packet of garlic around his or her neck, and then touching olive oil to his or her forehead. A related practice recommends rubbing olive oil on the victim's head to drive *malocchio* from the mind and on his or her chest to banish it from the soul.[54] One may burn or boil the victim's clothing to remove *malocchio,* burn feathers from the victim's pillow, pray over the victim's clothes, or fry a beef heart while continually pricking it with a fork.[55] Another remedy requires the curer to obtain a garment from the possessor of the evil eye which measures at least two-and-a-half times the length between the victim's elbows and fingertips. She should measure the garment three times while saying appropriate prayers. The victim wears the garment until the ailment disappears.[56]

Since *malocchio* may often result from inadvertent action on the part of the possessor of evil eye, such as a failure to add a blessing after offering a compliment, Italian Americans seldom attempt to retaliate for falling victim to this ubiquitous threat. However, occasional practices for turning *malocchio* back on the perpetrator have been used. For instance, giving him or her a lock of the victim's hair may have that effect.[57]

The current status of *malocchio* belief is hard to assess. Certainly many people still fear the threat of evil eye and take appropriate prophylactic or remedial measures. But others claim to have only vague knowledge of it or not to have heard of it at all. Overt belief in the power of overlooking by acculturated Italian Americans is limited and, like folk supernaturalism in other cultures, may surface only at times of crisis—in the case of *malocchio,* instances of mysterious illness.

Monsters

In addition to their beliefs in saints, guardian angels, mischievous demons, and the serious threat of *malocchio,* some Italian Americans have retained belief in a variety of supernatural beings which their ancestors had known and feared in the Old Country. Principal among these was the *lupu manaru,* or werewolf. Most often males, people become werewolves by being born on Christmas Eve at the stroke of midnight and are most likely to experience the transfomation from human to lupine form on that date each year. Being born during a full moon may also cause one to become a werewolf. If so, the monstrous change may occur at each climax of the lunar cycle. The transformation may be complete—the person becoming utterly a wolf physically and psychologically—or it may involve only the growth of hair and a psychological change. Someone with this curse can be cured if blood is drawn from his forehead while in the wolf state. He may be killed with a silver bullet or by being pricked three times with a pin.[58]

Most stories of werewolf activity told by Italians in this country are set in Italy. For example, a woman told folklore collector Michael Brunetti about a man who had been born at midnight on Christmas Eve:

> When this man got married he told his wife that when he went out on Christmas eve, she was not to let him back in the house until he had come to the door and knocked for the third time. On one Christmas even [sic] his wife fell asleep. When the man, still a werewolf, banged on the door for the second time, his wife awoke.

Thinking it was the third time her husband had come to the door, she let him in and was killed.[59]

One recourse that might have saved the woman's life was for her to stand on the third step of a church.[60]

Other supernatural threats recalled from Italy included the *mamm'Adraia,* or hydra; the *stajaga,* the spirit of the dead which returns to punish its enemies; and the *fiammetta,* or will-o-the-wisp.[61] About the last, an immigrant from Lombardy noted,

> They almost died when they saw the *fiammetta* in their fields. In the daytime the priest would come with his holy water and bless all the ground where it had been, but then he would run away. He was afraid too. And the ground where it had been—no one wanted to work there anymore.[62]

Unlike *malocchio,* most monsters of Italian folk supernaturalism did not make the Atlantic crossing, perhaps because in many cases they were associated with specific sites in or near a particular *paese.*

Luck

If a propensity toward fatalism lies at the foundation of much Italian-American folk supernaturalism, it finds its most prosaic expression in beliefs and practices focusing on luck. The old peasant world view of limited good meant that everyone would have a share of misfortune and could expect only a minimal amount of good luck. Whenever something good happened, the lucky person should expect unhappiness in the near future. Among southern Italians in Brooklyn, this bleak view has applied especially to lucky gamblers:

> We all faithfully believed that a bettor never ever wins completely; there always is a piece of bad news coming down the pike to let him have it in the teeth.... There wasn't a kid in the neighborhood who didn't believe this tit-for-tat philosophy. We may not have had any religious credence, but we certainly felt that there was some force afoot to balance any luck we might have had. Something good has happened—hold your breath, here comes the bad.[63]

Those who win at numbers or at some other gambling pursuit, though, may be able to avert the bad luck that will follow by sharing their winnings.[64]

No such notion of limits informed beliefs about bad luck. Immigrant laborers early in this century, for instance, assumed that if a worker had an accident, it was *destina* that other accidents would follow—a fear that inconvenienced employers when entire Italian-American work gangs would leave a job after some mishap.[65] Various omens forecast imminent bad luck: hearing a dog baying while one prayed at night, having a bird fly in a window, hearing a bird chirping at one's window, encountering a female hunchback, dropping scissors, finding an open safety pin, or spilling wine or olive oil, for instance.[66]

One can also bring bad luck on oneself by committing such traditional blunders as pointing at a star, crossing one's eating utensils, killing a spider, buying a new broom in August, or sweeping house dust outside especially at night.[67] Dreams may be particularly reliable prognosticators of coming misfortune. Often an Italian American would expect bad luck if he or she dreamed of old wood, descending a ladder, tooth loss, babies, an enemy, raw meat, rats, a wedding, muddy water, a banquet, floods, storms, coal, or money.[68] While dreams of these subjects indicated general bad luck, other dreams were interpreted more specifically: snakes meant that one was a victim of gossip, and teeth or an egg forewarned of the loss of a friend, for instance.[69]

Fatalistic pessimism may account for the relative paucity of ways to avert the misfortune which these omens predict. But one can ward off bad luck and perhaps encourage a somewhat positive future in a more general sense by sprinkling a house with salt, especially after an indicator of potential misfortune has occurred. Use of amulets that protect against the evil eye and of objects associated with official religion such as holy water and pictures of saints can also assist a household in attaining what little good fortune is its due.[70]

While omens of good luck are fewer than those which predict bad, Italian Americans might become optimistic upon seeing a male hunchback, a shooting star, or a lizard, butterfly, or moth in the house.[71] Dreams which foretold a fortunate future might deal with a funeral, running horse, swimming fish, priest, or bright red.[72] More specifically, dreaming of lice meant that one would soon receive some money, while dreaming of fire indicated that a letter was on its way.[73] One could encourage good luck by bringing a broom, bread, and salt into a new house, carrying salt in one's pocket, and, if a fisherman, placing palms blessed on Palm Sunday aboard ship.[74]

Weather conditions often seem to be the product of luck. Italian Americans, especially those whose occupations place them at the mercy of the weather, have often tried to affect weather through folk supernaturalism. For example, Sicilian-American fishermen along the Texas Gulf Coast have feared that a storm is brewing when shrimp turn red. To break up a waterspout, a tradition which their ancestors brought from Sicily suggests making the sign of the cross with a white-handled knife while reciting words that can be learned only on Christmas Eve. Dwellers on land have used a similar procedure to dispel a tornado. One can also gain protection from a storm by lighting blessed candles or burning palms blessed on Palm Sunday.[75]

While these and other evidences of folk supernaturalism survive among some Italian Americans, they figure less prominently in the lives of children and grandchildren of immigrants than they did for people born in Italy. Partially due to the general influence of Americanization, the lessening hold of traditional spiritual beliefs also stems from developments in the Catholic Church in the United States. An Italian-American clergy, increased official acceptance of some form of traditional piety, and the more visible role of the Church as a focus for ethnic identity on a pan-Italian rather than a regional basis gave Italians in America a religious institution with which they could feel comfortable as early as the 1920s. In Greenwich Village, for example, the second generation became active participants in the life of the parish, devoting themselves to its patron instead of the saints of their *paesi.* The parish, in turn, introduced a festival in the patron's honor which resembled the familiar *festa.*[76] Elsewhere, charismatic clergymen were able to attract Italian Americans by reactivating the folk piety that the Irish- and German-dominated Church had stifled.[77] The heritage of traditional supernaturalism may endure, but with much less exclusivity than was once the case.

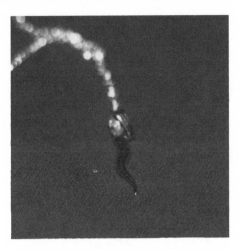

For constant protection from **malocchio**, *some Italian Americans have used the* **corno**, *an amulet shaped like a horn. The* **corno** *may be worn on a necklace or keychain, hung from an automobile mirror, or pinned to clothing. The meaning of this symbol has expanded to include good luck in general or simply Italian-American identity.*

CHAPTER SIX

Folk Medicine

IN APRIL 1892 A NEW YORK newspaper reported a court case involving several Italian Americans. One of them, Joseph Libertino, was charged by another, Pasquale Siessone, with "violation of the medical law." Ill with pneumonia, Siessone had sent for Libertino and his brother Vincenzo, who said "he needed an overhauling, and they overhauled him." First stripping the sick man and blowing in his face, they then made cuts "about his legs and toes" which bled freely. They wet their hands in the blood and rubbed it over his body. Next they cut off a lock of Siessone's hair, placed it in an envelope addressed to "the Prince of Hades," and consigned it to the fire.

The Libertino brothers repeated this last procedure four times and then demanded $120, an amount that would increase by $380 should Siessone actually be cured. The judge in the case fined all parties for their participation. Vincenzo Libertino "declared that he possessed supernatural powers, but W. A. Purrington, counsel for the County Medical Society, said he was an arrant fraud."[1]

While a century later we cannot know enough about the motivations of the Libertino brothers to contradict categorically attorney Purrington's assessment, we can guess that it was produced as much by ethnic and professional prejudging as it was by a dispassionate consideration of Siessone's case. We can also suggest that some folk medical method existed behind the apparently chaotic procedures which the Libertinos performed on their ailing client.

The most dramatic of these, the series of razor cuts that caused profuse bleeding, was most likely an example of the practice of "cupping," which was supposed to produce flows of blood to drain noxious forces from the system. Though it had become obsolete in the professional medical science of the late nineteenth century, it and other methods of bloodletting remained part of the folk medicine of Italian immigrants. For example, Josephine Fastuca reported that older Italian Americans "used to lance people in the back and this was supposed to take the poison out. Then they had leeches, and they believed when the leeches died, they were dying from the poison they took out of the sick person."[2]

Combining this folk science with supernaturalism—as the Libertinos did by invoking diabolical forces—also represents traditional practice, since very often folk etiology for illness suggested causation from both natural and supernatural worlds. Quite possibly, then, the defendants in this court case were merely carrying out medical procedures that they had learned through traditional channels and that they believed to be entirely efficacious.

While southern Italian religious views were often the bane of representatives of official Catholicism in the United States, health professionals had to deal with attitudes and practices toward health, disease, and curing brought from Italy that often seemed to have little real merit. A social worker writing in the 1920s, a generation after the Libertino case, characterized the fears that Italian immigrants still typically had regarding hospitals and other institutions associated with modern medicine. As she noted, "The average Italian immigrant dreads the hospital as a lonely place where one is sent to die, not to get well; where one must submit to unpleasant foods and odors; where all sorts of experiments are tried on unwilling victims, and where the 'black bottle' is passed when doctor or nurse want quietly to put a troublesome patient out of the way."[3] Instead, many Italian Americans then and now have preferred to place their medical needs in the hands of traditional healers.

Many Italian-American women have had knowledge of folk prophylactics and cures which they use for the daily health of family members. At the same time, folk medical specialists, individuals with special knowledge and gifts, were available for serious ailments. Particularly when an illness lasted for some time or when its cause was uncertain, Italian Americans went to folk healers, usually women, who could diagnose the source of an ailment, perform the necessary procedures for curing it, and prescribe additional remedial activity as needed. Such healers usually had to be versed in two kinds of medicine: one based on a folk pharmacopeia of herbs and other natural ingredients, and one requiring expertise in magical counteractants to illness. The latter often overlapped with cures for *malocchio*, but it also included magical responses to ailments whose causation was purely natural. Sometimes the healer would rely on only one kind of medicine, but sometimes she had to combine the natural and the magical to effect the required cure.[4]

Some communities had folk medical specialists, such as the *spilato* among Sicilians in Buffalo, New York. This person, blessed with an inborn healing gift that became honed through instruction traditionally by a relative, could use his or her hands to cure sprains, strains, stiffness, bruises, and other skeleto-muscular disorders.[5] Generally, specialists in magical healing were able to practice their skills in the United States much more effectively than those who relied on natural remedies, since the ingredients for the latter were often unavailable in the New World and might be replaced by relatively inexpensive patent medications that were available to anyone.[6] Usually the herbal remedies that have endured in Italian-American folk tradition are those requiring no specialized healer status within the community. They are truly "home remedies."

There is also an interplay between scientific and magical folk medicine, seen in some ways in which Italian Americans have traditionally promoted good health. These include drinking holy water, eating a bowl of grapes on New Year's Day before rising, putting blessed palms from Palm Sunday beneath the mattress, sprinkling clothes with salt, wearing garlic or camphor in a pouch around the neck, or having a priest bless one's house.[7]

The lack of clear distinction between magically and naturally induced illness is further suggested by health omens in the culture's medical folklore. Spilling wine or dreaming of coins means that one will enjoy good health, but sickness is forecast by dreams of a snake, snow, or paper money or by spilling olive oil while cooking. Future health can be predicted by breaking open a walnut on Christmas Eve. If it is good inside, good health will occur during the next year, but a rotten nut forecasts poor health.[8] Moreover, the blurred distinction between natural and supernatural in the cause and treat-

ment of illness can be seen in such prophylactic measures as having
children wear copies of the black habit of Saint Anthony to protect
them from chronic ill health.[9]

The Folk Pharmacopeia

Italian-American folk medicine attributes the cause of most
ailments to natural factors. While a germ or viral theory of illness
may not be a part of this belief system, and cause-effect relationships
between natural phenomena and illness may not always be clear,
usually such a relationship is believed to be the source of a specific
sickness or of ill health in general. For example, "night air," a natural
phenomenon, has been assumed to be particularly injurious to
health. Consequently, one should always close windows at night
"even in the hottest weather." Night air, according to Rosa Cavilleri,
will "make you sick if you let it get in."[10] Some sort of remedy
derived from nature—based on "folk science"—would be the appropriate treatment for an illness brought on by such a natural
threat.

While, in seeming contradiction to the fear of "night air," fresh
air was thought to be a general cure-all, especially for minor ill-
nesses,[11] most preventives and remedies in the realm of scientific
folk medicine have come from plants. Italian Americans, especially
women, have traditionally used a variety of plants with healing
properties in a variety of ways. One list of the wild plants that figured
in the pharmacopeia includes fennel, deadly nightshade, wild mallow, mullein, dock, and sorrel. To these were added the domestic
herbs basil and rue. All these might be dried and combined, then
mixed with powdered palm leaves and salt. Worn in a pouch around
the neck or soaked in olive oil, the mixture served to treat a variety
of discomforts.[12] Another relatively general medication was the
mustard plaster. Joanne Terranella Burleson described how it was
used: "They made this big goo out of the mustard and put it on your
chest, and then you put a rag on top of that. And then you just lay
there in bed until you knew that that was going to make you well."[13]
A poultice made from cooked linseed had similar general uses:

> Now I remember if you got a cold and, you know, like your chest
> would be real thick with congestion, she [Francesca Capello] used

to use flaxseed and heat it in water, I guess. And then they'd put it between the two cloths and put it on your chest to draw out the—it felt good. And they did the same thing if you had the mumps. Of course, I remember having the mumps, and if you'd hold that, well, it reminds me of today using a heating pad, you know.[14]

Whiskey and linseed poultices were used as preventives by Italian Americans during influenza epidemics early in this century.[15]

General cures more distinctive to Italian-American folk medicine included the camomile plant. Its blossoms were made into a soothing tea used to alleviate several complaints. Camomile tea could be given children for indigestion and might be administered to infants in a baby bottle. It was also efficacious for menstrual cramps and as a mild relaxant: "If you had the bellyache or if you couldn't sleep or something like that, the camomile tea was brewed."[16] Leaves from the camomile plant when soaked in hot water provided some relief from pimples or boils.[17] Tea could also be made from the small, round leaves of the malva (or wild mallow). Its main use may have been as a cleansing tonic; Pearl Malpezzi remembered prunes being added to malva tea for that purpose. It also had soothing effects on swellings of the jaw and on stomachaches.[18]

Though the curative and prophylactic powers of chicken soup may be more often associated with other ethnic groups, some Italian Americans also believed in its medical efficacy, especially *stracciatella,* a "soup of documented therapeutic and recuperative virtues." A whole chicken, including head and feet, was boiled for two hours. Then salt, peppercorns, parsley, small carrots, the leaf end of a celery stalk, half an onion, and ripe or canned tomatoes were added. After boiling for another hour, the broth was strained and the fat removed. Beaten egg and parmesan cheese were mixed into the broth. According to one testimonial, "If you are a matron with young ideas, take *stracciatella.* If you are a gentleman in whom performance and desire are in disequilibrium, *stracciatella* is your soup. If you are an infant and anemic, put *stracciatella* in your little stomach. If you are a convalescent, *stracciatella* is your dish."[19] Vincent Panella's grandmother would make a similar brew every Monday, saying, "It washes away the sins of the weekend."[20]

Garlic has figured prominently in the scientific folk medicine of Italian Americans. It has been used to correct high blood pressure, rheumatism, bronchitis, and swooning. Mixed with butter in hot milk, garlic may be ingested to counteract the symptoms of a cold. A garlic poultice relieves stomachache, and garlic draped around the neck prevents sore throat. Worn around the neck or applied to the navel, garlic relieves children of worms.[21]

In John Fante's novel of the life of immigrants from Abruzzi, *Wait Until Spring, Bandini,* the title character recalls a winter when he almost died of influenza and pneumonia. Disgusted with the pills prescribed by a physician, he eats a half-dozen garlic bulbs, goes to bed, and sweats the illness out.[22] Lucia Matera Ferraro believed firmly in the health benefits of garlic, even if it meant social difficulties for her children. According to her daughter,

> I think we had the remedy of all remedies. I can remember as a little girl. Now we were five children attending school. Five of us. If one came down with a cold, five of us came down with a cold. We were two girls and three boys. The minute one of us had a cold or a little cough or a little sneeze, my mother would go down the cellar where we kept our—we had a root cellar. Because my grandfather who was a gardener took care of it for us.
>
> So she would get the garlic. And this was all home-grown garlic. Get the cloves, string them on a piece of store string because my mother saved all the string that came into the house. She never threw anything away. So she strung up—and we had beads of garlic that we wore to school everyday of the winter time. We were not popular children. No one wanted to sit near us. However, our teacher could do nothing about it. I remember one teacher trying to discourage my oldest brother. He was in the fourth grade, and he went with a necklace of garlic. She did not get too far because my grandmother insisted that her grandchildren be healthy, and if no one could stand the smell of garlic, it was just too bad. And it worked. We never had colds, and we were healthy children.[23]

Other components of Italian-American traditional foodways also had healing properties. The hearty red wine that accompanies the typical meal is efficacious for several disorders, particularly when heated and seasoned with black pepper. Cold symptoms find relief from this drink, as they do from a wine toddy. Red wine would be boiled with cinnamon sticks, cloves, sugar, and a cut-up orange

Basic items in the Italian-American folk pharmacopeia include garlic, red wine, olive oil, and camomile. While the last is primarily an all-purpose sedative, the others—either alone or in combination with other ingredients—are used for a variety of ailments.

(including the rind). A person suffering from an especially severe cold would drink the heated mixture and go to bed immediately to sweat out the sickness.[24] Olive oil has also figured prominently in traditional remedies.[25]

Specific complaints have been addressed by specific remedies. Relief from arthritis, for example, could come from eating grapefruit or the core of a green apple. One could prevent the crippling ailment by drinking alfalfa tea.[26] A common cure for backache required that one wrap a coin in a cloth that was soaked in oil. After a flame was touched to the cloth, it was placed on the back. When a glass or cup was inverted over the burning cloth, the ache was supposed to enter the glass or cup with the smoke. Sprained and injured backs also responded when a coin was taped to them.[27] Cures for boils included applications of a paste made from rancid lard and fine stone dust, bread which had been boiled in milk, and a poultice of bread, sugar, and soap.[28]

In addition to mustard plasters, garlic, and wine, Italian-American folk healers have prescribed a variety of remedies for the common cold. Curative drinks have included a mixture of sugar and sour clover, the juice of boiled onions, and honey mixed with hot milk or whiskey. Fried onions applied to the chest or Vicks on the soles of the feet also provided some relief. One could complement these scientific efforts with a couple of apparently magical practices: wearing a horseshoe nail that had been bent into a ring and placing a pail of hot water under the patient's bed. For minor symptoms such as sniffles or sore throat, rock candy might be recommended.[29]

Minor cuts were treated with rabbit fur, cattails, or a white cloth soaked in lemon juice and sugar. If the cut became infected, briar leaves, an onion heated in olive oil, or a poultice similar to that for boils (made from warm milk, bread, sugar, and soap) could be applied.[30] Eating fried eggs was supposed to cure diarrhea, as was a procedure similar to that for backache. One wrapped a penny in a cloth which had been soaked in olive oil. When the cloth was lit and placed on the navel, the smoke was caught in an inverted glass.[31]

A panoply of cures existed for earache. Drops of breast milk or beet juice might be introduced into the ear; a bag full of heated salt could be placed on the ear; steam from boiling vinegar and water or smoke from a burning piece of cotton which had been soaked in oil could be wafted into the painful ear. Another possibility was to make a cone from paper, insert the point in the ear, and light the other end.[32]

Gold was regarded as a prophylactic for eye troubles. Beginning in infancy, young children wore gold earrings to prevent future eye problems, and the practice continued throughout life. However, if problems did occur, a wash of wine or beaten eggs could be used.[33] A gold ring might cure a sty when placed upon it. Other Italian-American folk remedies for sties have included stabbing them with pillow feathers or making a cross with a needle over them.[34]

Eating dried figs on the first of May was thought to prevent fevers, as was carrying an onion in one's pockets. Fevers could be relieved by placing a raw potato on the sufferer's forehead.[35] One found solace from aching feet by resting them in a pile of cow manure or washing them with epsom salts. Pearl Malpezzi remembered her mother's harvesting the flowers of Queen Anne's lace, boiling them, and soaking her sore legs in the water.[36]

To counteract the effects of a sudden fright, Sicilian Americans suggested a drink made from rhubarb. Should a headache result from a fright or other natural cause, it could be cured by rubbing urine on the forehead, wearing a crown of lemon leaves, placing a mixture of potatoes and coffee grounds on the head, or pouring oil over the head.[37] A plaster made from egg whites beaten until stiff and spread on surgical cotton could be wrapped on a sprain or a simple fracture.[38] Urine would quickly heal raw skin.[39] Gastric ulcers could be soothed by drinking goat's milk or the juice produced by boiling chestnuts. Other kinds of stomach distress might respond to the application of a cup over a burning rag or to a dose of warm water in which bay leaves have been soaked.[40]

This listing only samples the vast quantity of scientific folk cures that have been a part of Italian-American medical lore. Remedies which relied upon plants found growing wild were often associated with a particular region or even *paese* where the needed plant could be found. Valued medicinal plants might be brought from the old country and established in the New World, but often substitutes had to be found among plants indigenous to the new environment. Frequently, such cures were forgotten and substitutes found among the many patent medicines available. As members of the first generation and their descendants became more trusting of medical professionals in the United States, other cures went by the way, their function being taken over by medications purchased at pharmacies. But scientific folk medicine continues to operate for many Italian Americans as a first line of defense against illness. They may turn to the medical community or to magical folk medicine only if traditional scientific remedies fail.

Magical Healing

Anthropologist Bronislaw Malinowski hypothesized that the Trobriand Islanders, a society in the South Pacific which he studied early in this century, turned to magic only when more down-to-earth measures failed to accomplish whatever they wanted. They resorted to magic after other kinds of activity had been tried and proven ineffective—when, in Malinowski's words, people recognize that "science has its limits and that a human mind and human skill are at times impotent."[41] Students of cultures in other parts of the world have found Malinowski's theory applicable, and it seems to offer one way of interpreting Italian-American folk medical practices. Typically, when someone becomes ill, he or she will turn first to medical science. If the illness is a common, relatively minor complaint such as a cold, one consults folk medical science as embodied in modern patent medicines or traditional botanical remedies. Should the problem be unfamiliar or of a serious nature, the scientifically trained medical professional will be sought out. But if scientific remedies—whether they come from folklore or the medical establishment—fail to provide relief, the sufferer may turn to magic, which is usually the province of the folk medical specialist. Magic may also figure in the medical process as a complement to scientific healing, the magical healer performing his or her art as reinforcement for the efforts of the scientist.

The Reverend Enrico Sartorio reported an incident that demonstrated primary reliance on magical healing without initial consultation of someone practicing scientific medicine:

Some time ago I was aroused in the middle of the night to call on a sick man who had, for a short time, attended religious services at the mission. When I arrived at his bedside, it was to hear this man beg me to go to the nearest city and ask a certain old woman to come at once to his rescue. When I asked for the explanation, the man said that once before when he was tortured by the same disease, a form of rheumatism, this old woman, a powerful "maga," had stretched herself at full length on his body, murmured certain magic words, blown seven times on his face, and, behold, he was well.[42]

Sometimes an easily accessible magical healer—a family member, for instance—might be consulted for even the most commonplace ailments. That seems to have been the case with Marie Marchese's Sicilian-born grandfather, who offered relief from his grandchildren's stomachaches:

When you had a stomachache, my mother would take us to Grandpa. Grandpa would get some cooking oil, heat it, and rub it on our stomach. And then he would say—and still today I don't know the prayer. But he would say a prayer, and maybe an hour later your stomach would stop hurting. And that's just the belief. You had to believe in it.

He would use a similar procedure for discomfort in other parts of the body, rubbing the painful area with oil and saying prayers specifically for that area.[43]

This is apparently *mettere la mano al ventro,* which Angelo Bertocci recalled from his years growing up in Boston. When one of the children became ill, an elderly lady was consulted. She

inserted her hand wrinkled and worn, but gentle and so cool, under our clothing and on to our stomachs, and for a quarter of an hour silently transmitted the kindness and calm within her to our fevered little bodies. Then she left, bearing her present, and the next day we were well—invariably, it seems.[44]

Sicilians in Buffalo, New York, used much the same procedure for curing children of timidity. Then they would open windows to allow evil spirits to escape after the prayer had been said.[45] This Sicilian practice resembles the Calabrian *fushunate,* a prayer recited while rubbing the forehead of someone with a headache. The words to the prayer can only be revealed on Christmas day, and the one who passes them on loses his or her healing power.[46]

A similar cure from the Piedmont seems to have been used in much the same way, though it might also supplement scientific procedures. Comforting a sick child, a Piedmontese woman—not necessarily a healing specialist—would chant:

> *Maizina'd bo, maizina'd vaca,*
> *Chi la mal a slu grata.*
> *Maizina'd vaca, maizina'd bo,*
> *Chi lal mal, le tut so.*

Translated from the Piedmontese dialect, this means, according to Pearl Malpezzi, "Medicine of bull, medicine of cow, / Who has a pain can snatch it. / Medicine of cow, medicine of bull, / Who has a pain, it's all yours." Malpezzi, whose mother used this charm and who may still recite it for an ailing great-grandchild, emphasized its psychological rather than supernatural function. She related what she would tell one of her grandchildren who frequently suffered from stomach pains:

> "These are magic words. They'll make you feel better." And she'd be so impressed she'd say, "You know, it does. I feel better now." She would tell me. I forget if I ever told her it's just a—wasn't so. It was just the thing we said.[47]

Similar reliance on magical recitation characterized a cure for erysipelas practiced among Ligurian miners in California. The healer should circle the afflicted area with a silver coin headside down while saying,

> Pain that beats
> With the fury of dragon's blood
> For the love of all the saints
> Leave this body,
> Remove thy taint.[48]

These same Ligurian miners practiced an especially elaborate magically based remedy for stomach problems. The sufferer brought the healer an article of clothing which had been worn for at least twelve hours. The healer tied a string to the garment and placed its end at the pit of the sick person's stomach. Three arms' lengths of string and garment were measured while the healer recited a charm. The process was to be repeated on three consecutive days.[49]

Magical responses to physically induced ailments often lacked the intensity associated with remedies for diseases caused by sorcery and magic. Fears of witchcraft as a cause of disease and even death have been very real for some Italian Americans. For example, a widely known case in Buffalo, New York, in the 1950s concerned an old woman, reputed to be a witch, who discovered she was being cheated by a young man to whom she had entrusted some of her business dealings. She angrily exclaimed to him, "I'm crying tears now, but tonight Saint Cecilia will make you cry blood!" Later that evening the young man was boasting in a tavern to his cronies of having outwitted the old woman, when he collapsed with blood gushing from his eyes. Death ensued shortly thereafter, according to legend.[50]

Though similar to *malocchio,* witchcraft differs from the former practice in that it is always intentional. Usually one becomes a witch *(strega* or *maga)* by being born at midnight on Christmas Eve.[51] Italian-American folk tradition includes a number of activities that will provide immunity from the negative influences of sorcery and witchcraft, the most common being sprinkling salt around one's house or placing red ribbons over the doorways. To remove a spell that has already been cast, a particular prayer learned on Christmas may be efficacious. In some cases, it will remain in effect for six generations in a family, the spell reappearing in the seventh. To prevent further spells, it is a good idea to have a *maga* anoint the clothes one was wearing when the original spell was cast.

It is also a good idea to plug the keyholes to one's house, since an open keyhole provides easy entry for a witch. A witch can be removed from a house by putting a broom behind the door. The witch will count all the straws before leaving or risk having its identity revealed. If the broom is placed outdoors, the witch will not enter the house because he or she will be compelled to count the straws. Mass on Christmas Eve provides a context for detecting a witch, since he or she will be the last person to leave the church. The witch's power may be destroyed by gazing at him or her while holding a broom, sickle, or crucifix. Or if one substitutes water for the magic ointment which witches rub on themselves to gain the ability to fly, their power will dissipate.[52]

Should such preventives for magically induced illness fail, one will usually have to consult a specialist in magical healing. A social worker for Chicago's Hull House in the 1920s reported several cases of Calabrians in the city who attributed diseases that did not respond to scientific remedies to witchcraft and consulted someone reputed to have magical powers. One case involved a family whose father and eldest son had become mysteriously ill. Consultations with a *maga* pointed toward the mother's stepsister, who had cursed the father's wine and had bewitched the younger man by putting three hairs on his coat sleeve. The *maga* relieved their suffering with prayers, "but not Christian prayers."[53] Another young woman became ill through the passion of a rejected suitor. Hoping to win her love, he enlisted the aid of a *mago*, who first prescribed a love potion. When this failed, the suitor secured a collar the young woman had worn. The *mago* stuck pins in the collar, thus bewitching her. She could find relief only by marrying her former suitor.[54]

A similar case has been reported among Italian Americans living in Philadelphia:

> A woman had been wronged by a man who refused to marry her. She told him that she was going to compel him to marry her by the power of the "fattura." On Christmas Eve at midnight she went to mass and before going to the altar rail to partake of the Holy Communion, she spat thrice on the floor on the church and repeated the formula of the renunciation of Christ:
>
> *Cristo, Cristiello,*
> *Tu buono, ma e piu buono quello.*
>
> ("Thou art good, but he [the Devil] is better.")
>
> Then she went forward, kept the wafer in the mouth till she was out of the church, put it in a little bag, tied it up with a string containing as many knots as the years of the man's age, and then deposited it in a vessel full of water. The idea was that the man would gradually sicken as the string became decomposed in the water and would eventually die when the knots of the string were all broken by decomposition. Of course the man, knowing what

she had done and fearing evil results, began to feel sick by the power of auto-suggestion and proceeded to marry her.[55]

Pins stuck in a doll caused the death of a young Calabrian man in Chicago, and an infant in a tenement in that city succumbed to "a death stroke" sent by a woman still living in the mountains of Calabria:

> She did not need a doll to do the deed; a lemon was enough. In the Chicago tenement were her eldest son and the girl he married against his mother's will. So, for revenge, when news came to her of the birth of a baby, the old woman took a lemon and stuck it full of pins and as it withered and shrank, the baby pined away and died.[56]

A recent account from a second-generation Sicilian American who grew up in New Orleans suggests the survival of the attitude underlying such events from the 1920s:

> I had this lady who was giving me a hard time. And my mother said, "If you can," she said, "send me something of hers, and we'll take care of it. You know, anything of hers." And I said, "Like what?" "Just send me something." But I never did because I couldn't get that close—I never got that close to her.[57]

While the results that might have ensued had a possession been obtained are not specified, presumably its owner would have suffered some sort of discomfort that could have been relieved only through the processes of magical healing.

The Italo-American Citizens Club of Masontown, Pennsylvania, formed in the 1920s to provide a focus for general Italian-American identity. Though providing services for families, it has been primarily a place for men to get together for informal recreation and more regularly scheduled events such as Columbus Day dinners. Photograph courtesy of Guido Malpezzi.

Recreation and Games

AT A FOURTH OF JULY CELEBRATION in New Haven, Connecticut, in the late 1940s, someone had extended a greased telephone pole with an American flag attached to the end from a pier over the cold waters of Long Island Sound. The object was for the "blades and bloods of the Italian quarter" to walk to the end of the pole to retrieve the flag, an exercise that deposited many of them in the icy waters.[1] Walking or climbing a greased pole has been a traditional contest at many Italian-American *feste* and other get-togethers. It represents one example of the folk recreation, often rooted in the Old World heritage, that has flourished among *paesani* and the general Italian-American community.

The traditional pattern of recreation in Italian-American families has produced a fairly rigid gender separation. Women have usually spent their leisure time in or near the home or at church, socializing with family members and neighbors. Men, though, have been more likely to congregate at public locations: street corners, bars, parks, and Italian "clubs." The last kind of site, an important institution in Italian-American culture, usually emerged from the needs of regionally based immigrant communities to provide organized services that members felt they could not receive from a mainstream society they viewed as unsympathetic.

In urban areas with a large Italian population, clubs usually focused on regional identity. For example, the Augusta Society in Boston's West End has accepted as members only those whose ancestors came from the village of Augusta in eastern Sicily.[2] Early in this century, most of the 110 Italian societies in Chicago included Italians from the same province or *paese,* the most popular organization being the *Unione Siciliane* with twenty-eight lodges in the city.[3] In Cleveland, a number of hometown societies developed in the

1880s and 1890s, including the Italian Fraternal Society in 1888 and the Sicilian Fraternal Society in 1896. In the mid-1970s, a sampling of Italian clubs in the city revealed several whose emphasis was still on a particular region or *paese:* Noicattarese Club, North Italian Club, Baranallo Women's Auxiliary, Calabrese Club, Imerese Club, Ripalimosani Men's Union, and The Trentina Club.[4]

In smaller communities, clubs have been more likely to include all Italian Americans in their activities and to promote an Italian identity which may coexist with the regional cultural differences that tend to persist away from the urban Italian concentrations. For example, Italian immigrants from Abruzzi and the Piedmont in Kiel, Oklahoma, where they had come to work in the mines, jointly organized a Columbus Society in 1881, an early date for the founding of an interregional society.[5] The Italo-American Citizen's Club of Masontown, Pennsylvania, was established in 1927 to reflect the general ethnic heritage of all Italians who had settled in that mining community in the southwestern part of the state.[6]

Sometimes clubs that began as regionally oriented societies merged to form organizations emphasizing general Italian ethnicity. This occurred in Hibbing, Minnesota, when the Marconi Lodge of the Order of the Sons of Italy combined the *Societa M.S. Guglielmo Marconi* and the Cesare Cantu Lodge, OSIA, both founded some years earlier to represent Tyrolese and Piedmontese loyalties.[7]

Most such organizations had service as their original goal. The clubs in Cleveland assisted with burial expenses, cared for widows, and sought jobs for their members.[8] In the 1910s Chicago's *Unione Siciliane* provided members with weekly sick benefits ranging from eight to twelve dollars per week and would cover funeral expenses up to ninety dollars. All members of the organization were expected to attend funerals, and, according to one contemporary observer, "A band of musicians is always provided" by the *Unione.*[9] Originally designed to help the single men who comprised the overwhelming majority of the immigrant miners, the Kiel, Oklahoma, Columbus Society later became a focus for family-oriented activies such as band concerts and Sunday afternoon picnics.[10] The *Lega Fratellanza,* founded in Globe, Arizona, in 1905, provided inexpensive health and life insurance and sponsored gala dances on the Fourth of July and Columbus Day.[11]

Most clubs offered services and entertainment for the entire family. The Central Society, a New York City Italian-American organization that promoted ethnic unity in the face of the city's 150 separate regional organizations at the turn of the century, scheduled a range of activities, including a summer picnic "with or without a parade" and a masked ball each winter with a "hurdy-gurdy orchestra" providing the music.[12] Pearl Malpezzi recalled what the Italian club in Rillton, Pennsylvania, had to offer during the 1920s:

> And they made their own wine in the club too. They would stay there all night. His [her husband's] father would be there all night. He'd just come over to us and call me and say, "Make me a sandwich. I'm hungry." He wouldn't go home any because he lived way up on a hill. He'd come over to our place asking to make him a sandwich. They played cards all the time, and they had dances there every Saturday almost. We had our school plays there. I was in the school play. I could dance the tango when I was twelve. Had an Italian fellow there taught me how to tango. Oh, we used to be pretty good at it. That was during the Valentino days, you know. It was—tango was the dance, and the Charleston. Then the Charleston came in.[13]

Sam Gennuso noted that the Amicus Club in Beaumont, Texas—open only to Italian families—"had dances and parties" to which his married sisters and their families would go.[14]

As Malpezzi's memories suggest, despite the clubs' scheduling of family activities and perhaps even of programs especially designed for women (usually by a ladies' auxiliary such as the one she helped to found in Masontown, Pennsylvania, in 1934), men have used club facilities more regularly, often spending substantial portions of their leisure time drinking with cronies, exchanging gossip and other verbal folklore, and playing traditional Italian games such as *bocce, morra, passatella,* and card games.

Bocce

Italian-American children may be comforted when it thunders by being told that the sound is only Saint Peter playing *bocce.*[15] Pearl Malpezzi remembered that the Rillton Italian Club had three *bocce*

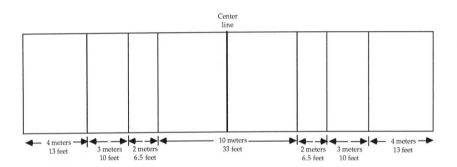

Center
line

4 meters
13 feet

3 meters
10 feet

2 meters
6.5 feet

10 meters
33 feet

2 meters
6.5 feet

3 meters
10 feet

4 meters
13 feet

*A standard **bocce** court measures twenty-eight by ten meters. Diagram by Carl Lindquist.*

courts, where Italian-American men could play their most popular folk game—the only Italian traditional game to have achieved a significant following outside the ethnic group. A bowling game usually played in its traditional manifestations on a permanent outdoor or indoor court, *bocce* requires two teams, usually of four men each. Actually, any number of men can play the game as long as they can be divided into two equal sides.[16]

The court, surfaced in clay, measures twenty-eight by ten meters, has a low wooden boundary on all four sides, and may have a distinctive tilt which players must "read" to play successfully. Such courts exist in public parks, as adjuncts to commercial establishments such as bars and restaurants, and—as was the case in Rillton—on the grounds of Italian clubs. Nine balls are also needed for *bocce:* eight wooden balls of about six inches in diameter colored to identify those of each team, and a two-inch target ball of stainless steel called a *pallino* or *balline.*

The game begins when a bystander or player selected by coin toss rolls the *pallino* toward the center of the court, thus providing a target for the *bocce* players, the first of whom tries to roll his ball as near to the *pallino* as possible. The next man (an opponent) executes a similar rolling shot, called a *punto,* either to get closer to the target, to knock the first ball out of contention, or ideally to do both. Players from the two teams alternate shots, designed to accomplish one of these purposes, until all eight balls have been rolled. A determination, which may require use of a tape measure, reveals which team has the most balls closest to the *pallino.* That team wins the round. After several such rounds, one team is declared winner of the game.

In addition to the *punto,* some *bocce* players have perfected a shot called a *volo.* A hard drive slightly above the surface of the court or a lob which arcs to come down on top of an opponent's ball, the *volo* is used late in a round when a player is blocked from his target by balls surrounding the *pallino.* Should they be from his own team, he may want to avoid hitting them—hence the need for a shot that will pass over them. A spectacular shot, the *volo* receives an ovation when successfully executed. Guido Malpezzi, who like many Italian-American men has continued to compete successfully at

The object of **bocce** is to get one's ball as close as possible to a target ball called a **pallino**. Usually this is done by means of a rolling shot, or **punto**.

bocce into his eighties, laments the absence of the *volo* from recent games in which he has participated.[17]

An older form of the game has persisted in some rural and small-town Italian-American communities. Four to eight men form two teams and set a finish line at some distance. They take turns rolling or throwing stones down roads and across fields until someone crosses the finish line. The winner can be the man whose stone first crosses the line or who crosses the line with the fewest throws.[18]

Bocce has often been an informal affair conducted with "great interest" in empty lots and backyards where temporary courts might be laid out.[19] Stakes are often small, the losers usually being required to buy drinks for the winners. In *bocce, morra,* and other folk games, Italian-American men often play a brief, supplementary round or draw lots to select someone as *"padrone"* or "boss." This person has the responsibility of distributing the drinks that the losing team must buy—either to the whole group or only to the winners.[20]

Formal *bocce* play may occur at tournaments scheduled as part of the entertainment at an Easter celebration or a saint's *festa.*[21] Sometimes *bocce* leagues have been organized. Joseph Capello recalled an intercity (and apparently interethnic, since one of the teams was sponsored by the Belgian Club in Charleroi) league in southwestern Pennsylvania several decades ago,[22] and his brother-in-law has played in a league composed of teams sponsored by local clubs and businesses in Masontown, Pennsylvania, in the 1980s and 1990s.

Bocce also is played frequently at family picnics or reunions without fixed courts. Often younger Italian Americans, who may have previously dismissed the game as suited only for older people, participate in *bocce* for the first time at such gatherings.[23] That the game has enjoyed a resurgence in popularity that transcends its ethnic roots is indicated by the political objective of former Minnesota governor Rudy Perpich, a Croatian American, to provide a *bocce* court for every community in his state.[24]

An unusual variant of *bocce,* probably no longer played in Italian-American communities, is *palla di formaggio.* Instead of using balls, players throw disks of cheese sometimes weighing as much as eleven or twelve pounds. The object may be to hit a target or simply to throw the cheese as far as possible. In either case, the game requires both strength and skill. Occasionally the cheese may be spun out on a rope like an unsecured yo-yo. The successful competitor must have the requisite athletic abilities as well as some cheesemaking skills, since firm, smooth cheeses can go greater distances than their less well made counterparts.[25]

Morra

While *bocce* requires special equipment, a playing field, and some degree of organization, *morra,* another traditional game favored by Italian-American men, can occur less formally and more spontaneously—in fact, whenever at least two men are present. Quite simple to play, *morra* involves two competitors' simultaneously extending some fingers of one hand and loudly guessing what the total number will be.[26] Joseph Capello explained the play as follows:

> And then you throw the finger down. You have to guess what's fallen. You understand? If I put three and you put two and I call five, that's my number. If you call five, that's a tie. That don't count. You have to guess what's coming up.[27]

If neither player calls the correct number of fingers, that also does not count.

Characterized by one observer as a game "played with outflung fingers and a lot of emotion,"[28] *morra* may go on for hours and can be played in teams. One procedure for involving teams divides a group of men into two parties and sets a winning point total, determined by multiplying the number of persons on each team by four and adding one. A member of each team squares off. They display their fingers and shout their guesses. The winner earns a point for his team and will continue to take on opposition players until one of them outguesses him. The play usually progresses rapidly and rhythmically, and guesses are often accompanied by ritual insults. Theoretically, one person could win the entire competition for his team by defeating each opposing team member four times.[29] A young Italian American from Boston's North End described a game of *morra* played by teams:

We had a game of La Mora [*sic*] ..., with three men on a side. I was anchor man on my side, against Chick. The game was to twelve points, and when I came up, the score was eleven to three against us. I took nine points in a row and won the game for us. Chick was sore. He was calling me all kinds of names. But I only laughed. I thought it was a big joke.... After a while I went over and sat down in a doorstep on Norton Street. Chick came up and slapped me in the face.[30]

Winning at *morra* requires some strategy as a player gauges his guess of any number from one to ten in relation to the number of fingers he plans to extend and his educated assumption about his opponent's intentions. Opponents who have faced each other for years often seem to be able to "read" the number of fingers each will display. Also, the successful *morra* player needs a loud voice so that his guess can be clearly heard. Descriptions of the game often emphasize the noise involved: "You could hear them scream and holler up Main Street," for example.[31]

Stakes in *morra* generally remain low. The story about men playing the game with the agreement that the loser would have to cut off one of his fingers is probably an exaggeration.[32] But even if—as in *bocce*—the stakes in *morra* only involve the purchase of drinks by the losing team, feelings can run high, as the young Bostonian slapped by Chick testified. Joseph Capello recalled the intensity and excitement generated by playing the game:

> We used to go sometime like picnic in summertime, you know, in the park or something. They have Italian Day. Man, there'd be gangs going all the way back. They'd be from one club to the other—you know, from one gang—from one town to the other, you know. "Come on, Masontown, come on." I mean that—buddy, they used to play for blood. Don't fool yourself. Hard losers.... We had good players up there. One time we went to Perryopolis, you know, where they had that club. We went down there to see the building.... I think it was—think it was about ten of us. Nine or ten. So this guy says, "How about a game of *morra?*" Said, "Yeah, come on." So they played their side, and we was all from Masontown, you know. We went down there. By God, we played *morra*.[33]

Even *morra*, though, has become subject to formalization. *Morra* tournaments sometimes represent part of the activity at a *festa*, where men from various ethnic groups compete against Italian-American teams.[34]

Passatella

Bocce and *morra* are generally known throughout Italian-American society. A more regionally based game is *passatella*, from southern Italy, whose social structure the game seems to portray. Also called *sopra e sotto, tocca,* or "boss and underboss," *passatella* is a drinking game reflecting the inequalities inherent in southern Italian peasant life.

The game begins with eight or ten men playing a round of *bocce, morra,* or cards to create a financial pool from which drinks will be purchased. A *padrone* and *sotto-padrone* (underboss) are chosen by drawing lots, cutting cards, or rolling a *bocce* ball at a *pallino*. The *padrone* orders a tray of drinks. He downs the first drink in a single gulp and offers the second to the *sotto-padrone*. Then the *padrone* offers drinks to other players as he chooses, but each must ask the *sotto-padrone* for permission before he can accept. If permission is granted, the player gulps the offered drink. The process continues until the tray of drinks has been consumed.[35]

Passatella can offer a variety of scenarios. If both *padrone* and *sotto-padrone* treat all the players equally, then everyone will receive his fair share of the drinks. But either one of the game's leaders can exclude whomever he chooses, thus creating—or perhaps reflecting—a system of status among the players. Often the *sotto-padrone* will refuse to give anyone permission to drink. This results in the *padrone*'s drinking an inordinate amount: "The understood object is to get the boss drunk."[36] The only potential equalizer in the game involves the selection of *padrone* and *sotto-padrone*. If someone who has been neglected by the game's leaders in a round assumes one of those roles for a subsequent tray of drinks, then perceived mistreatment may be avenged.

Card Games

A turn-of-the-century observer of Italian life in the United States disapprovingly noted, "A strong racial taste for gambling expresses itself in the frequent groups of players in tenement courts, cafes, and card-rooms."[37] Whatever taste for gambling Italian Americans might have has traditionally been satisfied not only by *bocce, morra,* and *passatella,* but also by a number of card games. The deck used in most of these games consists of forty cards in the conventional four suits. The eights, nines, and tens have been removed from the fifty-two-card deck with their numerical places being taken respectively by the queens, jacks, and kings. The ranking of the cards may differ from game to game.

The card games generating the most enthusiasm among players are partnership games such as *briscola* (or "brisk"), *tresette,* and *trumpscopa* (also simply *"scopa"*). The first begins with a deal of three cards face down to each of four players, who constitute two teams. The thirteenth card, placed on the table face up, determines the trump for the hand. The player to the dealer's right leads with any of the cards in his hand. The other players follow with any card they wish; they do not have to follow suit. A trump card takes the trick. If more than one trump is played, the highest is the winner. If no trump is played, the highest card of the suit played at first wins the trick. After a trick has been completed, the players replenish their hands with cards that had not been previously dealt so that each again holds three cards. Play continues until the deck has been depleted. The winners are the team that scores either sixty-one points in one deal or 121 points in two deals. Points are determined by predetermined values assigned to the cards.[38]

Tresette begins with ten cards being passed out to each of the four players. The first player puts down a card of his choice. Everyone else must follow suit, the highest card of the suit taking the trick. This method of play continues until all ten tricks have been taken. Scoring is determined by whether the two partnerships have declared that they hold sequences of cards in the same suit and by predetermined point values for the cards which turn up in the tricks they take. The winning team is the first to reach a total of thirty-one points, a feat that will take several deals.[39]

In *trumpscopa,* four players receive three cards each, and four cards remain face up on the table. The game's object is to add and match these four cards. For example, a jack in the hand may pick up a jack on the table, or a nine in the hand may pick up a seven and a deuce. *"Scopa"* (worth one point) occurs when a player is able to pick up the last card from the table. Play continues until one of the teams reaches a score of twenty-one.[40]

All three of these games are enlivened by traditional gestures that allow partners to communicate what they hold in their hands and to offer commentaries on each other's play and that of their opponents. For example, touching the thumb to the index and third fingers with the palm held up suggests disappointment in the cards one has been dealt. An average hand might be signaled by spreading one's fingers, holding the palm down, and shaking the hand slightly. A partner could indicate his confidence in victory by running the backs of his fingers under his chin.[41] Customarily, men have played these partnership card games for small stakes, often just a glass of wine. Their enthusiasm has stemmed from the play itself, not from the anticipated rewards.

Except for *bocce,* most of these Italian-American folk games and recreations have given way to Americanized forms of play, and even *bocce* has lost much of its exclusive connection with a particular ethnic group. As Italian Americans became increasingly involved with life in the United States, their interests shifted from the games their ancestors had brought from Italy to such American pastimes as baseball and poker. While all of these games continue to be played by Italian Americans, for many of them they represent relics of an earlier stage in their cultural lives.

Meanwhile, young Italian Americans, especially in urban areas, have developed a recreational style that blends their sense of ethnic identity with elements of popular culture. Called "Guido" or "Cugine," this youth subculture finds expression in a variety of ways. Hairstyles for both sexes, for example, reflect Guido identity. Young men wear their hair close-cropped and slicked back, while young women affect "tall" hair which is teased and arranged high on their heads.

These "Guidettes" complement their tall hair with heavy make-up and long, brightly colored fingernails. Young men and women also announce their Guido identity through clothing, the former wearing athletically oriented apparel for casual situations and a turtleneck shirt, cardigan sweater, and black pants for other occasions. The Guido costume for women consists of tightly fitted spandex pants, oversized blouses, ankle bracelets, and large earrings.

Automobiles figure significantly in Guido culture, and "cruising" in fancy cars decorated with such insignia of ethnicity as Italian flag decals and red, white, and green streamers constitutes an important Guido pastime. Participants in this youth subculture also frequent dance clubs where they perform contemporary dance steps.[42] The Guido subculture represents ethnic identity through recreation for contemporary Italian-American youth just as games such as *bocce, morra,* and *passatella* did for their grandparents.

Many Italian immigrants and their descendants (like the Cenatiempo family, who made the trip back by ship) have paid return visits to their homes. Stories about those visits figure prominently in their personal narrative repertoires and stress the lavish hospitality they received, the familiarity of people and places about which they may only have heard, and the close ties that have continued between family members in the Old World and the New. Photograph courtesy of Lucia Peek.

CHAPTER EIGHT

Stories and Storytelling

AMONG THE PEOPLE WHOM Clementina Todesco remembered from her youth in the Venetian village of Faller were Patrizio Zampieri and Giuseppe Todesco. What stood out in her memory was their ability to tell stories: *Märchen*, the tales of wonder which are popularly known as "fairy tales," fables with humanized animal characters, funny stories about clergymen and other authority figures, and legends about supernatural experiences. Todesco described Zio Bepi to an interviewer:

> He had a little of the clown in him, you know. He gave grand importance to all these little stories. He had a way of attracting our attention. Everyone watched him. There in Faller, there was nothing else to do. Bepi had traveled a little around the world, had read some books, and had heard and read lots of stories which he told.[1]

Zio Patrizio, according to Todesco's recollection,

> had something special. Not everybody was like him .... He always had something to say. He knew everything—how many inhabitants were here and there, what this or that country was doing, what they produced, all this.[2]

People as talented as Zio Bepi and Zio Patrizio were part of the Italian migration to America; in fact, Clementina Todesco continued to relate some of their stories after her immigration in 1930. But, in general, conditions in this country worked against the perpetuation of story performances such as those she knew in Italy. One negative influence was the loss of a traditional context for such performance.

In Todesco's Faller, the stable provided a setting for storytelling. Each night from November through March, several families would gather in one of their stables. From about five o'clock until nine people would gossip, do handwork, and spin the hemp that they

had harvested from their fields. The last occupation gave the occasions the name *filo*, from the verb for "to spin." When a storyteller
such as Zio Bepi or Zio Patrizio was present, he or she might assume
the "stage" and "perform" for the assembled audience, "spinning"
tales of magic and fantasy that delighted not only the children
present but the adults as well.[3]

Life in the United States, however, provided fewer opportunities of this sort. Todesco continued to tell tales of magic and
wonder to her children on picnics or during the winter when it was
too cold to play in the streets. Other Italian Americans also have
evocative memories of hearing their forebears tell Old World stories
in New World settings. For example, a Sicilian American described
the context for his mother's narration of tales from the same
Carolingian cycle which provided material for puppet plays:

> How can I recapture the sense of warmth and love, as on a cold
> December night in Auburn, New York, we huddled around the
> coal stove, with hot faces and cold backs. Then, impatiently waiting
> for a few chestnuts or filberts to roast, we would urge her to tell us
> another story. Ah! the smell of orange peels toasting on a hot lid
> and the thought of Bayard champing furiously as he waits for
> Roland to mount him and ride furiously again. Ever victorious
> Roland, our shining champion!
>
> Seated around my mother we listened and by listening grew
> wiser. We fashioned, woven from the fabric of many a winter's tale,
> some permanent values to guide us through this labyrinth we call
> life.[4]

In Roseto, Pennsylvania, home to immigrants from the Apulian
village of Roseto Valfortore, the custom of traditional storytelling
enjoyed more vitality than in most other Italian-American communities. A second-generation resident of the community recalled
the context for story performance during his childhood:

> Well. My father, in wintertime, we used to sit around the stove.
> That's when we had all our work done, and he would tell us the
> story. When it was about eight o'clock, he'd say, "Now, tomor-
> row." He'd do certain jobs, my sisters had to do their jobs and
> tomorrow night we would continue the story. So, we would wait
> for that night to come and we used to sit wait … and wait … what
> would be the end of the story.[5]

Such occasions, though, were rare in this country and, more importantly, had not become institutionalized in such forms as the Fallerese *filo* or the Tuscan *veglia*.[6] What storytelling did occur had to depend on irregular contexts such as that remembered by Daniela Gioseffi: "My grandmother told them [family members around the kitchen table] Italian fairy tales while they sewed the covers on ... baseballs for a few cents apiece."[7] Without a regular, traditional context—one that would endure longer than the need for supplementary income sewing baseballs, for instance—the performance of long, involved traditional narratives was bound not to flourish.

Another reason that traditional performance of *Märchen* and similar narrative forms, a practice known in most regions of Italy, did not persist with as much strength in the New World may be the stories' connection with the peasant way of life that the immigrants had abandoned. The "permanent values" learned from the Carolingian cycle around the coal stove in Auburn, New York, were in many cases connected with an existence that had been abandoned. While those values might, in the abstract, still be important, they could be conveyed in much more relevant terms with the kinds of stories which in the repertoires of many performers replaced the wonder tales, the sagas of immigration and adjustment to life in the New World.

The storytelling that flowered among Italian Americans involved their own experiences and those of their family members who had gone through adventures which, though not as magical as the events that befell the heroes of *Märchen* and the protagonists of supernatural legends, involved just as much peril and had the advantage of immediacy and obvious relevance to those in the audience. Moreover, personal-experience stories and family sagas did not require a formal storytelling context. While an effective narrator could invest them with dramatic intensity around the dinner table at a Sunday gathering of family and *paesani*, they could also be injected into casual conversations to illustrate points. It seems a safe claim that, in general, personal-experience stories replaced *Märchen* and other traditional story types that flourished in the traditional Old World storytelling contexts.

One might also argue that the traditional narrative forms were too tied to language to survive effectively in a setting where quite often efforts were being made to convert immigrants' children to exclusive use of English. While particular language was not as vital to the narration of a *Märchen* as it was to the articulation of a proverb or the singing of a song, the formulaic nature of some aspects of the wonder tale (for example, openings, closings, magical spells recited by characters) made language of some relevance. As verbal art, *Märchen* narration required linguistic skills that storytellers who had learned how to narrate in a regional dialect might not have in English. To tell a *Märchen* effectively, one needed to know the subtleties of the language he or she was using. Especially when their audiences consisted of second- and third-generation Italian Americans, Old World storytellers might not be able to make themselves understood in the language in which they had learned their art.

When people did attempt the stories in English, the result might not be as satisfying for either performer or audience as they would hope. The same would, of course, hold true for other immigrant storytellers whose native language was not English. But the Italian-American case may have been exacerbated when the plethora of dialects that had provided the original language for storytelling were abandoned in favor not only of English but also of standard Italian or some other *lingua franca* within the Italian communities of the United States.

Finally, one must take into account the availability of entertainment forms other than storytelling in the New World. Folk entertainments such as puppet plays and popular theater in large Italian communities joined mass cultural offerings such as motion pictures, radio, and later television to supplant the performance of traditional tales of wonder. Although the mass media do not always weaken oral tradition, in the case of storytelling, particularly the longer forms that had been valued in the *filo* and *veglia,* they clearly had a deleterious effect.[8]

Despite these factors, some storytellers like Clementina Todesco did find an audience for their Old World tales of magic and wonder after coming to the United States. One such performer of traditional tales was Carlo G. Silvine, who immigrated from the Alpine village of Visoni in 1905. Settling in eastern Tennessee, he worked as a miner and farmer and told stories to his four daughters. In 1956 his daughter Rosa wrote out several of the stories which her father, who had died in 1949, had told her twenty-five years earlier. One of these she entitled "The Black Sheep":

> Little Carlo was an orphan boy who lived with foster parents. His parents were good to him but one day his foster mother became very ill. In a few days she was gone and Carlo was very sad. He tried to be helpful but he seemed only to get in his foster father's way, especially when the father started dating a woman who everyone thought was wicked.
>
> They finally married and then everything was different. Little Carlo had to take the sheep and goats to the woods every day and all he had to eat was a slice of cold mush and old cheese. He slept many a night just inside the cemetery wall in a vacant space ready for some one to be buried in it. His sheep and goats would huddle close beside him. At daylight he would take them in home, stay a couple of hours and then leave again.
>
> One day he was crying because he was so hungry. The little black sheep that wore a tiny bell came up to him and suddenly began to shake its bell. As he did, Carlo looked up and saw food coming down from the sheep's bell. Carlo ate to his heart's content. He kept this up. No one paid any attention to him, so things went along well until the owner of the sheep decided to sell a few of his flock.
>
> Carlo became sad and begged his foster father to let him keep the black sheep. This he didn't get to do. The last day in the woods was a sad one. The black sheep came up to Carlo and for the first time talked to him. The black sheep told Carlo that he wouldn't need to worry because all that he needed to do was to remove his bell from the collar, carry it in his pocket, stuff it so it wouldn't ring unless he wanted it to. He was doing all this because Carlo had saved the little black sheep's life from the cliffs up on top of the peak where he had so carelessly wandered.
>
> All went well until one day Carlo had grown into manhood and soon he would be in the service. Carlo lost the bell as mysteriously as he found it. Some said the black sheep needed it to wear as it wandered over the meadows at night to remind him that he must not forget to return to his resting place before midnight. Some would say they heard Carlo's bell high up on the Alps; others

said they heard it wander around the cemetery or around the old farmhouse where he lived so many years.[9]

Silvine's narrative seems related to the general story outline which folklorists have identified as Aarne-Thompson Type 511A, "The Little Red Ox."[10] The sheep's bell as the remarkable source of food is somewhat unusual among other versions of this story that have been reported. The passing references to the custom of dating and to Carlo's entering the service may reflect what the storyteller or his daughter, who provided this tale text, had encountered in the United States, but the boy's occupation as shepherd and the localization of the narrative in the Alps certainly tie the story to the storyteller's homeland.

Another story in Carlo Silvine's repertoire resembles the Cyclops episode in *The Odyssey* (Type 1137), but probably represents an oral tradition independent of the Homeric epic. Rosa Silvine entitled this story "The One-Eyed Giant":

> Each country I guess likes to make believe that the one-eyed giant lived some where in one of its hidden caves on some lofty mountain. This giant lived in a cave in a mountain that is covered with ice three-fourths of the year and contains an icecap on its peak the year round. He lived all alone in the Alps high above a path known as Pass de Gial. He owned some goats which furnished him with milk, cheese and meat, also skins for shoes and clothing. He, like all other giants, was supposed to raid the village gardens, vineyards, and orchards and no one dared stop him.
>
> One cold blustery winter morning a boy wandered into the cave to shield himself from the wind for just a moment. He hears the earth shake; it is the giant coming out of the cave with his goats. The boy was so frightened he leans against the wall as close as he can. The giant thunders out of the cave and then suddenly turns around and begins to look in all directions. He spies little Gildo, who runs far into the cave.
>
> The giant laughs as he continues to drive the goats out to pasture. After the last one is out he pushes a heavy stone slab over the entrance. He continues to tend his goats until evening and then he returns to his cave. He prepares himself a fine meal and decides that in a couple of days he will have a different kind of meat, as soon as he can fatten little Gildo and put some meat on his bones and tight-drawn skin.

Gildo finds the food on a rock left for him by the giant. He eats it a little at a time, afraid it might be poisoned. He feeds the rats a little of his food. He looks for a way to escape but the giant is lying half way across the path and the entrance is barred for the night. Gildo explores the cave and plots on a way to get out. He has made friends with all the creatures in the cave, from the least to the biggest ones. One old rodent is very poor; the giant wouldn't even let him have a crumb when he could help it and he often tried to kill it. This cave rat would rub his nose against the giant's feet and tickle him until he would go into a rage.

The giant decided he would have goat meat for his meal one night, so he picked one old goat out and prepared him for his supper. He ate enough for a dozen men. He left Gildo a plate full but he would not touch a bite of it; he fed it to his pets. The old rodent, whom Gildo called Gobo [sic] because it had a hump on its back, would do all kinds of tricks for him. Gildo spied a huge dagger up on a side wall in one of the inner rooms inside the cave. He couldn't reach it so he thought and thought how he might get that dagger. He gathered some clay, put some cheese in the clay, and threw it at the dagger. Some of his cheese and clay stuck all around the dagger and on it. The old rat, Gobo, decided to have fun too so he went after the cheese in the clay. As he landed on the dagger down it came. The sound awoke the giant. He yells out, "What happened there!"

"I dropped my plate," replies Gildo. The giant resumes his snoring. His hot drink is still brewing in its pot. Gildo creeps up slowly to the giant. With one quick stroke of the dagger he cuts the chain around the giant's neck. The key he carries around it flies past Gildo. Gildo lays the dagger on the hot coals to use later, but the giant, though a sound sleeper, awakens. Gildo pours all the boiling drink in the giant's one eye.

The giant roars and rises to pursue Gildo. He feels his way along the wall of the cave. Gildo with the key runs off to the far corner of the cave. He puts the skin of a dead goat on and huddles close to a few stray goats in the interior of the cave. The giant's pains are unbearable but he must reach the room where he has his keg of gold. He pushes all the rocks away until he finally reaches the treasure room and finds it locked. He runs to the entrance to keep Gildo from escaping.

When morning comes Gildo shambles out when the other goats are called and is counted as a goat. He carries the old rodent along in the dead goat's skin. When the giant discovers he has an extra goat he races to the entrance. He feels of the goats again.

When Gildo comes along the old rodent takes a nip on the giant's finger and he yells and chases the goat out of the entrance.

He was blind when he removed the stone slab that morning and so he didn't do a good job; he only partly moved the stone. In running out of the cave he hit the stone so hard he knocked it over. And as the stone went over the threshold and down the valley the old giant was right with it. He landed first and the large stone flattened him out at the foot of the steep ridge.

Gildo returned to the cave in a few days with his father and a few other men. He knew how to open the door to the treasure room, but when he did they found only a deep round well. In the midst of it they saw a huge keg but could not reach it. Gildo finally located another narrow hole which led down by steps to the water's edge. He found that the keg was fastened to a rope which he pulled and brought the keg ashore. When it was opened it contained only the jewelry the giant had stolen in the village.

Gildo rid the valley of the giant, and the dagger he owned would cut into metal, wood, or flesh as quick as lightning. This brought him good luck for he was feared at home and away. The chain and key were gold and sold for a considerable sum of money. The stories he told about the one-eyed giant made him welcome in any court. He never had to wander any more nor was he ever cold again in a cave or in need of food.

He was known far and near as a giant killer, when really the giant killed himself.[11]

Both these stories from Carlo Silvine exemplify the *Märchen*, but like most traditional storytellers his repertoire contained other kinds of narratives, including moralistic religious stories. Probably told as much for the lessons they teach as for their entertainment value, such stories communicated some of the values which folk religion shared with official Roman Catholicism. An example told by Silvine is "The Deaf and Mute Sisters":

A farmer, his wife and two daughters lived in a humble cottage by a fishing lake. He farmed and made charcoal and fishing nets for a living. He and his family were happy but poor. His two daughters were deaf and mute. The family were never dissatisfied with their meager living. The daughters learned to embroider, crochet and do all kinds of fancy weaving. At night the family were never too tired to pray. The father and mother prayed for the safekeeping of their daughters.

One morning Agnes went upstairs to dust the bedroom. In a niche in the wall she kept the picture of a religious lady whom the family admired very m[u]ch. She lifted the picture up to dust it. She noticed that the picture was damp. She wiped it off gently and placed it back in the niche. That night she placed a candle at the foot of the picture to dry out the dampness.

The next morning Florence went upstairs to dust and make up beds. She noticed by the flickering candlelight that tears were dropping from the face in the picture. She wiped them off and kissed the picture. Then she ran down the stairs and for the first time in her life she heard her feet hit the stone steps.

She ran into the kitchen where her mother and sister were busy making dough to prepare some cooked macaroni. She told her mother and Agnes just what had happened. The two ran upstairs and found that the picture was again weeping. All at once she too could hear and talk as freely as anyone else.

When the father returned from work he was told the whole story. The next day he decided that maybe he should take the picture and put it in a church. This he did. But the next morning the picture was again in the niche in the wall. The family didn't know what else to do, but in a dream one of the girls saw a beautiful church standing in place of her humble cottage.

The family began to use their humble cottage as a place for the deaf and dumb to pray. Some were helped but others were not. Later it became a sort of church and more like a monastery where men of all walks of life could come in time of need, especially those who were seeking shelter as well as spiritual need.[12]

The lack of specificity in this religious legend is unusual, since often such narratives will clearly identify such factors as the being in the picture (probably a saint) and the exact site of the cottage that became a shrine.

Carlo Silvine also included in his repertoire at least one example of a romantic tale or novella. Distinguished by their complexity and relatively realistic tone, novellas differ from *Märchen* by placing less emphasis on magic, by taking place in the real world, and by pitting human protagonists against human, rather than supernatural antagonists. They often emphasize pathos and sentimentality. All of these qualities characterize the story which Silvine's daughter entitled "The Mysterious Locket," a complex novella involving intrigue, travel, and a highly sentimental conclusion:

Once upon a time in a tiny village at the foot of the Alps lived a poor villager with his wife and small daughter. They were poor but happy. The small girl lived too far from school to attend regular classes but she was taught at home. Her mother spent the long winter evenings teaching her daughter to read, sew, and make baskets. The father spent the early dark evenings making fishing nets.

In the spring the peasants of the small communities nearby paid some young men to take their goats and cows to the mountain pastures. Some among the young shepherds would take a younger brother or two with them. A family or two would also move to the mountains to tend to the milk and see to it that the cheese were made and aged just right. These families and little boys lived in temporary shelters with the exception of the cheese maker who lived in a room made of stone. This room was large enough for everyone to gather for songs, games, or church at night when the day's work was done. The rooms in which the cheese were made and aged were small and made to extend into a hillside in the fashion of a cellar.

Little Madeline looked forward to late spring when company came to the Alpine pastures. Of all who came Madeline liked Deno the best. He always brought her some chocolate candy and he didn't eat most of it before he came to her house like the others did. He always brought her a package from his sister Lena, who did up her clothes that she had outgrown and sent them to Madeline.

Year after year the summers went by too fast and the winters dragged by too slowly. Her father told wonderful stories about the adventures he experienced in his escape journey from Turkey through war traps and enemy territory. He would tell Madeline and his wife that some day they would go back to Turkey and inherit their family's wealth.

Ten years passed but they were no closer to his family's wealth than they had ever been. He always carried on a tiny chain around his ankle a golden locket supposed to have been his grandmother's. Madeline asked for it but she was told that it must always remain on him until he returned to his homeland, that it was his passport.

One bitter cold day Madeline's father failed to return with the sheep. The flock came home led by the leader, Chicko. It was too cold and dark to search the woods for him that night. The next day the sheep were left at home. Madeline's mother ventured before daybreak to the nearest house down in the village to spread the sad news. Many friends came to search but no trace of the shepherd who had disappeared could be found.

Madeline and her mother moved to a small town where Madeline went to school and her mother did house work for a wealthy wine merchant and his family. Madeline longed to go to their mountain home, especially in the spring, but her mother always told her she didn't have the money to take her. Their home was practically torn apart after they left it and strangers would ask Madeline about her father's jewelry, to which she always replied, "Papa had no jewelry." She didn't consider the locket jewelry and so she always answered no. The family for whom her mother worked promised Madeline a trip to the mountains just as soon as their son and his family came to visit them. It would be a good trip for all of them to take.

Madeline was finally in a landau drawn by six horses and on her way to the mountain village. The trip to the mountain home was very disappointing to all but the children. Madeline saw Deno and he was now a handsome young shepherd who planned someday to be a great musician. He sang and played a mountain flute or was dancing some new step he had made up when the day's work was done. Madeline had inherited her father's fairness, blond hair, and pale blue eyes, more like the Greeks than the Turkish. Deno was of a dark complexion. The children went far up the mountain and picked many wild flowers. Deno made Madeline and her girl friend a daisy chain to wear around their necks. Deno wandered far out on ledges that were dangerous, or to the edge of ice crevices without fear.

The next summer was Deno's last to wander up in the woods because he had reached the age to enter the army for three years. He had been secretly looking for any trace of Madeline's father. One day while far out on a rocky ledge he noticed in a deep ravine a bed of scarlet flowers, a sort of wild poppy flower. He couldn't get down to them that day, but on the next day he had a pick and stout rope. He tied the rope to a large pine and descended to a lower ledge where he could climb down from rock to rock and reach the flower bed. Once down to this strange bed of flowers he discovered a cabin under shelter. In this cabin he found a few household materials, all home-made. Some digging tools were found of a different kind than any he had ever seen. He walked around and found the frayed end of a rope that had been cut in two by the sharp rocks. Someone had descended on a rope but because of ice or some other mishap had fallen when the rope's fibers had been cut by the rocks. The bones lay in a heap below.

He searched farther and found at least three more skeletons and evidence of a struggle. Their knives, usually carried for protection, were rusty and lying around opened. A rusty old ring lay in the corner of the rocky ledge above the fireplace. He recognized the ring as one that was worn by Madeline's father. He also located a hand but none of the skeletons he found had a hand missing. He looked the cabin over and looked out at the beginning of a small brook from the melting ice. He looked and looked but found no other skeleton and decided to pick some flowers and return home. He stepped over into the flower bed a way and his foot sank deep. He tried the opposite corner and the same thing happened. He would just dig one or two flowers and plant them down in the valley to start new flowers. The more he looked at the flowers the more they reminded him of something he couldn't describe. He dug at the roots of one large cluster of flowers just at the end of the long bed. As he dug them up it suddenly dawned on him that the flower bed was in the shape of a grave. He dug and dug until he came to some bones. Dark came on and he slept there and resumed digging early the next morning. Around nine o'clock he uncovered the skeleton with the missing hand and it was Madeline's father's skeleton, for the locket was still on the chain around his ankle. He removed the locket, which resembled a round watch or disk. He was brushing it when the inside of the locket came out leaving a thin outer shell. Inside the locket were tiny crosses, or X's, fourteen in the second circle, one lonely cross in the center, and the outer circle, which was a little soiled, contained twenty-one crosses.

The next day he told his adventures to no one. The more he thought about the locket the more he felt drawn to it and he wanted to keep it. Maybe after his army term he would tell Madeline all about his experience in the ledge cabin up in the Alps. She would be older and would understand it better in three years.

In the service he traveled to other small villages and cities. He saw Madeline only once during his stay in the army and met other girls, one or two that he liked as well as Madeline. After he left the army he decided to travel. He applied for a job with Madeline's mother's boss. As a worker on the wine merchant's vessels he went to Spain and Portugal, Greece, Persia, and also Turkey. And he always went out into the villages when he had a chance to travel from port. He remained in Turkey for seven months. In the vineyards he learned from the older men that many an old estate was being ruled by men who could get the most soldiers to fight for them. One old castle and all the village around it was stolen from an aged ruler. All of his family were supposed to have been killed along with the faithful servants.

He learned from an old gardener who lived nearby that a son was supposed to have escaped by hiding in a wine cask that was being returned to another country. The gardener told him that many men had lost their lives searching for the secret map to their treasure, as well as for the rightful emblem belonging to the family who should and would rule this estate.

Deno traveled and saw the world as far as traveling at this time permitted. He received less and less news about Madeline and for a period of about three years which he spent in an India[n] port checking exports for a company he had heard nothing. Time passed quickly because Deno had a good time. He finally began to wonder about home. He would go back and give Madeline the locket and help her to recover some of her father's wealth or his estate. He was beginning to long for a home of his own, as well as to see his friends and relatives.

He left one spring morning with a crew in the most expensive vessel. They met only with rough weather and storms until they found themselves nearing a group of unknown islands. They bribed the natives with wine and spices for food as well as pearls. The natives looked upon them as gods since their weapons were the best they had seen and the travelers knew how to use them. One old sea-going member played all sorts of tricks on the native[s] and this made him a sort of leader among them. After a time they prepared to leave, but several accidents occurred which made Deno suspicious of the sea captain. Deno believed the captain knew something about the locket for he had asked questions about it.

Deno and his few faithful members left unexpectedly for home. Home was far away and with only second best steering they drifted farther away from home. Some several years passed before the ragged hungry crew reached an island on a route of passing vessels. Their owners' sons, who were in charge of these merchant vessels, sent gladly for them thinking that their stories would provide entertainment for years to come.

The first person Deno began to look for after landing and cleaning himself up to look like a respectable citizen was Madeline's mother. The servants were reluctant to tell him anything but finally an old gardener told him what had happened. Madeline had married a young farmer she met at a church program in town. Her mother had gone to visit them when a contagious disease broke out in the village. Madeline, her husband, and mother were all gone, but their nine or ten-year-old son and a little daughter were in some orphanage.

Deno left again for Turkey. This time he applied for a job as keeper of the gardens at the "Coastal Chana" estate. He looked it over carefully; he noticed that the flower plots were surrounded with rocks. The center circles reminded him of a wheel. He counted all the rocks and they corresponded to the X's in the locket. He weeded the beds and examined the rocks but found nothing unusual. In the center stood an old bird bath or fountain, long ago out of use. In draining the fountain base he discovered a large square hole of water. After removing the water he found a tiny opening at the top just below the ground. He removed some stones and found a passage-way to the castle cellar. He worked on the fountain for a couple of weeks, until he had the information he needed.

He returned to Europe and to the mountain orphanage where he hoped to locate Madeline's children. He had to pretend to be their grandfather in order to get them. He left for an island near the country in which a home of their own awaited them and left the children in the care of a school master and his wife while he made the necessary journey to reclaim their property. When the new owner asked for evidence he produced all kinds of papers, emblems, and the locket to prove he was the long lost son and he demanded his rightful estate. Since the law permitted no fighting for land at this time due to the fact that many rulers were Christians, he was given the keys to his home. Thus he passed as the children's grandfather and they swore to it because they didn't know their mother's father and they were willing to stand by Deno.

In la[t]er years when both were married, Denena to a prosperous farmer and little Christopher to a beautiful woman, and in charge of the estate, Deno would sit by the open fireplace and tell them true stories of his adventures, which they all enjoyed. He often would fall melancholy and would sing songs of his lost lover. Little did the children know that it was their mother of whom he sang. Of course it was his fault for not returning home sooner, or staying at home. He was repaying them what their mother should have had.

Denena kept the jewels found in the castle and some of the gold. She was as happy as any princess and lived as a queen in her village. Christopher carried on the old tradition of the family by marrying someone who not only owned as much as he but knew how to live and rule such a place.[13]

Another traditional storyteller who continued his art for at least awhile after coming to the United States was Rocco Pantalone, who immigrated to work in the mines of West Virginia from his native Buggi in 1906. His repertoire included *Märchen* like those told by Carlo Silvine as well as other types of traditional tales such as the following which folklore collector Ruth Ann Musick, who wrote it from Pantalone's dictation, called "The Priest and the Three Suitors":

> One time a priest had a niece, a nice looking girl who kept his house. A young fellow came along who was stuck on the girl and she on him. He asked the priest for permission to marry her. This was about eight o'clock at night.
>
> The priest said, "What kind of a boy are you? Are you strong? And have you got good courage?"
>
> The boy thought that he did.
>
> Then the priest said, "You'll have to make out like you're a dead man. You'll have to have the courage to stay all night in a casket. If you're afraid, then—nothing doing."
>
> The boy agreed to try it. About an hour later a second fellow came along. He was stuck on the girl too, and she liked him. She said he was even better looking than the first one. But he had to talk to her uncle, of course, before they could think of getting married.
>
> Again the priest asked if he had courage and was a strong man. The priest said, "If you do what I want you to do, then we'll talk about marriage."
>
> "Well, what do you want me to do?"
>
> The priest said, "I have a dead man in a casket. I want you to pray all night by the casket. You come; you've got to pray all night."
>
> At about ten o'clock a third boy came along. The priest told him the same thing. He said, "You've got to have a lot of courage. If you do what I want you to, and show a lot of courage, that's all I ask. Another boy is praying all night by the side of a dead man in a casket. You'll have to pretend you're the devil and try to frighten him away.["]
>
> The ten o'clock boy said, "All right."
>
> The eight o'clock boy had flour on his face to make him look like a dead man. The nine o'clock boy was supposed to pray all night by the dead man's casket.
>
> At ten o'clock the devil came in. He had put chains around one of his legs, as the priest had told him to do, and all night long he was supposed to walk around the church and down the aisles. The

man who was praying, he looked around, and said, "Say, what the devil is that?"

All three were scared, but none wanted to give up. The fellow who was praying couldn't stand it any longer. He started to run and the one in the casket did too. After a while the boys had upset the whole church. They were all running around, trying to get away from the rest—until they all fainted.

When they came to, they all began to talk at once. "Are you really a dead man?" "Are you really the devil?"

When the priest came in the morning none of them were there. None of the three had the courage the priest had demanded.[14]

This story includes some widely known motifs, including H310, "Suitor Tests," and H1461, "Test: sitting up with corpse," which Pantalone weaves together to develop a story of seemingly comic emphasis.[15]

Moralistic animal fables represent another type of story which would have been told in traditional settings in Italy. Depicting familiar creatures, both wild and domestic, in human form, these tales often had explicit messages which the storyteller might state at the conclusion. Rocco Pantalone also told Musick several such stories, including one which she called "The Bird and the Fox." The fox's fabled cleverness is overshadowed by that of the dog in Pantalone's story. The moral for the fox is clear, but obviously the storyteller is concerned with the entertainment value of his narrative as well as with any lessons his audience might learn:

In Italy there is a bird called *cotagi* that has a color like a canary, but is as big as a pigeon and with a long tail.

They were going to plant a crop, this bird and the fox, so they agreed to go partners.

The bird said, "It's time to plow."

The fox said, "No, I'm busy now. You plow, and when time comes to sow, I'll sow."

So the bird plowed, but when time came to sow, the fox didn't show up. The bird came down to the fox and reminded him.

Fox said, "I'm busy. You sow; I'll thresh."

But the fox didn't show up. When the bird went after him the fox said, "You go ahead and cut and then I'll thresh."

The bird said, "O.K."

After this was done, the fox said, "You go ahead and thresh, and I'll come in and divide 'em up."

So the bird did the threshing too. Then he went to the fox, and said, "Come and divide the crop."

He said, "O.K. I'll come in."

When the fox came, he said, "You take the straw and I'll take the wheat, *or* I'll take the wheat and you take the straw."

The bird said, "I'm going to a lawyer. If the lawyer agrees, then I'll agree."

So the bird went to the lawyer—the dog was the lawyer—and the dog said, "You'll get the straw and wheat both."

The dog said, "I'll cover up with a measure (a bushel-basket) and you can go and get the fox. But for my pay I want one *meal,* one *lick,* and one *laugh.*"

So the bird brought the dog to the place, covered him up with the bushel-basket measure, and called the fox to come and get the wheat. But when the fox went to get the bushel basket, the dog took after him and the fox left.

Then the dog said, "Now I want my meal."

A woman was to bring dinner to the men who worked on the farm, and she carried it on her head. The bird flew up to her head and kept darting and fluttering around until—well, she spilled the food. So the dog got his meal.

Olive oil was kept in an old courtyard in copper containers. So this woman went out to carry olive oil home in a container. Again the bird started to fly around the woman's head—darting here, darting there—until the woman spilled the olive oil on the road. So the dog got his *lick* (that is, he licked it up).

The dog still had to have his *laugh.* The bird studied and finally, he thought he would get the dog to go to church. When they went into the church, the priest came out to say the mass, and the bird lit on his bald head. When the stick was brought in to light the candles, the bird took it and hit the priest on the head. This made the dog laugh, so he got his *laugh* too.[16]

More typical of the *Märchen* is a tale told by Carmela Teresa Maiolo, born in Pennsylvania but brought up in Italy, where she apparently learned to tell stories. She later moved to Shinnston, West Virginia, where her daughter Melia Rose Maiolo recorded "Fafuzza," which seems to be a variant of Type 881**, "The Poor Girl Pretends to Wealth and Wins the Prince":

Fafuzza was a peasant's daughter. She always worked in the garden. Now, it happened that her garden was near the king's palace. One day the prince went to the window, and as he looked down over his father's kingdom, he noticed Fafuzza, and because of her great beauty he immediately fell in love with her. He went to his mother and said, "Mother, I want to get married."

"That's fine," his mother said. "Go and see what daughter of king, emperor, or nobleman that you want to marry."

"Daughter of king, emperor, or nobleman that I want!" said the prince, imitating her. "I want to marry Fafuzza."

"What! What will the people say if a prince should marry a peasant girl? She may have beauty, but does she have wealth? No, she doesn't have anything. She doesn't even have a decent dress to wear. They are all patched."

"I don't care. If I can't marry her, then I'll kill myself."

The next day he again looked out of the window and saw Fafuzza. She was picking peas. "Fafuzza, will you throw me two pea pods?"

"Two and more if you want," she said. "But how will I throw them to you? Come down and get them." She didn't throw them to him because he was on the eighth floor of the palace.

"Catch me, Fafuzza. I'm going to jump down."

Fafuzza held out the apron she was wearing and caught him in it. His mother had tried to catch him, but the shirt remained in her hands, and she was afraid to look down. She knew, almost, that her son would be dead, but, to her surprise, when she looked, she saw him laughing and talking to Fafuzza.

He helped Fafuzza pick peas, and while they were picking them, he asked her to marry him. She answered him by saying, "Why would you want to marry a poor, peasant girl like me, when you can have any princess you want?"

"I don't care for any princess. I love you, and I want you to be my wife and queen."

"Well then, I'll marry you if Mother and Father say I can."

So he went home with her to ask her parents for her hand in marriage. When her parents saw her coming, with the prince, they were ashamed. They had on old, patched clothes, and they were dirty from having worked in the field. Also, their home was not well furnished, for they were so poor that they just barely made enough to eat. Therefore, they couldn't afford to buy much furniture.

Well, it so happened that Fafuzza had magic powers like the fairies. Before they entered the house, she turned the inside of it into a magnificent mansion. In fact, it was even more luxurious than the prince's home. When the prince entered and saw this, he was amazed, for Fafuzza had told him that they were poor, but now, it looked as if she were wealthier than he was.

When they entered the dining room, a table with costly dishes of food appeared before them. They sat down and ate, and afterwards the prince left, saying that he would have his parents come and ask for Fafuzza's hand in marriage, as was the Italian custom.

That night he told his father and mother that he wanted them to go to Fafuzza's parents and ask them for her hand in marriage, for him.

"Are you out of your mind, Son?" the king asked.

"Just think! A prince marrying a dirty, ragged peasant girl. You ought to be ashamed of yourself."

"Me ashamed of marrying her? Well, I'll tell you I'd be ashamed to have her come and see our home after I saw hers."

"We can imagine what kind of home a peasant girl would have," sneered the queen.

"Go ahead and make fun of her. If you'd see her home, you would realize that you aren't the only ones with wealth."

The prince begged them so hard that the king and queen decided to go the next day and do as he asked. When they saw Fafuzza in the garden, they went down to talk to her, and later went home with her.

Again Fafuzza's parents became ashamed of their poverty, when they saw the king and queen coming, and again Fafuzza turned the house into a magnificent mansion.

The king had brought a beautiful basket filled with gold, and offered it to Fafuzza. She took it and said, "I'll accept it as a gift, but not because I need it, for we have more than enough gold."

While she was saying this, she opened a door to a room, and there they saw the room practically filled with gold pieces.

They asked for Fafuzza's hand in marriage and left, saying that they would return later to arrange the wedding date.

When the king and queen got home, they talked about Fafuzza's home and how much finer than theirs it was.

A few days later, when they went back to set the wedding date, Fafuzza saw them coming, but this time she did not change the house as she had done before, but left it bare and poorly furnished as it was. When the king and queen saw this, they left. They refused to let their son marry her.

The prince had not gone with them, and therefore he had not seen the house as it was. He was determined to marry the girl, regardless of her poverty.

Finally the king and queen gave their consent, and the prince and Fafuzza were married.

Fafuzza had the wedding at her home, and, since she had not transformed it as she had done twice before, the house was dingy and ugly. The prince was unhappy about this.

He wanted to take her to the palace to sleep that night, but she wouldn't let him. She said that she wanted to sleep in her room.

A little while before dark, the prince went out for a walk. As soon as he left, Fafuzza transformed the house into a magnificent palace, and did not change it back. And so it remained a palace for always.

When the prince returned, he thought he had lost his way. But Fafuzza came out to meet him, and they lived happily in their palace from that day on.[17]

Another story told by Carmelo Maiolo exemplifies the distrust of clergy that stereotypically has characterized Italian expressive culture. Her daughter used the title "The Blind Man Can Still See" for this tale, a version of Type 1380, "The Faithful Wife," which hints at traditional Italian anti-clericalism by casting a priest as the adulterous wife's lover:

There was a married woman who had lived happily with her husband until she met a very handsome young priest and began to have an affair with him. She had to be careful that her husband did not catch her, and since the priest came to her home frequently, she had to be on guard at all times.

One day she got to thinking and said to herself, "If only there were some way that I could make him go blind, then he wouldn't see what we were doing."

That evening she went into the church to pray. Her husband followed her into the church and hid behind a statue, so that she would not see him. He heard her praying out loud to a saint. He heard her ask the saint what she could do to make her husband go blind. A voice told her to kill a chicken every day and give it to her husband to eat, so that he would get so fat that his cheeks would puff out, and he would no longer be able to see. She went home and began to do as the voice had told her to do.

By the time she had killed all the chickens, he began to get fat. She went back to pray to the saint, and her husband again followed her and hid behind a statue. He heard her tell the saint that she had fed him all the chickens, but still he could see.

"Well," said the voice, "go home and kill the three kids and cook them for him to eat, and by the time he has eaten them, he will be so fat, that his cheeks will puff out so that he cannot see."

One morning after several weeks, when his wife called him to come and eat, he told her to get him a stick and help him go to the table because he could hardly see.

That night she went back to the church to pray, and again her husband followed her and hid in the same place. This time he heard her tell the saint that he could still see a little. The voice told her that in a day or two he would be completely blind, and if she wanted to get rid of him, she could tell him that the priest had died during the night, and ask him to go with her to throw him over the cliff. "But," said the voice, "when you get there, you put the priest down and shove your husband over the cliff."

Two days later she told her husband that the priest had died during the night, and asked him to walk up the hill with her, so that she could throw the priest over the cliff. He replied by saying, "I'll go with you, but you will have to walk slowly so that I can follow you, for I can't see."

In the meantime, he had a needle and some thread ready to take with him. On the way he sewed the priest's clothes to those of his wife, and kept saying, "Three are going, but one will return."

"What are you saying, Husband?"

"Oh, I'm just saying that three of us are going up the cliff, and that one of us will return."

"How is that?"

"Well, the priest is dead, and you're going to throw him over the cliff, and I am blind and can't see, so I'll remain, but you will return."

When they got there, the wife started to set the priest down, and turned to push her husband off the cliff as the voice had told her to do. However, she didn't know that the voice had been that of her husband, and he knew what she was going to do.

So, when she turned to push him from the cliff, he gave her a shove, and she and the priest went hurtling into space. Then the husband returned home, for he could see well enough, and had only pretended that he could not.[18]

As late as the 1960s immigrants from the Campobassan community of Guardiaregia in the Abruzzi Mountains who had settled in the Syracuse, New York, area were still telling traditional tales which they had learned in Italy. Rosemary Agonito recorded several of these during the summer of 1962. Among them was a short version of the familiar *Märchen* known usually as "Hansel and Gretel" (Type 327A), which transforms the familiar witch into a bear (motif G211.2.1). The storyteller, Filomena Giambattista, had spent her childhood in Guardiaregia and immigrated in 1920. Her names for the two children in this folktale are the masculine and feminine forms for what might be translated as "Curly Top":

> Once upon a time there was a brother and sister, Riccitello and Riccitella, whose mother was dead. Their father had remarried and the stepmother did not like the little children. Each day she kept telling the husband, "Make them disappear or me!"
>
> One day the children heard this and went to their godmother, telling her everything they heard. She told them to carry some flour in their pockets. "If your father should bring you into the forest, drop some of the flour at spots along the way so that you may find your way home."
>
> Then one day their father told them to get ready to go into the woods with him. They hid some flour in their pockets and together with their two pet dogs followed their father into the woods. Riccitello and Riccitella dropped flour along the path as they went. When they were deep in the woods, the father told them, "Wait here. I will chop some wood below."
>
> As the children sat they heard a constant banging similar to the sound of wood being chopped. When they tried to find their father, they discovered that a pumpkin had been tied up in a tree and was banging in the wind. They looked all around but could not find their father.
>
> Then they returned to their trail of flour and found their way home. When they got home, they waited by the door, frightened. But then they heard their father say, "My poor children; if only they could have some of this soup!" So when they heard that, they knocked. Father was overjoyed and let them in.
>
> But the evil stepmother again began to say to her husband, "Make them disappear or me!"
>
> So one day their father again took them and their two dogs out into the forest. Riccitello and Riccitella dropped flour along the path as they went, but this time a bear came along and licked it all up.
>
> When night came, they could not find their way home. They were lost. They walked and walked and soon came to a house which was filled to the brim with delicious sausages, hams, salami, breads, and all types of wonderful foods. The children went in and

ate and ate. They put the dogs into a shed by the house and went to sleep contented.

Suddenly, the bear came home, for it was his house. He discovered the dogs and the children. While the dogs were sleeping, he crept into the shed and stuffed their ears with cotton and locked the shed door. Then he went into the house and grabbed Riccitello and Riccitella. The children cried out to their dogs,

> Break the chains and open the door,
> Your masters are in danger!

But the dogs could not hear them.

The bear growled, "Now I shall eat you!"

The children begged, "Oh, please, let us call to our beloved dogs before we die." The bear agreed for he was sure the dogs could not help. So the children cried out again,

> Break the chains and open the door,
> Your masters are in danger!

They cried this out three times and whistled three times.

Immediately the dogs sensed the danger and shook their heads until the cotton fell out of their ears. When they heard the three cries and the three whistles, they broke the chains and opened the door. Then they rushed at the bear and devoured him.

So the children and the dogs lived happily ever after in the wonderful house in the woods.[19]

Another storyteller from the Campobassan community in central New York had come to this country at the turn of the century at the age of seven. But Mariangelo Giambattista had heard traditional tales during his Italian childhood and told one of them for Rosemary Agonito in 1962. His version of Type 1030, "The Crop Division," is entitled "The Devil and the Woman":

There was a woman who had a piece of land a little way from her home. One day she stood in the doorway of her home and saw a big fire on her land. She hurried over and saw the devil sitting on a heap of burning red hot coals. But she was not frightened by anything.

She asked, "What are you doing with those coals on my land?"

He replied, "Hah! That is not coal! That is all gold. There is so much gold here you never saw so much and you never will see so much!"

The woman said, "Get out of here. This is my land."

The devil said, "No, I found the gold and it's mine. I'll never go."

She argued, "Go or there will be trouble here!" He refused. Then she said, "If you go, I'll give you half of what I raise on this land for two years." He agreed.

"I want the food of this earth," he said. "I have all the money I want."

She said, "Before you go any further, let us get something straight. Whatever, I plant, I will give you all above the earth." He agreed so they signed a contract.

In the spring, she planted beets. In the fall, she picked them. The devil came, and she gave him the leaves from above the ground when he demanded his share. The poor devil had to take the leaves.

Then the devil said, "You fooled me once, but next time I will get all below the earth." She agreed, and they signed a contract.

Next spring she planted corn. In the fall, she picked it. The devil came and demanded his share. She gave him the roots from below the earth. This time the devil got so mad he jumped into a big hole, and nothing but fire came from the hole in the earth.

The woman became richer than anybody in town with all the gold.[20]

Stories such as these tales of wonder, magic, and adventure, though, have given way to less formal kinds of oral narratives, ones which address more directly the social and cultural immediacies of Italian-American life. Personal narratives and family stories also have the advantage of fitting into the everyday contexts of conversational interchange and of being performable by anyone who engages in talk.

One summer afternoon Frank and Guido Malpezzi paid a visit to their brother in a nursing home. The talk turned to the enormous tuition Frank's grandson was paying to attend Notre Dame University. After much discussion, Frank concluded that the whole issue was irrelevant because "You can't take it with you." He reminded his brothers of how their father had said a rich man could be distinguished from a poor man after their deaths: the former by the sour expression on his face and the latter by the peacefulness thereon.

The memory reminded him of a story. When their father had first come from his native Tuscany to the New World, he had earned only a dollar a day as a porter. So the offer of two and a half dollars per day to work in the coal mines of southwestern Pennsylvania seemed like a golden opportunity. He would now be rich enough to bring his wife over from Italy. But two or three children later, miner's wages didn't seem so high. The older Malpezzi consequently went to work in a funeral home. One day a very wealthy man died. When they laid him out, his family followed tradition by adorning his body with rings and other gold jewelry. However, Frank's father noticed that when he was buried, all of these treasures had disappeared. The austerity of this rich man's burial in contrast with the riches displayed on his body in the funeral home graphically demonstrated the truth of the adage which Frank Malpezzi had used to justify his grandson's tuition expenditure.

Personal and family stories commonly emerge in contexts such as that in which Frank Malpezzi related this narrative about his father. During the give and take of conversation, people often recount appropriate tales from their own experience and about their forebears to reinforce points that they may be making. Sometimes such stories occur in slightly more formal contexts, as when an older person has the ear of someone younger who is willing to listen and perhaps absorb some of the family history. Many people develop extensive repertoires of stories about themselves and their families which they relate whenever the opportunity presents itself, while others may tell such stories less frequently and only in direct response to specific conversational situations.

The telling of personal and family stories is certainly not exclusive to Italian Americans, but some of the themes that recur among Italian-American storytellers represent the distinctive experiences of the ethnic group. Subjects such as leaving their homeland, making the Atlantic crossing, arriving in the United States, and getting established remain central even in the tales related by Italian Americans several generations removed from the immigration experience.

For those immigrants who were old enough to remember their life in Italy before they crossed the Atlantic Ocean, tales of the old country may comprise a significant part of their narrative repertoires. Sometimes stories about Italy consist of little more than generalized descriptions of what life was like. In some cases, Italy has been portrayed in glowingly positive terms, as a "static paradise" which contrasts with the sometimes disturbing features of life in America. In Italy, as opposed to the United States, for example, women "knew their place," intimate family relationships were the norm, and people lived close to nature and to God. Among Italian immigrants in New York City early in this century, stories of an idealized life in Italy were told to American-born children "to reveal to them how far they had fallen from it and how impossible it would be for them to live up to its standards."[21]

Other Italian-American storytellers may stress some of the negative features about life in the Old World that account for the decision—their own or their ancestors'—to come to America. But even tales emphasizing poverty, lack of opportunity, and social repression in Italy may strike a positive note by focusing on the almost heroic responses of family members in dealing with such problems. For example, Rocco Capello had come to the United States from Monteu da Po in the Piedmont in 1913, expecting to send for his family after working as a miner for a couple of years. However, World War I interrupted trans-Atlantic travel, so his wife and two children were not able to immigrate until 1920 when commercial shipping routes were restored. For seven years, then, Francesca Capello had to see to the needs of her family. Among the family stories in the repertoire of her daughter Pearl, who was ten years old when the family came to America, is an account of the risks braved by a mother to provide for her children:

> Yes, my mother during the World War Two, during World War Two. We couldn't get any food. No, World War One. What am I saying? "Two"? World War One. We couldn't get any food. We weren't getting any—anything except what we could get out of the garden. And somebody confiscated some rice or something from somewhere. But it was across the Po [River]. And she wanted to go get some rice for us, you know, to—that was something to eat. And she didn't know how to swim. So she walked as far as she could with a cow. Then to cross the river she hanged on the cow's tail. Told the cow to keep going. And that's how she got across the river to get the rice. And came back the same way. That was a rough way to do things. Yes, she worked so hard.[22]

Despite their hopes for richer opportunities in the New World, most immigrants looked back on their departure from Italy as an extremely distressing experience. They and their descendants have preserved narratives of their final actions in Italy and their last impressions of the homeland to which some of them would never return. Even Italian-American families who have not kept other memories of existence in Italy alive may preserve a story treating the final separation from Italy. Christina Falaricco left her home, the village of Castagna in Calabria, in 1906 when she was four years old. Although she spoke little about her early life to her descendants, her grandson knew a story about the family's departure:

> But there are very few stories really that my family told of the Old Country. Most of them came through my mother. My grandmother didn't talk about these things much with the grandchildren. One was about leaving home in Castagna. My grandmother remembers, of course, being a very little girl— probably vaguely remembers that her mother on leaving the house for the last time left a candle burning on the eating table and left a crucifix on the wall. I think to sort of keep it as a home perhaps— who knows?—so the children wouldn't be sad thinking that they would really be leaving home for the last time.[23]

For many immigrants, personal narratives about the actual trip across the Atlantic loom particularly large in their repertoires of tales. Such narratives may be complete sagas beginning with the departure from their *paese,* continuing with embarkation from an Italian seaport such as Genoa, Naples, or Palermo, lingering over the ocean voyage and first New World contact at Ellis Island or other American port of entry, and ending with arrival at their new home in the United States. The recounting of such sagas, which may often assume "the air of an epic tale,"[24] requires a more formal setting than casual conversation, and the storyteller assumes the role of performer for the duration of his or her narrative.

As he grew older, Joseph Capello, who was sixteen years old when he, his mother, and his sister Pearl traveled from the Piedmontese village Monteu da Po by train and then aboard the Cunard liner *Dante Alighieri* to Irwin, Pennsylvania, frequently told the complete story of their trip. His audience might consist of family mem-

Joseph Capello (1904–1991) immigrated from the Piedmont region of northern Italy in 1920. As he grew older, he relished telling long personal narratives, including accounts of his immigration experience and of a visit home in 1969.

bers or acquaintances, and he was careful to ensure that they followed the details of his narration. Having a tape recorder running while he spoke did not seem appreciably to affect his storytelling style:

> We left Italy at Genoa. You've heard of Genoa, Italy? That's a port. It's not far from us. Probably a hundred miles—something like that. You got it [the tape recorder] on? [Interviewer: Yeah, it's on.] We went by train to Genoa. Then we get on the ship and then make the rest of it on the Mediterranean, you understand? [Interviewer: Yeah.] Then we stop at Naples. They load people at Naples. And then we stop in Palermo, Sicily. They load some there. And then we come through the Rock of Gibralter. We come through the Straits of Gibralter into the Atlantic Ocean. We was supposed to get here in thirteen or fourteen days. Took us eighteen days to get in. We had storm all the way to New York. In fact, they went out of course. Then they had to come back, so it took us eighteen days to come across. Five days longer. And where my mother was sleeping, they had those big rooms of double beds, or bunks, you know. They had still the same thing that they had during the First World War that they use for the troops, you know. That's what we come on. And where my mother was sleeping, it busted the door and the water went down. And they had suitcases and clothes bag. It just knocked it over. We had a suit that shrunk, changed colors.
>
> Then we got in New York on the—well, we left Genoa on the fifteenth of November—sixteen. And we got in New York on the second—on the third day we dock of December. That's how long it took us. And then we had to wait there three days to get unloaded. There was three ships ahead of us, and they take one ship at a time to get to Ellis Island, you know. So you know my sister Pearl—she had a rash on the ship already. When we come in, they stop her and they check her and they put her in quarantine. So I had my own passport, but I had guided us, you know. When you went up there—when you pass the examination, you know, to check, they ask me—say, "Who's with you?" Says, "My mother. Where's she at?" They got an interpreter. I don't speak English, you know. When they come, a guy says, "Well, they stop her down there." Says, "I don't know." He says, "Well"—says, "I know what it says. There's something wrong some place. Come on." So I went down there. They was down there. They quarantine her. We was there for three days. Then they let her go. She just had a rash. She had that on the ship already.

Then we left. We come—we got in Irwin [Pennsylvania] on the twelfth. That's when we come in. We got in on the twelfth. We was there ten days altogether in New York on the way over here. [Interviewer: Came on the train?] From New York, yeah. That guy that punch your ticket, you know—they had a big—on the Pennsylvania Railroad, see, we come right in Irwin. It was right on main line, you know. But I already know where I have to get off. You know, guys come over—they just come over—says, "When you come down," says, "you get in Johnstown. Then next it's—when you come to Greensburg—there's a place they call 'Greensburg'— there's three more stops. There's Jeannette—yeah, Jeannette. Three more stops: Jeannette, then Penn—no, Manor, and then Irwin. That's where you get off. At Irwin." You know, when I got to Irwin, that guy—ready to get off (I was stopped)—said, "That little shitass knows where he's going."

Then I saw my dad. Was there waiting. He was off two weeks from work. Every morning would go down and wait on that train. You see, that's where we were coming in. They're immigrants. They put a number there where you get off, you know. That the way it happened.

[Interviewer: He was already here then?] Huh.

[Interviewer: He was already in America?] Well, my dad come here in nineteen-thirteen. See, we was supposed to come in nineteen-fifteen. And then they stop all the passage. They come the war on the Atlantic, you know, and we had to wait there until after the war. And it took us a long time to get passage because after the war, they had to overhaul the ship, you know. They paint them and clean them and everything. They run errands during the war, you know. And it took us a long time. It took us six months to get passage till finally we got it.

And, you know, when I got the citizen's paper, you know—to make a story short, you know. I went to the examination, and they asked me when I come to this country. I told them when we dock in this country: on the third day of—it was my birthday. The third day of December. The guy said, "You come on the second day." Well now, after that I thought, "You know what?" When you come in the twelve-mile limit, the American pilot come in, and they'll pilot the ship into the dock because it's secret, you know— the channel, you know. All the countries like that, you understand? Then I said, "That's when they get on—come over the twelve-mile limit. Was on the second." And that's when I come to this country: December the second, nineteen twenty. That's what my records are. But I says, "How in the heck?" Then I says, "Ohhhhhhh."

When you're in the twelve-mile limit, you're in the United States already. That's when we come, yeah.

We were supposed to come in nineteen fifteen, but we couldn't make it. I didn't want to come that time. But in 'twenty I wanted to come.[25]

While a complete recital of this saga would require special circumstances, Capello might introduce parts of it to make a point during conversation. His sister's brief quarantine at Ellis Island for a minor skin disorder or his learning that his arrival in the United States actually dated from the time the *Dante Alighieri* entered the twelve-mile limit might fit into discussions of the picky precision by which bureaucracy must operate, for example.

Getting adjusted to life in America has provided substance for Italian-American personal narratives and family stories. Difficulties with language seem to be an especially favorite theme. Some stories deal with personal discomfiture at not understanding the subtleties of American English. Pearl Malpezzi could relate an embarrassing experience from her attempts to fit into American life linguistically:

But when I was fifteen, I graduated from the eighth grade then. I knew how to speak English pretty well then. Even learned some things I wasn't supposed to learn. I thought it was great, you know. Like, used to hear these guys—I don't think I should say it. "S.O.B." I'll say that. Gee, I thought that was something beautiful to say. It was a good word. Say, "Gee, you're beautiful or something." So I was at a dance one time. They used—we had a clubhouse right next to our house—Italian club, and they had dances there all the time. I remember there was a guy playing a banjo, and boy, he was really good. And I said, "Boy, he's really an S.O.B., isn't he?" Oh, that was really embarrassing because they looked at me, and then they told me what it was and not to say that. Oh, that's terrible.[26]

Italian Americans may also tell family stories about experiences with the images of Italians in American popular culture. The stereotype of the Italian, fostered by late-nineteenth-century anxieties about the economic effects of mass immigration from southern Europe and perpetuated in almost all the commercial popular media since then, has created problems in self-image and in interethnic contact. Joanne Terranella Burleson tells of her own family's sensitivity to how the media have portrayed Sicilians:

> My name is Joanne Burleson. And my mother's name was Genaro, and my father's name was Terranella. So I grew up as Joanne Terranella, of course. But my father came from a little town in Sicily called Campofelice, which means "happy land" or "happy country." And my mother's family came from a town called Corleone, which is rather familiar to Americans now at this point in their lives. And all my life I heard about Corleone, and I heard about how pretty it was, and I heard about the family history and about Grandpa coming from there and the family and how they lived and so forth. And Mother was always saying, "You know, they weren't poor; they weren't poor." And so I always got the impression that the Genaros were rather well-to-do people, not *very* well-to-do but well off. So many years ago *The Godfather* came out at the movies, and it was a great hit in the United States. And my mother went to see it with my father, and after she came away from seeing it, she told everybody that she was from Palermo. And she wouldn't—she would come—she wouldn't say she was from Corleone any more. She's never said it any more. It embarrassed her so much—it hurt her so much that she just could not stand it as an Italian—you know, as a Sicilian.[27]

The fact that ties with Italy have remained important for immigrants even after they have lived in this country for many years and that family in Italy figures prominently in the social network even for Italian Americans several generations removed from the immigration experience finds expression in trips back to Europe and in the prominence of stories about those trips in narrative repertoires. Invariably, accounts focus not on the grandeurs of Rome or Florence but on a visit to the tiny *paese* from which the individual or his or her forebears emigrated. While there, returnees receive royal treatment from members of the family who have remained in Italy. Joseph Capello often recounted how he and his wife Rose had been received when they returned to Monteu da Po in the Piedmont after an absence of some fifty years:

> I went in 'sixty-nine after I retired. Me and Rosie. That's the best thing I ever did: bring Rosie over there. She didn't want to go. She was scared, but she said all the time she never forgot. Them people were so good to her, honest to God. She had cousins she'd

never seen. She was the only one that went over. There was family there. I didn't know them, but I know other families that were related because I know Rosie's parents. We come from the same village, you know—the people. But she came here when she was two or three years old. And there was a family there—when I went in, I asked in the city [Turin]. I know one of them—he had a cleaning plant. Cleaned—washed, you know, the laundry. So when I come to Turin, I asked my cousin—I said, "There's a family here, Trombetta so and so, and they're Rosie's uncle. I don't know if they live here, but they got cousins over here." I said, "Where are they?" "Hell, three blocks from here." So went over right away.

So they—the man wasn't home. See, the old man die. Now it was a son and two daughters. They run—they had a business. They were pretty well-to-do, you know. So in the evening, you know, he come over right away. Says, "I'll come get you. We go down my house." And we went down to his house. And he says, "Now you go down there"—this town, you know: Chivasso. He says, "There's an uncle lives so and so." He says, "You cross the bridge. There's a place they make gravel right there off the Po River." He says, "You go over there. The son's working there. His son works there." And he says, "Think you can find that place?" I said, "Hell, I know that place. When I was a kid, I used to go there all the time."

So we went there, and I didn't know those people. They were in South America, you know, for years, and then they come back, you know. That's why I didn't know them. And that old man in there—I think we were there for three days. I was busy, you know, and he was watching all the time. So we come in on the afternoon. We was over where we was born. We was eating some place because, hey, I never went into a restaurant because we had to eat some place all the time every day. So I come back. And I come down there. There was a guy waiting for trucks, you know, where they load the gravel. And they get the gravel off the river, and they treat it and, you know, screen it. So I asked—I said, "There's a guy here named Trombetta." See, my wife's maiden name is Trombetta. He said, "Yes, he just went up to the supply house right there." Says, "Can I go?" Says, "Yeah, you go ahead and go." Says, "You're allowed to go." I went up there. I went up the ramp, you know. When I went up the ramp, that cousin—he saw me through the window, and he jumped up. He come out and met us right there. He said, "Where the hell you been?" I said, "We got stuck some place." So I never noticed, you know—I had a car with a German license on it because I got the car with the [plane] ticket, you know. And I never noticed, and Rosie noticed it. She noticed the license is different than the other ones. We got a light[-colored] license. Over here they got a dark one. I says, "I don't pay no attention." He says, "By God"—he says, "I been looking all over for a German license and could never find it." So he says, "I'll find it." I remembered because we had to come on the train that way close, you know. Right down in front of the house.

Rose's uncle—he was ninety years old. He was in the bed, and he was shook up when we come in. So as soon as we come in, well, another girl come down with a bicycle. It was about three miles. She almost beat us down there. See, this guy went over and told his sister lived in town there. Says, "They're over here. They go down." She come over on a bicycle puffing like hell. That was something.

So we went to one of them girls. The girl was there. Well, the boy was working—the son, you know, and the grandson. So she told the girl—said, "You go down the cellar." Says, "Get a bottle of wine." And says, "No, come back. When you go down there, there's three bottles of wine buried in the sand in the cellar. You get one of them bottles." The other girl says, "I'm not going to go down there. I went down one time." Says, "It doesn't matter" (the one come with the bicycle). "I'll go get it." And that wine—this was 'fifty-nine ['sixty-nine]. That's from nineteen forty-six. Had that wine in that bottle.

Boy, he was shook. He died about a month after we left there. He had—a year before, you know, he went down on the land, you know. And he was walking along the irrigation canal and the ditches, you know. And he had a new hat. It fell in the ditch, you know. That water's swift like hell, you know—going like hell. He jump in, and he got his leg frozen. He didn't ever catch the hat. So that's what happened. That's what messed him up, and then he died after that.

So he said, "Now wait a minute." When they brought that bottle, opened it up, and then he tasted it first. "This is the one." He says, "This is from nineteen forty-six." So I drank a glass, and I drink a second. Said, "Go ahead. Drink. *Bevi, bevi.*" I said, "I don't want no more now."

Oh, we had a nice—them people—they weren't rich. They just work the land in there, and they work in there. They just—they not starving, you know. They doing pretty good. Boy, they were good to Rosie. Man, she never—Rosie never forget them people. Once in awhile she says, "Joe," says, "I never thought we'd meet people like that."[28]

Capello's richly detailed narrative includes several elements that frequently occur in stories about return visits to Italy: for example, the unforgettable hospitality of the people, his own keen memory of specifics of the landscape even after a lifetime's absence, and the instantaneous recognition between kin who may not have seen each other for many years, if at all. His attention to such dramatic devices as dialogue suggests the importance of this personal narrative in his story repertoire.

Personal narratives and family stories may not really seem like folklore. After all, they lack the generations of anonymous oral tradition that may lie behind the tales of wonder and magic that represent what we often consider folk narrative to be. But stories such as these do have many elements of tradition. They are told in traditional contexts and require that the storyteller employ many traditional performance techniques. The effective teller of personal narratives and family stories will invest his or her accounts with dialogue, vocal inflection, body language, and other devices to make the events come alive in the same way as a raconteur telling ages-old wonder tales. Moreover, even though narratives of personal experience may be unique in their details, they often follow stylized patterns which mold their content into traditional forms. Repeated tellings of the same story will often produce a formulaic style for certain portions of the narrative, which are told in virtually the same words each time.

The Italian Women's Circle of Masontown, Pennsylvania, staged all-female versions of popular theater, some of which stressed Italian-American subjects. **Love and Duty** was their offering for 1937. Photograph courtesy of Pearl Malpezzi (costumed as the groom in this "wedding" scene).

Drama, Music, and Dance

LIFE IN THE ITALIAN COMMUNITY on New York City's East Side seemed very exotic to Caroline Singer, who wrote an evocative description of the sounds, sights, smells, and—most importantly— people encountered there one Saturday in 1921. Among the individuals who particularly impressed her was a representative of a type who had become a part of the conventional image of urbanized Italian Americans well before the beginning of the twentieth century. The organ grinder, a musician who wandered the streets of "Little Italy" often accompanied by a child or by a monkey while playing simple folk tunes on his machine, came to stand for the pleasure-oriented life to which Italian immigrants, according to stereotyping, were thought to aspire. By the time Singer was writing, though, the organ grinder had already become somewhat obsolete:

> He is seventy, and has looked so long with hope at the upper windows of the prosperous that his head has taken on an everlasting backward tilt, which exposes his Saturday smile, and leaves his old eyes blinking in the sun. If there is no room [on the sidewalk], he stays in the street, screened by mounds of tomatoes and green peppers, with only the top of his dusty hat visible from the sidewalk. Of his presence every Italian is aware, for he and his music-box on its wobbly wheels have not traded *"Fenesta che lucive e mo' nun luci,"* as have the grander wheeled pianos, for a potpourri of jazz and Presbyterian hymns. They are true to the songs which, when he was young and carried an organ as lightly as one wears a flower on the coat, made children dance and called Madonna-faced women to the balconies in Italian streets. Perhaps those who listen to-day are the children who danced and the women who gazed long ago in the Mediterranean town.[1]

As representative type, the figure of the organ grinder, even in his twilight years, highlighted one of the traits most often imputed to

Italian Americans in stereotypes from the nineteenth century through the present—an interest in and aptitude for the performing arts, especially drama, music, and dance. The association of Italians with grand opera and other forms of "classical" music has contributed to the perpetuation of the image on a more lofty plane, and successes of popular Italian-American entertainers such as Frank Sinatra, Tony Bennett, and Madonna maintain it.

On the folk-cultural level, the "performance genres" that Italian immigrants brought from their home villages took only precarious root in the New World. Dependent as they were upon specific language traditions and upon the peasant way of life, drama, music, and dance fared more poorly than other forms of Italian-American folklore that were more adaptable to the American context. But at least for the first generation, all three of these art forms enjoyed some success in Italian-American communities.

Folk drama, extant primarily as puppet plays, was perhaps the first of the three to yield to other forms of entertainment as the Italian audience became more Americanized and as mass cultural entertainment forms such as motion pictures, radio, and later television became more important for everyone. Folksong, which as much as any folklore genre was tied to particular regional and linguistic heritages, has endured longer, but has generally been replaced by Italian music more rooted in mass popular culture than in folk tradition. Folk dance has gone much the same way as folksong, for while Italian-based dances such as the *tarantella* maintain some vitality, they have generally yielded to dances such as the polka adapted from other ethnic heritages or, especially among contemporary Italian-American youth, disco and other popular culture forms.

Drama

At the turn of the century New York City boasted several Italian theaters, at least one of which was devoted to the tradition of puppet plays. The Teatro delle Marionette, seating perhaps 175 persons who paid admission of fifteen or ten cents, offered serial dramas based upon stories that dated back for centuries and often derived from identifiable literary sources. One favorite was based upon Tasso's *Jerusalem Delivered* and required four months of nightly performance to be completed. The masterpiece of the theater was the story of Charlemagne's knight Orlando (Roland), derived loosely from Ariosto's epic *Orlando Furioso*, which would run in nightly installments for fourteen months. On a stage only six feet high, "gaily-tinselled wooden puppets, dressed as Saracens, Turks, crusaders, knights, nuns, maidens, [and] warriors" performed the heroic stories with high seriousness.[2] The Carolingian cycle also provided the principal subject for the plays given in Boston's marionette theater, where during Holy Week the New Testament account of Jesus' Passion was also enacted by puppets.[3] The puppets, called "Orlando puppets" after the principal character in their plays, might be as tall as three feet and weigh nearly a hundred pounds. Costumed in silk and velvet, they were valued at a hundred dollars apiece.[4]

By mid-point in the first decade of this century, more than one puppet theater was active in New York City. In addition to the Theatro delle Marionette, one could find places where puppet plays were aimed especially at speakers of the Neapolitan dialect and of the Sicilian dialect. A writer who visited a puppet theater at that time depicted the scene frequented by "these swarthy children of pleasure":

> The bare brick walls are painted with Italian villas, with flower gardens stretching wide before them—a mass of roses and lilies in wild profusion. From one corner, a piano of ancient lineage and a guitar, quite its contemporary, are pouring forth in unison dulcet melodies and gay waltzes in turn. In the front of the room a tiny curtain adorned with warriors in armor gives promise of the marvelous performance to follow.[5]

After the audience had gathered, the play was ready to begin:

> The curtain rises and enter *La Bella Rosanna*. In sweet, plaintive tones she mourns her father's death; no sooner has she prayed to Heaven for a[n] avenger than enters an armored soldier and pledges his life to her cause. With a speech of gratitude she withdraws, showing a swarthy hand and battered cuff from above as she makes her graceful bow. So the play runs on for a while, working up to the climax of the evening, which is always, time without end, a fierce battle.[6]

Many in the audience might leave after the battle scene, but those who remained were treated to scenes of sentimental love before the evening's entertainment ended.

This theater dramatized only one story per year, beginning in October and ending in June. During the summer shorter pieces were enacted. A half dozen men and boys took charge of manipulating the puppets, sometimes having to handle as many as forty in one night. The master of ceremonies recited all the dialogue in "deep, much inflected tones" and "with unstinted emphasis." Patrons of this puppet theater paid no admission, but were charged fifteen cents when they left, a policy that allowed mothers who had to leave early with fretful infants to avoid having to pay.[7]

Puppet theaters were not confined to the big cities with populous Italian neighborhoods. In Tontitown, Arkansas, for example, puppet plays provided regular entertainment for the Italians who had settled in this small community in the northwestern part of the state. According to an observer who visited there shortly after World War I, the repertoire was more varied than that at the east coast puppet theaters and tended more toward farce than bombastic or sentimental melodrama:

> They had *Rosaura* here, of wholesome Goldoni fame, as she filled the *campielli* of Venice with her twittered *bon mots;* and *Pulcinella,* the facile Neapolitan; *Stenerello,* the timorous and salacious Florentine; *Arlecchino, Brighella, Doctor Balanzon*—all the time-honored types and caricatures, all the characters, fundamentally true or simply plausible to the student of human nature, in which live and are handed down from one audience to another, young or merely mentally unsophisticated, the history and romance of a historical and romantic land.[8]

The puppet theater as an institution, though, seems to have disappeared from Italian-American communities by the early 1930s. As early as 1919, a commentator on Italian-American culture predicted its demise: "But the deeds [of knighthood depicted in the puppet plays], alas, have lost their flavor, or the imagination needed to enjoy them has been jaded or found other delectation."[9] Imported virtually intact from Naples, Palermo, and other southern Italian cities, the puppet theater had limited relevance to an Italian population that was becoming more and more Americanized. However, at least one company, Manteo's Sicilian Marionettes, survived into the 1970s in New York City. Begun by Agrippino Manteo, a native of Catania, Sicily, who came to this country via Argentina shortly after World War I, this company flourished throughout the 1920s, giving nightly performances as well as Sunday matinees of episodes in the Carolingian cycle. By the mid-1930s it was the only permanent puppet theater still extant in New York City.

Manteo's puppet theater closed in 1939, but was reopened by the founder's children in 1950. Although performances did not occur as often as they had in the twenties, most of the traditions of southern Italian folk puppetry endured, including the use of material from *Orlando Furioso*. Agrippino Manteo's scripts—called either *copione* or *manuscritti*—were still being used. The scripts consisted of bare plot outlines which indicated basic action and determined the setting. Occasional set speeches were also included. Much of the actual dialogue apparently was improvisational. Mike Manteo, Agrippino's son, described the company's use of scripts:

> Sure, Ariosto wrote in cantos but who's gonna listen to poetry? The common people on Mulberry Street, they want to see *action*. My father used the exact plot and characters from Ariosto; we never recited it as poetry. Here's an example; here's a beautiful little story—where Roland meets the [C]hristian sorcerer Malagigi in the forest. Roland needs help, so the sorcerer helps him by rowing him across the river; says he doesn't want any reward for doing it. Let's face it even Roland was helped by sorcery ... Actually, we know it by heart; we don't even have to look at the script, understand? *We never rehearsed.* We learned by going on, knowing the action. Sometimes a couple of set sentences.[10]

The Manteo company's performances required six people to manipulate the puppets as well as someone to provide musical accompaniment. Dialogue was provided by several people, who took the parts of various characters in the narratives.[11]

Folk drama in the strictest sense involving human actors apparently enjoyed little if any vitality in Italian-American communities. However, amateur and professional theatrical companies, some of which focused on regionally homogeneous audiences such as Neapolitans or Sicilians, performed popular melodramas and farces at social clubs and mutual benefit societies in many American cities with large Italian populations. Their performances provided appealing Sunday afternoon entertainment for families for whom the enthusiasm and volume of the actors weighed most heavily in assessing performance quality.

A few Italian-oriented theaters existed in major metropolitan areas early in the century. A typical example was Manhattan's Teatro Garibaldi, which flourished from about 1910 until 1920. Seating about five hundred, the Teatro charged an admission of ten, twenty, or thirty cents for men and admitted women without charge. The bill, which changed nightly, emphasized vaudeville, character sketches, and comedies.[12]

One of the most popular figures to emerge from such theatrical contexts in New York City was Eduard Migliaccio (1892-1946), who specialized in character sketches called *macchetta coloniale,* comic turns which relied heavily on Italian-American folk speech for their effect. His creation Farfariello, "the archetype of the poor southern Italian immigrant," represented "the street vendor, the rag picker, the organ grinder, the pick-and-shovel man, the uneducated 'greenhorn,' who murdered the English language as well as the Italian."[13] Migliaccio's act was so popular that he took it on tour not only to various Italian communities in this country but to Italy as well. Popular Italian-American theater also found audiences at Italian clubs in a number of communities. For example, the Italian Ladies Circle of Masontown, Pennsylvania, made such performances a regular part of their annual round of activities.

Music

Italian regionalism, an influential factor in most of Italian-American traditional culture, acted with special force upon musical traditions. In broad terms, the Italian south and the north represented markedly disparate musical customs, the former having drawn upon the musical heritages of the Mediterranean societies of Africa and the Near East, while folk music in the north reflected a kinship with the music of central and western Europe.[14] Because music, both melodies and words, is highly fixed in form, the regional traditions could not easily merge. A song in the Sicilian dialect, for example, would lose much of its impact when its distinctive sound patterns were translated into another dialect or into Standard Italian. It would also fare poorly when set to a new melody, accompanied by new instrumentation, or performed in a new style—all of which might happen if it crossed cultural boundaries. Consequently, although some songs with general Italian-American appeal—for instance, "Santa Lucia," "Funniculi, Funnicula," "Ciribiribin," and pieces from nineteenth- and early twentieth-century Neapolitan popular music—might now circulate in oral tradition, the strongest heritage in folksong has definitely not been Italian as much as Sicilian, Campanian, or Piedmontese.

Northern Italian singing differs in many respects from that in the southern regions. Choral singing in relaxed, smooth harmony has traditionally characterized northern folksong performance. Melodies are usually simple and unembellished. The words to the songs fit the relaxed style and emphasize such positive values as community and peace.[15] Southern singing style is more intense and emphasizes solo performances of a variety of song forms, many of which have not crossed the Atlantic to any marked degree. There is also considerable variety in southern Italian instrumental music. Favored instruments include those familiar in Italian-American and other ethnic communities such as the piano accordion, button accordion *(organetto)*, guitar *(chitarra)*, and especially the mandolin, but a number of instruments which are distinctive to particular regions in the south also exist. These include the Calabrian *zampogna* (a bagpipe) and the Lucanian *cupa-cupa* (a friction drum),[16] both of which find occasional audiences in Italian-American communities but seldom after the first generation.

Singing, like storytelling, depends upon the availability of appropriate, relatively formal contexts. Those contexts in the Old World included most festive gatherings associated with rites of passage or calendar customs, where solo and group singing might take place as part of the celebratory proceedings. In the north occasions such as the Fallerese *filo*, the nightly session of gossip, storytelling, and handwork that occurred during the winters,[17] provided opportunities for singing. Since singing may also have explicitly functional attributes, as when it is designed to accompany tedious, repetitive labor (worksongs) or to help to relax a fretful infant (lullabies), daily activities in some cultures may allow plenty of occasions for song performances.

In this country, the singing of traditional songs by Italian Americans endured as long as contexts with clear regional identities were available. For example, as long as social clubs served only immigrant families from one *paese* or region, they afforded settings for the performance of traditional song at Sunday-afternoon picnics or Saturday-evening dinners. Singing regional folksongs might even be part of the daily activities of such institutions.[18] Once such clubs became more broadly based to emphasize a general Italian ethnicity, the regional songs lost their pertinence. Or a *festa* in honor of a local saint might provide an occasion for singing songs from the relevant regional heritage. But when that *festa* became more generally Italian-American, those songs were likely to be replaced by material with no specific regional identity that might be as much the product of popular culture as of folk tradition.

Rites of passage, which remained more locally oriented within the confines of a particular family, have offered a more lasting context for the performance of regionally based folksong than community-based calendar customs. Southern Italian women in the United States, for instance, have still sung extemporaneous laments over the bodies of deceased relatives.[19] Most likely because they developed to accompany specific tasks, Italian worksongs do not seem to have had much currency in the New World labor setting, but lullabies such as those included in chapter 3 have continued to be sung in the relevant dialects by succeeding generations of Italian-American caregivers.

Traditional regional folksong, then, has clearly represented a survival from Old Country traditions. Often the singers have been first-generation immigrants who have not passed their repertoires on to offspring who lack the necessary linguistic skills in the dialect and who may find the songs of only minimal interest in an Americanized setting which emphasizes Italian rather than regional identity. Consequently, the performance of traditional songs in the United States often has operated principally as a tie with a romanticized homeland and has been one of the least persistent aspects of Italian folk culture.

Even so, examples of regional Italian folksong still occur in communities such as the Niagara Frontier area of western New York and southwestern Ontario where first-generation immigrants are continuing to renew the tradition. There, groups such as the Coro Alpino of Buffalo, New York, perform traditional songs from Trieste, Istria, and other parts of northern Italy. Begun informally in the 1950s to provide a social focus for immigrants from those regions, the group originally sang informally at dinner dances. Then in the late 1970s they began to perform publicly.[20]

Some immigrants from earlier in the century also retained and performed their musical heritage. Fragmentary variants of traditional songs remain in the memories of their descendants. For example, Antoinette Giglio, whose parents emigrated from Sicily and settled in Lake Charles, Louisiana, recalled a bit of a love lyric:

> *Mama, mi sita passa*
> *Cuo la catina ora.*
> *Si mi marita hora,*
> *Su mi marita cue.*

> (Mama, my boyfriend is passing
> With a gold chain.
> If I don't marry now,
> I never will marry.)[21]

Among the fuller versions of traditional songs collected from first-generation Italian Americans are several from the Piedmont region of northern Italy. In 1962, for instance, Francisco Musso, who had immigrated from there in 1907, performed a song associated with First of May festivities in his home village. Three girls, one of whom represented the "bride of May," went from house to house soliciting gifts. As they made their rounds, they sang the following:

Ben venga magg!
Ben staga magg!
Torneruma 'mezz' al magg
Se veuli non credi
Che il magg sia venu,
Affevite alla finestra
Lo vederai fiorì.

Refrain:

Ben venga magg!
Ben staga magg!
Torneruma 'mezz' al magg.

Antruma es la bellezza—
A tre, a tre, a tre.
Chiamuma la patruna
Se veu lassé canté.

Refrain:

Guardé la nostra spusa!
Che bei scarpin che l'ha!
Chissá chi l'ha donaje
Sará lo suo papá.

Refrain:

Guardé la nostra spusa!
Che bei orecchin che l'ha!
Chissá chi l'ha donaje.
Sará lo suo papá.

Refrain:

Guardé la nostra spusa!
Che bell'anel che l'ha al ditin!
Chissá chi l'ha donaje.
Sará lo suo marí.

Ringraziuma la patruna
Che n'avesse ben pagá.
Preghiamo Iddio e la Madonna
Che i daga la sanitá.

(Welcome, May!
May, stay well!
We will return in the middle of May.
If you do not believe
That May is come,
Look out the window;
You will see it while it is flourishing.

Refrain:

Welcome, May!
May, well stay!
We will return in the middle of May.

We enter where there is a beauty—
Three, by three, by three.
We ask the landlady
Whether she will let us sing.

Refrain:

Look at our bride!
What beautiful little shoes she has!
Who knows who has given them to her.
Maybe her father.

Refrain:

Look at our bride!
What beautiful earrings she has!
Who knows who has given them to her.
Maybe her father.

Refrain:

Look at our bride!
What a beautiful ring she has on her finger!
Who knows who has given it to her.
Maybe her husband.

We would thank the landlady
If she would pay us well.
Let us pray God and the Madonna,
Who give her good health.)[22]

Another Piedmontese American who continued to perform folksongs from her homeland after moving to the United States was Mary Fiorina, who immigrated from Turin in 1913. One of these was "La Monaca Sposa," a widely known ballad, or narrative folksong, which she sang for a folksong collector in 1952:

Giù per la via ie 'na filletta;
L'è tanto bella l'è 'nnamora.
Mentr' ei le deie le batitüre
Fin che l'amur le sia spassa.
Le süpare disse alla madre
Che le batitüre l'avria da fen.
Si compreremo 'na vesta grisa,
La bütteremo 'nt'al monister.
Custa filletta suva stanzietta—
Pià la puma el caramar.
S'ai a scriveie 'na letterina
S'ai a mandare al sü più car.

Gentil galanto più sta lettera;
La disigilla e pei la lee.
De 'na 'morosa che è nella via
L'è monighetta m'la veulu fè.
Du 'na 'morosa che è nella via
L'è monighetta la veulu fè.
Gentil galanto ve a la scuderia,
La scuderia dei soi cavai; remira uno,
Remira l'altro, büttà la sella al suvo più car.
Remira l'uno, remira l'altro;
I büttà la sella al suvo più car.
"O, levte su ti, caval muretto;
Se' el mio più bello, el più gaiard,
Que l'avrà da cure com 'na rondolina
Quanto spasügia traverso il mar.
Que l'avrà da cure come 'na rondolina
Quantu spasügia traversso 'l mar."
Gentil galanto se bütt'à curre,
Bütt'à curre e a speronen.
L'è 'rrivà là giust'a qull'ora
Ch'illa rientrava nt'al monister.
L'è'rrivà là giust'a qull'ora
Ch'illa rientrava nt'al monister.
"O, scuttes io, madre badessa;
'Na parolina l'avria da fe."
S'ai a spurgiie la man sinistra;
S'ai a büttaie l'anel al di.
S'ai a spurgiie la man sinistra
S'ai a büttaie l'anel al di.
"O, bondì, padre; O, bondì, madre;
O, bondì, tutti mei car parent.
L'è sü credeie a fermi mugna;
Son farmi spusa allegramente.
L'è sü credeie a fermi mugna;
Son farmi spusa allegrament."

(Down the street there is a little girl;
She is very beautiful and in love.
They [her parents] beat her
So that her love would pass away.
Her father told her mother
That the beating must come to an end.
We will buy her a grey dress,

And throw her into a nunnery.
This little girl went to her little room—
Took her pen and ink well.
She wrote [must write] a little letter
And sent [must send] it to her dearest one.
The gentle gallant took the letter;
He opened and then read it.
[It] is from the loving girl who is on the road
Because they are determined to make her a little nun.
[It] is from the loving girl who is on the road
Because they are determined to make her a little nun.
The gentle gallant goes to the stable—
The stable of his horses. He looks at one;
He looks at the other; throws the saddle on his favorite [horse].
He looks at one; he looks at the other;
He throws the saddle on his favorite.
"O, get up, you black horse;
You are my most beautiful, my strongest,
So that you have to run as the little swallow
When she flies over the sea.
So that you have to run as the little swallow
When she flies over the sea."
The gentle gallant begins to run,
Begins to run and to spur.
He arrived there just in the moment
When she was entering the nunnery.
He arrived there just in the moment
When she was entering the nunnery.
"O, listen to me, Mother Abbess;
I must have a little word."
She holds [must hold] out her left hand;
He [must] thrust the ring on her finger.
She holds [must hold] out her left hand;
He [must] thrust the ring on her finger.
"O, good morning, Father; O, good morning, Mother;
O, good morning, all my dear relatives.
You thought to make me a nun;
I am now happily a bride.
You thought to make me a nun;
I am now happily a bride.)[23]

Mary Fiorina also knew a folksong which illustrates the propensity for vocables (sometimes referred to as "nonsense syllables") in northern Italian singing. The text also suggests the ways in which animal sounds are traditionally imitated in the Piedmontese dialect:

La gata su la montagna
Sa l'ha perdì i gat[t]in.
L'è tut la nut che braia
"Mignin, mignin, mignin, mignin,
Mignin, mignin, mignin, mignin."

La gata su la montagna
Sa l'ha perdì i gat[t]in.
E la bela alla finestra
Ch'al guarda su e giù,
El maggio ritornato
Al canto del cucù:
"Cucù, cucù, cucù, cucù, cucù.
El maggio ritornato
Al canto del cucù.

(The cat on the mountain
Has lost her kittens.
All night long she is [m]ewing:
"Minying, minying, minying, minying,
Minying, minying, minying, minying."

The cat on the mountain
Has lost her kittens.
The beautiful one at the window

Looks up and down the road.
May [has] returned
To the song of the cuckoo:
Cuckoo, cuckoo, cuckoo, cuckoo, cuckoo.
May has returned
To the song of the cuckoo.)[24]

"Spazzacamino," a song about a chimney sweep who complains of being cold, hungry, and generally helpless, survived in the folksong repertoires of immigrants from northern Italy. August Franch of Lafayette, Colorado, who came to the United States fairly late in 1939, was still singing this song (which has also been reported from Tuscan immigrants on the West Coast) in the early 1960s:

Spazzacamino!
Spazzacamino!
Io ho freddo e ho fame.
Son piccolino [or picalino].
In riva al lago
Dove son nato,
La mia mamma
Mi ha abbondonato.
Come un uccello
Che lascia il nido
Per guadagnarsi
Qualche quattrino
Io vo gridando
"Spazzacamino!
Spazzacamino!"

(Chimney sweep!
Chimney sweep!
I am cold and hungry.
I am a little wandering child.
On the bank of the lake
Where I was born,
My mother
I have abandoned,
Like a bird
Which leaves its nest,
To get for itself
A half penny.
I go around crying,
"Chimney sweep!
Chimney sweep!")[25]

An observer's comment from the late thirties that "Among Sicilians, the only songs heard in the new country are those of the exile who thinks of his mother, [and] longs to be at her side once more"[26] remains an overstatement. "[R]omantically sentimental" music emphasizing mother and home "and having mostly Neapolitan rather than Sicilian origins" has been very popular with southern Italians, but other song types have also enjoyed some popularity. The *stornelli*, for example, apparently originated in Sicily but spread northward up the peninsula to cities such as Rome and Florence. The term for a single verse of one of these songs, *stornello*, also means "starling," an image suggesting the graceful irony that frequently characterizes *stornelli* lyrics.[27] As Charles W. Churchill found in 1940s Newark, New Jersey, *stornelli Romani* of southern Italian communities in the New World often were extemporaneous, "made up by two singers as they go along. The song," Churchill wrote, "frequently takes on an insulting character which even leads to physical violence only averted by the audience."[28] The novelist Garibaldi M. Lapolla reproduced some *stornelli* verses in English which, though lacking the competitive element, demonstrate the lyric richness of these improvisational verses:

Oh, flower of the fig, sweet you are,
But not the sweetness of my passion flower.

Oh, flower of the jasmine bush,

Her fragrance is the spring's, it never dies.

Oh, flower of the orange growing wild,
What, what do you know of beauty when she's by.[29]

In addition to *stornelli,* other southern Italian folksong types that have been recorded in North America include *canzone* and *mutteti* (lyric songs similar to *stornelli* from Reggio and Catanzaro), *canti per la questa* (holiday carols), and *romanze* (love ballads).[30]

From the rich tradition of Sicilian folksong, several songs dealing with courtship and marriage have endured in the Americanized life of Sicilian immigrants and their descendants. Perhaps because they deal with subjects related to marriage, a rite of passage involving a family heritage that might emphasize regional traditions, these songs have maintained their vitality longer than some other material in the Sicilian folksong heritage. An example is *"E la Luna Mezzu Mari,"* known to a general American audience from its use in the wedding scene which opens Francis Ford Coppola's film *The Godfather.* A text of this almost infinitely expandable song was collected from Sicilians in Tampa, Florida, in the late 1930s:

E la luna mezzu mari,
Mama mia, mi vogliu maritari.
Figlia mia, cu t'a dari?
Mama mia, penza ci toi.

Si ti dunnu lu pisciaru,
Iddu va, iddu veni
Sempri pisci manu teni.
 E s'iddu ci piglia la fantasia,
Figlia mia, ti pisculia.

(Chorus)

O mamá, pisci fritu e bachalá,
O mamá, va fatti la fari to!

Si ti dunnu lu carnizzeru,
Iddu va, iddu veni
Sempri salcizza manu teni.

E s'iddu ci piglia la fantasia
Figlia mia, ti salcizzulia.

(Chorus)

Si ti dunnu lu verduleru,
Iddu va, iddu veni
Sempri bonanni manu teni.
E s'iddu ci piglia la fantasia,
Figlia mia, ti bonannia.

(Chorus)

Si ti dunnu lu scrivanu,
Iddu va, iddu veni
Sempri lapizzi manu teni.
E s'iddu ci piglia la fantasia,
Figlia mia, ti lapizzia.

(Chorus)

This song begins with a daughter's questioning her mother about possible marital prospects. In successive stanzas the mother runs through the list of potential husbands: the fisherman, the meatcutter, the fruitseller, and the bookkeeper. She bawdily emphasizes the phallic nature of the objects (fish, sausage, banana, and pencil) associated with their occupations that they will always have with them. The song can continue indefinitely as the mother thinks of more eligible bachelors to list.[31]

Despite the general moribundity of regionally based folksong in Italian-American communities, recording companies during the first half of this century did document many of the traditions on commercial records. Early in the history of the record industry, companies realized that a market for recordings of folk music existed among the people who were accustomed to hearing that music in traditional contexts. Consequently, many immigrant and ethnic musicians made records intended for sale to the relevant ethnic communities. Recordings of Italian music for Italian-American audiences especially flourished. One count indicates that between 1894 and 1942 some 473 individuals and ensembles made records aimed at Italian-American record buyers. In fact, more records were made by Italian Americans than by any other non-English-speaking group in this country.[32] That most of these records emphasized regional rather than general Italian material indicates a continuing interest in this once-rich folk music heritage.

The development of a generalized Italian music derived from the "Neapolitan music hall of the early twentieth century" has been one of the hallmarks of pan-Italian identity in the middle and late twentieth century.[33] Yet that music, derived from and usually circulated as popular culture, represents a secondary level of musical tradition, one which has replaced the regionally distinct music that the immigrants had known through oral tradition in Italy but were unable to maintain effectively in the face of homogenizing and Americanizing influences.

Dance

Though revived through the efforts of folk dance enthusiasts, Italian-American traditional dance generally has suffered the same fate as regional folksong. Dances which immigrants brought from their *paesi* and villages have been replaced by interethnic dances such as the polka and the dances of American mass culture. A list of dances performed in the Italian community of Newark, New Jersey, suggests that a number of native Italian dances had made the Atlantic crossing: the *tarantella,* the Venetian *furlana,* the *mazzucca* (an adaptation of the Polish mazurka), the *ruggiera,* and the *siciliana.*[34] Of these, the most widely known—and the one about which most lore exists—is the *tarantella.*

Tradition, inspired probably by the similarity in name between dance and spider, holds that the *tarantella* has a connection with the bite of the tarantula. An account of the dance's origin emphasizes the connection:

> The Tarantella, an old Italian dance whose tune is known to every Italian boy and girl, started in a most peculiar way. Many hundreds of years ago it was believed that the only way to cure the poisonous bite of a tarantula spider was to dance oneself to exhaustion. During the Sixteenth, Seventeenth, and Nineteenth Centuries wandering bands of musicians roamed the Italian countryside

providing musical cures for what seemed to be an epidemic of tarantula bites.[35]

The *tarantella* also has traditional associations with the city of Taranto on the Apulian coast. That community probably gave its name to the disease tarantism, first described in the fifteenth century and, again probably through sound similarity, attributed in some cases to the bite of the tarantula. One of several "dancing manias" that swept certain parts of southern Europe during the fourteenth through seventeenth centuries, tarantism was thought to be alleviated by vigorous movement such as one might do while dancing a *tarantella*. By the mid-1700s tarantism had apparently disappeared, but the dance that had become associated with it endured as what some now consider the "national dance of Italy." Under that guise, the *tarantella* still enjoys some popularity at festive occasions such as weddings and especially at celebrations of general Italian ethnicity.[36]

Considerable regional variation characterized the *tarantella* in Italy. The standard form of the dance prescribes that dancers maintain a dignified posture by keeping the shoulders and hips relatively rigid. Otherwise, improvisation is the rule. When danced alone, the *tarantella* allows individual expression. When performed by dancers of the same gender, the dance encourages the juxtaposition and interplay of their personalities. When a male-female couple dances the *tarantella*, it may be openly sexual. Richard Gambino has described a couple's *tarantella* in which the pair acted out a range of attitudes—seduction, aggression, bravado, coquettishness, taunting, teasing, jealousy, feigned indifference, flirting, cruelty, surrender, and tenderness—all to the shouts of approval or disapproval of their audience.[37]

The esthetic appeal of these performance genres of Italian-American folklore make them particularly ripe for popular revival. While such a development would certainly contribute to the multicultural diversification of arts in the United States, it would not change the fact that in the natural development of Italian-American culture, drama, music, and dance as folklore have, for the most part, given way to entertainment alternatives available through the popular media.

A grape arbor is often a prominent feature of an Italian-American kitchen garden. Established by Joseph Capello, this one is now maintained by his daughter and son-in-law.

Foodways

"I KNOW I'M ITALIAN because I couldn't go for anything but Italian food," a resident of New Haven, Connecticut, told sociologist Irvin Child in the 1930s.[1] Observers of American ethnic groups have frequently noticed the correlation between traditional foodways and a sense of group identity. Many have, in fact, posited that patterns of food preparation and consumption have persisted longer than any other feature of Old World culture.

Such a generalization requires recognition that diversity in food habits and their retention occurs on individual, family, and—especially among Italian Americans—regional levels. But overall, loyalty to foodways remains a factor in the lives of many descendants of Italian immigrants who may have little other knowledge of their foreparents' culture. For example, Christopher Hodgkins, whose second-generation Calabrian-American grandfather actively Americanized his family by insisting that Italian culture be suppressed, retained traditional eating habits: "That was one area where my grandfather conceded and allowed Italian culture to prevail. That was around the table. The family table...was thoroughly Old Country. There was always a bottle of red wine—jug red—and plenty of pasta of all kinds."[2]

Similar testimony comes from other Italian Americans, such as Bruna Pieracci, an immigrant from Modena. Recalling the lives of coal miners and their families in Iowa, she noted, "[A]s the years went on, while they accepted other American ways and things their food preferences always remained Italian."[3] Or one can cite the prediction of researchers who extrapolated from their observation that second- and third-generation Italian-American women in Pittsburgh's Panther Hollow district usually served pasta even with American meals: "Even after Americans of Italian extraction abandon most of their traditions and dialects, their cuisine will remain an enduring link with the past."[4]

Food habits are steadfastly resistant to change—more so than most other aspects of culture. Not only do we—like the old parents in Joe Vergara's *Love and Pasta* who evince contempt for "American" cooking[5]—especially distrust the strange and exotic if we are expected to put it into our mouths, but we also remain faithful to certain foods because we associate them with the contexts in which we first ate them. Consequently, loyalty to what are perceived as Old World foods by Italian Americans may reflect dietary conservatism, a sense of group membership, and the symbolic values of "home," particularly the positive image of the tradition-oriented Italian woman as wife and mother.[6] While other features of Italian-American domestic life can perhaps evoke home as effectively, foodways (at least some of them) have the additional virtue of being positively regarded by mainstream society.

As early as the 1890s, American commentators were noticing the Italian diet. In 1897 a social worker observed in Boston's North End that the "dinner of the ordinary Italian is made up largely of macaroni, French or Italian bread, and usually some meat and potato.... Fruit or a few dried olives, which very much resemble a small prune, are sometimes eaten for dessert. Supper does not differ very much from dinner for the workmen. Some kind of vegetable food constitutes their principal diet."[7]

During the first few decades of this century, nutrition became a focus of contention between Italian-American women and representatives of the bureaucratic mainstream. Social workers as well as immigrant women viewed diet as a measure of Americanization, and the former promoted the adoption of American-style foods as a way to combat the malnutrition which they believed to be rampant in many Italian neighborhoods in American cities.[8] It was argued that while traditional Italian foodways met the nutritional needs of agricultural peasants in Italy, developments such as the substitution of coffee for milk, more reliance on meat and less on vegetables, more frying, and less outdoor exercise made them unsuitable for life in the United States. The increased consumption of sugar was regarded as particularly harmful.[9] Italian-American women were urged to avail themselves of canned and readymade food from the shelves of the grocery stores in their communities and to rely upon mass-produced, enriched bread instead of making their own in the traditional manner.[10]

However, Italian ethnic cooking prevailed, and since the 1930s and probably earlier in some parts of the country, what has passed for Italian food has become a regular feature of the mainstream diet. Child, for instance, characterized the situation in New Haven in the thirties:

> One of the most persistent traits of Italian culture ... is the cuisine. A major reason for its persistence may well be the frequently rewarding, and certainly nonpunishing, attitude of the American population at large. Dishes that are recognized by everyone to be of Italian origin are probably served occasionally in a large proportion of non-Italian households in the city. Italian dishes preserved in cans are a part of the standard stock of grocers throughout the city and are presumably bought by non-Italians rather than Italians. Many of the Italian restaurants secure a good part of their patronage from non-Italians. Italian families frequently invite non-Italian friends to their homes for an Italian dinner, and the usual response is enthusiastic appreciation. There is no other trait of Italian culture that receives anything like this treatment from the American population at large and that would, consequently, be so uniformly reinforced.[11]

Thus, one could assert Italian-American identity by eating Italian food without encouraging the negative reactions that other indicators of Italian-American ethnicity have sometimes produced.

At the same time, though, Italian Americans insist that Italian food from packages and most restaurants represents only a bland imitation of the real thing and point to the careful selection of quality ingredients and appropriate use of spices which characterize genuine Italian cooking. Hodgkins recalled his dismay at the "spaghetti" served at church suppers in suburban California in the 1960s and 1970s: "You know, it would just be these little chopped-up bits with flaccid meatballs soaked in fat, you know. That's not spaghetti, you know."[12]

A character in Rocco Fumento's novel *Tree of Dark Reflection* dismisses American cooking for its blandness: "Everything must be boiled or fried and with no spices, not even a bit of garlic, so that everything tastes the same."[13] The Italian Americans with whom Richard Raspa worked in Helper, Utah, believed that American cooking tended to obliterate "the dramatic contrasts in texture and taste" which Italian cuisine emphasizes through such combinations of salty *prosciutto* (ham) wound around a slice of sweet melon and accompanied by a sharp red wine.[14] These Utah Italians (mostly Calabrian) also tended to exaggerate ways in which their traditional cuisine differed from that of their Mormon neighbors by focusing on dishes that might seem particularly alien: squash patties made of chunks of squash and diced flowers fried in egg batter; *la rouinella*, chicken intestines and gizzards cooked in tomato sauce; goat intestines wrapped around *finocchio* (fennel) and simmered in sauce; and *sciungad*, a goat cheese.[15]

While a reflector of group identity on the general Italian level, food has had its most important symbolic value in the context of the family. Produced by the labor of both father and mother and representing the cooperative efforts of an integrated family, food has had almost sacramental significance. To waste or abuse food was seen as virtually a sin.[16] Food stands for wealth in the material and familial sense. To share food has been the consummate act of hospitality, and to refuse to accept offered food has often been regarded as an insult.[17]

Because Italian culture in the United States maintained much of the regionalism of the Old World, one would expect that regionalism in particularly pronounced form in foodways. It is certainly true that even after the disappearance of the often hostile *campanilismo* that characterized Italian-American life in the first generation, regional loyalties in diet have remained, "the Ligurian pesto sauce and the Sicilian use of anchovies" serving as "badges of regional identity within Italian-American communities and households."[18] Despite the development of restaurant fare—"pizza, pasta, red sauces, and cheap red wine"[19]—that reflects a pan-Italian identity, regional differences in foodways have actually become more pronounced with the trendiness of Italian regional cuisines in the 1980s and 1990s. Though such differences are subtle and some variance occurs from *paese* to *paese*, a major distinction can be drawn between the pasta-oriented cookery of southern Italian Americans and the *polenta–risotto* complex of northerners.

Pasta vs. Polenta

Shortly after the turn of the century, a social worker described the diet of Sicilians living in Columbus, Ohio. They ate beef or veal no more than two or three times per week and eschewed pork altogether. They also favored saltwater fish such as mackerel and bass, poultry, and eggs, but might substitute beans or pasta with tomatoes for these foods. Special luxuries in their diet included green vegetables, sardines, artichokes, and olives. They used prodigious quantities of olive oil and lard, but little milk.[20]

The lack of meat in the diet of Italian Americans from the south invited considerable criticism from the nutritionists who were trying to convert them from traditional foodways to a mainstream American diet. Social workers particularly singled out the meat-poor eating habits of citydwellers, not realizing that distinctive ethnic meat dishes did figure in their menus, if not on a regular basis then at least on festive occasions. For example, a "big treat" for Sicilians has been *brusciuluna:*

> It's the steak that you beat down, and then you make a batter. You make a thing with egg and bread crumbs and stuff, and you roll it. It rolls into a thing. You toothpick it and tie it and let it soak in the gravy to cook further. Pre-cook the steak very little, you know. But you got it down pretty thin so you can roll it.[21]

Other special occasion meat dishes include *cabutzel,* a lamb's head soaked in salt water, then roasted, and *lonza,* cured pork loin made each winter to be eaten throughout the year.[22] Italians from the south have also eaten a considerable amount of sausage on a daily basis, purchasing some from groceries featuring imported foods and making some on their own. Sausage-making can be a serious undertaking. It certainly is for Federico, a character in Guido D'Agostino's novel *Olives on the Apple Tree:*

> "You raise one pig just for me. For nobody else. I show you how to make the sausage from my part of the country. You chop the meat, plenty garlic, strong pepper, the lilla red ones, salt—and I forget what else, but I remember. Then with the pipes from the

inside the pig wash clean and the funnel, you push, push, push, like this," forcing the thumb of one hand into the fist of the other.[23]

Italians who lived in rural communities in the United States could raise their own pigs to provide sausage, lard, and *prosciutto*. Sara Vittone's father, for instance,

> would kill pigs and make those big hams, those *prosciuttis*, and lard and sausage. And he would hang them, smoke them first, and then hang them in there. They would keep. And he would make lard, and he'd get some of that sausage and put it in the lard while he was pouring this, you know, and then they would get like the lard. Then when you pick your lard, you'd get one of them sausage and fry it, and it was good. That's the way we'd get our meat for the winter.[24]

While traditional eating patterns among southern Italians have changed in reponse to—among other factors—nutritional trends such as those advocated by the early-twentieth-century social workers, even the typical meal cycle based on Old World models was not as devoid of virtue as critics suggested. Breakfast was admittedly a simple affair: chunks of crusty bread used to soak up coffee and milk. Occasionally, cereal or meat might be added, and some Italian Americans have had soup as a regular part of their breakfast menus.[25]

But even if bread provided the main course for breakfast, it was usually home-baked with considerable attention to quality. Bread-making skills served as an important measure of a woman's domestic worth. Occasionally in rural areas, tradition would govern bread-making to the extent that it was done in outdoor ovens. The wives of Italian-American coalminers in Thurber, Texas, for instance, baked fifteen or more loaves per week in outdoor ovens shaped liked beehives and made of brick, stone, and clay.[26] Sara Vittone remembered the twenty-five pounds of flour that was used to mix the bread dough for her family's weekly supply. As a girl of thirteen, she had the chore of manipulating the cumbersome mass of dough under her mother's direction.[27]

Perhaps because of its sacramental significance as the Body of Christ in the Mass, the preparation and consumption of bread have been attended by numerous prescriptions and taboos. For instance, some believed that Monday was the only day suitable for breadmaking. Performing this culinary chore on the first day of the week meant good luck until the following Monday. Each loaf should be marked with a cross. Should one sneeze while mixing the dough for bread, it will not rise. Once bread had been baked, one should be careful not to turn a loaf upside down. If a piece should drop onto the floor, it should be kissed and blessed with the sign of the cross. It was considered sinful to waste bread, to stab it with knife or fork, or to eat meat without it. Any leftover bread should be kissed before being discarded. If a housewife borrowed bread from a neighbor, she had to return it or risk a hundred years in purgatory.[28]

The almost sacred significance of bread made it a good luck charm: one of the first items brought into a new home should be bread, perhaps in combination with salt.[29] According to Jerre Mangione, who grew up in a Sicilian household in Rochester, New York, bread carried considerable symbolic weight:

> Aside from its traditional association with the body of Christ, bread to my relatives was a daily reminder of the hardships they and their ancestors had endured to survive, a symbol of man's humbleness. They regarded bread as some God-bequeathed friend who would keep their bodies and souls together when nothing else would. And when times were bad, they said to each other, "As long as God grants us a piece of bread, we shall get along."[30]

Ideally, lunch *(collazione)* was a family affair. As late as the 1970s, a Cleveland, Ohio, high school reported problems in keeping its Italian-American students on campus during lunch time. Despite regulations, they were going home to eat with their families.[31] If their mothers followed the old ways, they might encounter *lentiche e pasta* (lentils and macaroni), *pesci di vuova* (an omelet with romano cheese), and black olives, a typical southern Italian noontime meal.[32] Or perhaps they would have *pasta e fagioli* (pronounced "pasta fazool"), bean and pasta soup, or escarole soup such as that prepared for her children by Lucia Ferraro:

> Another thing I used to like was the escarole soup with the little small meatballs in them and the pasta. And it would be the fresh escarole. And you would bring the soup to a boil and drizzle in the

egg and put it on with nice fresh grated cheese, a nice piece of fresh Italian bread. And we all made pigs of ourselves.[33]

If they should have to eat lunch away from home, school-children might pack a lunch of bread, salami, and cheese. Although some children, interested in becoming Americanized, might be embarrassed by the "bulky sandwiches of crusty Italian bread heaped with salami, cheese or Italian sausage," most eventually came to value their foodways over the "white-bread-and-ham" fare of their classmates.[34] Perhaps their fathers might eat as well away from home as Joe Vergara's shoemaker father, whose usual lunch consisted of a half loaf of sliced bread stuffed with leftovers such as veal cutlets, eggplant, or meatballs. Sometimes he might have a few pieces of chicken cacciatore with roasted peppers. Always there would be black olives and, in season, a ripe tomato. He would wash his lunch down with a glass or two of red wine from a bottle he kept under the counter.[35]

Family would definitely be expected to be present for the evening meal *(pranzo),* at which pasta would figure either as the featured attraction or as a side dish. In the former case, it would certainly be served with "gravy," the tomato- and possibly meat-based sauce for which southern Italian cuisine is famous.[36] The foundation for most southern Italian gravies is the tomato, grown with considerable care in home gardens or purchased in bulk from produce vendors and supermarkets. A family from Almalfi living in New Haven, Connecticut, reportedly purchased forty bushels of tomatoes each year, a quantity that would be typical for tradition-oriented households.[37]

For families that used only their home-grown tomatoes, methods for preserving the summer harvest for year-round use were essential. One possibility was to convert the tomatoes into *conserva* (paste). To make *conserva,* an Italian-American woman would boil masses of tomatoes ripe from the garden. Then the mashed, cooked tomatoes would be suspended in a linen bag so that the juice might drain from them. The remaining pulp would be mixed with olive oil and dried in the sun.[38]

Conserva produced in this way comprised a principal ingredient for sauce throughout the year. A typical recipe for pasta sauce begins with frying a pork chop in olive oil and butter. A bay leaf, parsley, some sliced tomatoes, and water would be added, the mixture stewing for a couple of hours. Then the cook adds a tin of *conserva*, salt, and pepper and allows the sauce to simmer for another half hour.[39] Today even tradition-oriented cooks such as Sara Vittone may avail themselves of readymade ingredients when they make sauce for pasta:

> I put a big can of crushed tomatoes and a twelve-ounce can of tomato paste and cook that, simmered, you know, real low. Then I put salt and pepper and garlic, you know. And before I make my meatballs—first I make my meatballs. I never fry—like a lot of people fry their meatballs on the stove. I bake mine. First I put them down and then brown them on the bottom. Then I turn them up to broil, and I stand there and watch them, you know, and then I take them off. A little bit of that grease I get and put it in a skillet, and I fry like a handful of ground meat, mash it up and fry it, and then I throw that in my sauce first. Yeah, and I always put a stalk—one piece of celery in my sauce.[40]

Some cooks may add some sugar to counteract the acidic quality of the tomatoes. Sauce made according to these—or a multitude of variant recipes that endure as family traditions—can be ladled over pasta of many shapes as a staple meal.

While most today buy prepackaged pasta or make it using a convenience such as a "spaghetti machine," Italian-American women used to roll out pasta and cut it into strips using either a knife or a device called a "guitar," which cut dough into several strips simultaneously.[41] The manufacture of pasta could often be a major undertaking, according to Frances Gueri Byrd:

> And she [her mother] would work all day Saturday. And how she did this—she would be in the kitchen. She had a huge, wooden, thick wooden board to make this on, and she must have started with ten pounds or something of flour—started with that—and how many dozen eggs and all. So the mess would be in the kitchen. Then the dining room had the large—the long dining room table. And she'd have white sheets just covering the dining room table. And she would roll out this—you know, make this dough and roll it out.[42]

While some commentators have argued that the reliance on pasta as a staple in southern Italian households has developed in the United States, it has certainly been an important component of the diet of many Italian Americans. As Mamie Jo DiMarco Chauvin noted about meals in her Sicilian family, "Now no Italian meal is complete without pasta. I mean that's just a foregone conclusion."[43]

Pasta with gravy may be accompanied by an *insalata,* a salad made of fresh vegetables from the garden or of ingredients gathered in the wild, dandelions being a favored green.[44] Vegetables could include *lupini,* beans said to never fill one up because of a curse they received from the Virgin May when they pricked her legs on the flight into Egypt, or escarole, supposed to have cleansing properties.[45] Red wine would be the accompanying beverage.

Some southern Italian families carried on old-country ways of serving and eating pasta. For example, Sam Gennuso, a second-generation Sicilian, had heard his parents tell of the way a gravy dish might be served in their family early in the century:

> And we had a big round table. Big old oak table, according to them, that they would—they told me how they did it. They would cook the pasta and put it all in the center of the table. And around the pasta they would pour the gravy *on* the table.... And then they would be sitting. And this sounds kind of savage—kind of crude— but from what I understand that's the way they did it in Italy. They would pull the pasta. They would get their hand or their utensil and get the pasta and just pull it through the gravy in front of them and eat it that way. I guess they had forks and knives. Oh, I'm sure they did. They'd pull it to them like that and then eat it with a big thing of bread on the side.[46]

Gennuso also recalled the special Friday version of spaghetti his mother would make:

> She would bake her spaghetti. She'd cook the spaghetti and put a layer of it and then a layer of cheese and a layer of spaghetti and a layer of cheese. And have hard-boiled eggs cooked in the gravy. And instead of the meat, you know, we would have the eggs with the pasta.[47]

Generally, southern Italian-American cooks have prepared baked gravy dishes such as *lasagna* for special occasions.[48] Other special pasta dishes included ravioli, which might require the labor of four or five people. The filling for these pasta tarts might include leftover meat with spinach or cheese. Tortellini and cappelletti, both smaller than ravioli, also had a variety of fillings. All three of these pasta varieties might be served with sauce or in chicken broth.[49] Dessert might be fruit or nuts, sweets on a regular non-holiday basis being an American addition to the southern Italian-American cuisine.

The staple in the northern Italian diet was *polenta,* a cornmeal mush cooked until it was thick enough to congeal when poured from the pot onto a flat surface. When Joseph Capello came to the United States from the Piedmont at the age of sixteen, he was used to eating *polenta* on a daily basis. His sister Pearl Malpezzi recalled, "Like my brother always said, he couldn't eat *polenta* for years because he ate it every day before [coming to America]. He wanted to get away from it."[50] Sixty years after immigration, Capello—who noted that northern Italians were called *"Polentani"* because of their food habits—still expressed a lack of enthusiasm for the dish he had once eaten so frequently: "No more. I have too much."[51]

Actually, Capello's attitude toward *polenta* is somewhat unusual. Among many Italian Americans from the Piedmont and other northern regions—including some members of his own family—this once-daily staple, eaten so often because it was an inexpensive, filling meal, has become a treat to be eaten now on semi-festive occasions. Not really a holiday meal, *polenta* might be served for a Sunday family dinner, especially if relatives from out-of-town are visiting. It may be accompanied by a variety of meats and sauces. A favorite in Italy was roasted birds such as larks or blackbirds which would be eaten bones and all with a slice or two of *polenta* dripping in butter—a way of serving the dish occasionally reported among Italian Americans.[52] Or chicken stew might be ladled over slices of *polenta.* Sometimes it could be eaten with sausage and sauerkraut.[53] Another frequent accompaniment for *polenta* has been *baccala.* Bruna Pieracci noted this dish in the coal camps of Iowa during her youth:

> I especially remember the whole salted cod fish because it never spoiled winter or summer. The Italians call it *baccala.* My father

*Guido Malpezzi serves **polenta**. After the cornmeal has thickened, he pours it on a flat surface, allows it to cool and harden, and then slices it in the traditional manner with a piece of twine. Tomato sauce with sausage or **baccala** (codfish) will be ladled over the slices of **polenta**.*

would chop off a piece with a hatchet. It was soaked to remove salt, boiled until tender and tomatoes were added and simmered for a time. Meanwhile he would make a big golden yellow *polenta*. When done it was turned out on a board, cut into steaming slices with a heavy string and served with the *baccala*.[54]

Pearl and Guido Malpezzi try to have a hearty dinner of *polenta* (which is said to have "heating" qualities[55]) two or three times each winter, usually serving it with *baccala* or sausage, either one cooked in tomato sauce for several hours. The process of preparing *polenta* itself takes about an hour. Cornmeal, moistened with a little cold water, is dumped into a pot of boiling water at the proportion of one cup of meal for three cups of water. Salt and sometimes butter may be added.

The mixture requires constant stirring to disperse lumps and prevent sticking. As it thickens and the stirring becomes more arduous, Guido usually takes over and maintains a careful watch. The *polenta* nears readiness when the wooden stirring spoon can stand upright in the center of the pot on its own. Once he is convinced that the cooking has gone on long enough, Guido carefully pours the *polenta* onto a large cutting board. He allows the *polenta* to settle as he gradually dumps it out so that the result is a golden mound that suggests the etymology of its name—from the Italian for "pollen."

The *polenta* must set for a few minutes to ensure that it is solid and to allow the table to receive the other elements of the meal: the pot of *baccala* or sausage in sauce; a jar of mushrooms, picked by Guido and pickled by Pearl; a salad; and a bottle of wine. Guido serves the *polenta* in the traditional way. Like Pieracci's father, he grips the end of a length of twine in each hand and runs it beneath the mound of cornmeal. He lifts the twine to cut slices and uses a spatula to scoop them into each diner's plate. Tradition insists that the *polenta* not be cut with metal implements. With Pearl's assistance, he ladles sauce over the slices and perhaps sprinkles flakes of dried red pepper on top. Several slices of *polenta* with sauce washed down with as many glasses of wine produce a repletion that only the temptation of Pearl's berry pie, made from raspberries picked along the roadsides the previous summer and preserved in the freezer, can overcome.

The elevation of lowly *polenta* from everyday staple to center of festivity certainly suggests the symbolic potentials of food. For Pearl, who was only ten when she and her brother came to the United States, *polenta* evokes the idyl of childhood, as it does for Guido, a second-generation Tuscan, who had eaten it less frequently than his wife while growing up in Rillton, Pennsylvania. Joseph Capello's lack of enthusiasm for the dish probably stems from the longer duration of his contact with it on an everyday basis and his sharper memories of its associations with low income in their native village of Monteu da Po. *Polenta* can not only be eaten freshly cooked. Once it has congealed, it can be sliced and fried or stuffed with cheese and baked.[56]

The cornmeal dish's principal rival for supremacy in the northern Italian diet was rice, the short-grained variety grown in the Po River valley and nearby regions. Mixed with beans, rice provided a welcome alternative to *polenta*. As Capello noted, "I was raised with *polenta* and rice and beans. I'm telling you. Rice and beans. Man, I used to like that. I never got tired of eating it. But *polenta!*"[57] Like *polenta*, Italian rice dishes *(risotti)* endure as food for special occasions. Cooked with rich creamy or tomato sauces, a variety of vegetables, meats, and seafoods, the sticky Italian rice serves as a main dish. Northern as well as southern Italians have also favored a pasta variant called *gnocchi*, whose dough includes mashed potatoes as well as flour. The dough is rolled into small dumplings and eaten with red sauce.[58]

For second- and third-generation families, whether their ancestors had come from southern or northern Italy, the traditional cuisine has become more and more restricted to special occasions. The situation with Joseph Bernardin's mother is probably typical:

> Because her time was limited, Mother would prepare Italian food only on Sundays and holidays. During the week we would eat "American food," as she called it, because it was easier and quicker to prepare. Generally on Sundays, she would make various kinds of pasta, especially spaghetti.[59]

Yet appreciation for the regional and pan-Italian cuisines continues to mark ethnic identity.

Wine

During the first few decades of this century the urban settlement houses that tried to interest Italian Americans in their programs often failed miserably for the simple reason that they served no wine at their social gatherings.[60] The consumption of wine, particularly homemade, has figured so conspicuously in the Italian-American nutritional system that many have perceived it as a virtual staple. "To deprive a man of his vino would be like prohibiting the Englishman his tea or the American his coffee," a commentator on Italian Americans in Cleveland during prohibition has written.[61] Italian-American proverbial lore emphasizes the centrality of this beverage in the culture:

Un giorno senza vino e come un giorno senza sole.
(A day without wine is like a day without the sun.)[62]

Acqua fa male, il vino fa canta.
(Water is harmful; wine makes one sing.)[63]

Valued much differently than in mainstream American culture, where its use may often be a moral rather than a nutritional concern, wine has clearly been defined as food by most Italian Americans, who regard it as a natural accompaniment to a meal. A survey done among Italians in New Haven, Connecticut, during the 1950s revealed that winedrinking represented "a fact of life of almost the same import as the use of bread"[64]—a comparison strengthened by their both being used sacramentally in the Mass. Pearl Malpezzi recalled that in the Piedmont wine "was on the table all the time. It was a food. It wasn't a liquor for us." The same attitudes characterized wine consumption among her family after their immigration to southwestern Pennsylvania.[65]

The positive valuation of wine, "a natural food" that seemed the appropriate complement to the fresh fruit and vegetables that Italian Americans savored,[66] has made it a primary component of a hygienic system based upon food as a guarantor of strength, energy, and good health. The New Haven researchers found that their sources approved the largest quantities of wine for those engaged in heavy labor, suggesting the equation of the drink with vigor and stamina.[67] Such an equation could be interpreted indirectly since wine is believed to stimulate the appetite for strengthening foods, but since it was also considered to build blood, the equating of wine consumption with strength was meant quite directly. Its blood-manufacturing capacity made wine an excellent beverage to be given in small quantities to children who might be susceptible to winter chills.[68]

The novelist Marion Benasutti has a central character drink a wine and raw egg mixture each day upon returning home from work to compensate for the strength and energy he has expended.[69] By extension, winedrinking has taken on an aura of masculinity, an implied theme in one of Joseph Capello's favorite stories:

> My uncle, you know—he was my godfather. Her [his mother's] brother. He said when I was born, I was the first-born boy, you know, of the family, probably you know.... He says he put his finger in the glass full of wine. He said, "By God, he likes it." I was sucking it. Kids do that. You put it in, and they suck it. He said, "He likes it." He said, "Okay, boy, you be winedrinker like me."[70]

Wine may also restore lost vigor, so Italian Americans have prescribed its use by the aged and ill. A descendant of Neapolitan immigrants has claimed,

> We feel that wine can perform great healing miracles in all areas of life: medical, sexual, cultural. You name it, wine fixes it. If our neighbor Bellitti had cancer, which he did, and couldn't eat, the neighborhood advice was, "Have a drink of wine." It was magic stuff, pure magic.[71]

Drunkenness, however, is a sign of unmanliness, as a Sicilian rhyme suggests: *"La biviri non misurata / Fa l'uomo asinata"* ("Drunkenness makes an ass of a man").[72]

In addition to its practical value, wine has contributed signficantly to the maintenance of emotional ties with the Old World. In this respect, the production of wine in the home has been of paramount importance. For many Italian-American winemakers, this craft consciously follows patterns which have been a continuing component of family tradition.

The process, which may be a festive communal affair, begins in early autumn when grapes in bulk—sometimes shipped from California, sometimes locally grown—become available. Most Italian-American winemakers have preferred darker grapes which yield a "black" wine, the well-known "dago red" of ethnic stereotyping. This beverage is regarded as more healthful than white wine, which also retains some associations with the wealthy classes since white grapes were more expensive in Italy. Favored grapes include zinfandel ("California's alternative to Florentine chianti"[73]), Alicante Bouschet (a black grape with red juice that California growers often ship to eastern markets), and Carignane (a Spanish-derived grape used for bulk red wine by California commercial winemakers). The last may sometimes be mixed with white grapes to soften its hearty, sharp taste. The winemaking process is quite straightforward.

Once a winemaker has acquired a supply of suitable grapes, he uses a winepress to extract the juice. This is stored in barrels—perhaps castoffs from a distillery—in a cool place to allow natural fermentation to occur. Some winemakers may add sugar to augment fermentation, but others regard this practice as unnecessary and, in fact, adulterating. During fermentation, which continues as long as any wine remains in a barrel, the winemaker's primary responsibility is to ensure that the barrel remains airtight. This usually means only that he must keep it damp to prevent shrinkage of the wood and resultant cracks in the seams between the staves. Souring—the result of allowing air to enter during the fermentation process—may also be prevented, according to a Sicilian American who had observed his uncles making wine, by rubbing the sides of the wine barrel with "a mysterious plant."[74] Some Italian Americans see a correspondence between fermentation and the phases of the moon—the waxing of the lunar body paralleling an increased rate of fermentation and the rate decreasing as the moon wanes.[75] Others forbid the contaminating presence of a menstruating woman during any part of the process in fear that it will sour the wine.[76]

Although wine may be sampled at any time while fermentation is going on, it obviously will be stronger the longer one waits. A traditional date for tapping a barrel of wine for the first time has been Saint Martin's Day (11 November). If it is tapped under certain lunar conditions, according to some traditional winemakers, wine will turn to vinegar.[77] At the initial tapping, considerable ceremony may attend the sampling of the first glass, apprehension building until the winemaker and his "panel of experts"—family members and *paesani* who may have actually helped in the production of the beverage— signal their approval.[78]

A barrel of sour wine means real disaster for a family, since they will have to rely on the vintage of others or—much worse—commercially produced wine throughout the year. Moreover, since it is a masculine enterprise rooted in traditions perceived as having accompanied the *famiglia* from Italy, failure in winemaking can represent real loss of face and a blot on the family honor.

Italian Americans also make use of byproducts of the winemaking process. Some of the original grapes may be set aside to produce wine vinegar, for instance, and *sapa,* a conserve, can be made during the first pressing of the grapes. Unfermented juice is boiled with orange, nuts, and spices to produce a holiday pastry filling.[79] Some of the wine itself can be distilled for *grappa,* a strong brandy-like drink which some Italians may call "moonshine."

Grocery, Garden, and Field

Traditionalists sometime lament the adulteration of Italian foodways with American ingredients. Even Italians in Roseto, Pennsylvania, where ties with the ancestral *paese* have remained particularly strong, seem to have compromised their cuisine:

> What used to be the traditional pizza (a flat bread with some salt, tomatoes, or onions) now contains an amazing variety of additions: salami, pepperoni, sausages, ham, and even eggs. The same goes for all varieties of the so-called Italian spaghetti with meatballs (meatballs were totally unknown in the original peasant recipe) and sweets, most of which used to be quite plain and not sweet at all with the exception of the Sicilian sweets, which were honey-based. Not infrequently, Rosetan children in America make disgusted

faces at the plain *biscotto* made by their old grandmother for Christmas.[80]

Some of this change has occurred, of course, because of the lure of mainstream American cooking which offers convenience as well as the symbolic values of assimilation. At the same time, though, traditional cooking—like scientific folk medicine—has often been based on ingredients not easily available in the United States.[81]

One way of supplying Italian culinary needs is through the ethnic grocery store that has tended to flourish in urban neighborhoods and rural communities with high concentrations of Italian immigrants and their descendants. For example, in Providence, Rhode Island, several stores had been established on Federal Hill, the Italian-American district, by 1915. Stocking imported olive oil and pasta and offering spicy sausages, storekeepers tried to meet the needs of their neighborhood customers. One grocer from Providence explained the success of his venture: "I specialize in Italian grocery because Italians always eat Italian style."[82] But even Italian groceries were not able to offer the rich variety of freshly grown fruits and vegetables that Italian cooks and eaters desired.

Every spring Joe Vergara's Calabrian father, a shoemaker by trade, plowed up their yard and mixed bushels of sheep and goat manure into the soil. He would set out rows of tomato and pepper plants in the center and arrange beans, trained to climb up strings, along the fence. Eggplants and a grape arbor also contributed to the luxuriant growth, stimulated by ashes from the furnace strained and spread lightly around the plants, that by mid-summer engulfed the Vergara yard.[83]

The foundation of Italian-American cuisine, whether its roots lie in northern Italy or in the south, has been a kitchen garden such as that planted and tended each year by the elder Vergara. The raw produce consumed fresh in summer salads or preserved for use throughout the year by canning, drying, or another traditional process ideally comes from one's own backyard. While reliance on one's own garden may arise partially from economic reasons (it perhaps being less expensive to grow one's own produce than to purchase it at a supermarket), several other stimuli contribute to the place of gardening in Italian-American traditional culture.

Frank Malpezzi (in cap) shows off his garden to his brother, niece, and great-niece. Italian Americans have maintained kitchen gardens for a variety of reasons: to grow produce that may not be readily available in groceries, to provide their families with higher quality fruits and vegetables than may be obtained commercially, and to maintain ties with their agrarian past.

As noted, one factor affecting Italian-American interest in gardening has been the commercial unavailability of many fresh items important for traditional foodways. A list of the items found in Calabrian kitchen gardens in Helper, Utah, suggests that items which might seem exotic to mainstream American tastes were commonplace to Italian Americans: peppers, tomatoes, onions, endive, eggplant, beets, spinach, potatoes, fava beans, Swiss chard, zucchini, squash, carrots, garlic, parsley, basil, fennel, grapes, figs, and walnuts.[84] While all these items might now be sold in supermarkets even in small cities as well as in Italian-oriented grocery stores, some of them remain difficult to acquire in rural communities. On a very practical level, if Italian-American cooks wanted to use the ingredients to which they were accustomed, it has often been necessary to produce those ingredients themselves.[85]

Moreover, Italian Americans have a clear sense that produce from their gardens is of higher quality than that which they can purchase at supermarkets. As Sara Vittone noted, "I always had a nice garden. There was a nice ground there. Them peppers, I could have put a half a pound of meat in one of them peppers—you know, stuffed peppers."[86] Size, flavor, texture, color—all such determinants of the quality of a foodstuff—are perceived as enhanced in produce grown in one's own garden.

Gardening may also have had symbolic value as a microcosmic fulfillment of the *contadino*'s goal of owning land, a dream that had seldom been fulfilled in Italy. This symbolic dimension to gardening may explain the prevalence of fig trees in Italian-American gardens in parts of the country where the climate was inhospitable to figs:

> Behind each six-family tenement house was a handkerchief of fenced-in land on which every Sicilian planted a fig tree. In the winter-time, he covered it with rugs and linoleum so that the cold of North America would not kill that exemplar of his homeland, the symbol of Sicily.[87]

A writer who visited the Italian settlement of Tontitown in northwestern Arkansas shortly after World War I noted the "natural instinct of the Italian peasant to raise a little of everything on his own."[88] While gardening may not be instinctive, it certainly has represented cultural identity for Italian immigrants and their descendants—"a consistent marker of Italian ethnicity," according to one commentator.[89] As an analyst of the symbolism of ethnic identity in American literature has noted, gardening for Italian Americans represents a "metaphor for the ethnic encyclopedia" and operates as a "powerful locus of ethnic binding."[90]

Only such symbolic significance could explain why even in a community such as Roseto, Pennsylvania, where the high concentration of *paesani* would ensure the availability of most foods in markets and in neighbors' gardens, every household still has a garden of its own: "While little or no room is left between one house and the next one, all of them have long, narrow back gardens intensely cultivated by the oldest members of the families and still very reminiscent of southern Italian gardening."[91] Also, by including plants generally unknown outside the Mediterranean region in their gardens, Italian Americans can point to their cultivation of such vegetables as broccoli and fennel and of herbs used in cooking and healing as distinctive symbols of who they are in relation to members of other folk groups.

Italian-American gardening has involved both traditional and modern methods. The way in which gardens are arranged represents the methodical approach to the gardening process:

> A striking thing about such [kitchen garden] abundance, where every available slice of land is suffused with sprouting green leaves and stalks, is that while giving the casual observer the impression of randomness, the crops are actually organized generically into neat rows. One garden [in Helper, Utah] was sloped at the top in order ... to water vegetables in a specific order, tomatoes, potatoes, eggplant, and so on, giving more water to some and less to others.[92]

Folk beliefs have also figured into planting practices. For instance, a reliance on lunar cycles to schedule setting out certain kinds of plants (generally, root vegetables in the dark of the moon and leaf vegetables in its light, or vice versa) is a widely known practice which governed the gardening schedules of some Italian Americans.[93]

The tradition of the Italian-American kitchen garden has adapted to various situations in the New World. In crowded cities where a yard for a garden may be unavailable, a few herbs grown in a flower bed or window box may fill the symbolic role of garden.

Some Americans of Italian descent have built upon their gardening heritage to create businesses for themselves. For example, in Depression-era New York City some Italians had established "market gardens," which provided needed income as well as food for their own tables, on "areas of unused or marginal land which landowners lend out or lease ... for a limited period of time." Most of these plots were no larger than fifteen acres, and the growers themselves sold the produce in open markets.[94]

Italian Americans on the West Coast have carried out this process on a larger scale. By the 1870s Italian farmers in the San Francisco Bay Area were producing enough from their gardens to require the opening of a market exclusively for their wares. Elsewhere, they began to specialize in particular crops such as onions, cabbage, broccoli, and cauliflower and to establish major produce growing and distribution operations.[95]

The availability of fresh produce direct from the kitchen garden has translated into traditional food specialties such as *la giardiniera*, a mixture of tomatoes, zucchini, summer squash, peppers, onions, and fresh herbs simmered together and eaten cold or warm with hunks of bread, and *bagna cauda*, a "hot bath" of garlic, olive oil, and anchovies, into which one might dip a variety of fresh vegetables, including mushrooms.[96] These last usually were picked wild by Italian-American men and women knowledgeable in mushroom lore. Guido Malpezzi has been an avid harvester of mushrooms. According to his wife Pearl,

> He picks the morelles in the springtime. They're like an ice cream cone. It comes on a stem. It's hollow. It's hollow inside. The stem and the top. And the top is like a sponge. It comes to a point. That's the first mushrooms they pick, and then there's the field mushroom. They'll be starting now [mid-summer]. And then there's the sheepheads. And there's a purple mushroom. It's delicious. You get that mostly around woods. There's a brown mushroom that grows in the woods. It's real good. But you have to get it when it's small. I like them when they're real small. But then there's another kind that's called "elephant ears" and seashells. I think that's about it that we picked. You have to know your mushrooms.[97]

Her last comment emphasizes the critical factor in mushroom hunt-ing, for eating the wrong mushroom can be fatal. Like many Italian-American mushroom hunters, Guido Malpezzi has relied upon his experience to distinguish the edible from the toxic. Those who eat what he has picked assume the attitude that Christopher Hodgkins voiced regarding the mushrooms gathered by his Calabrian-American uncles in the foothills of the California mountains: "You trusted your uncles, so you ate their mushrooms."[98] More skeptical individuals might try a traditional test for poisonous mushrooms: dropping a silver coin into the water as they boil. The coin will turn black if they are poisonous.[99]

If "Traditional foods and ways of eating form a link with the past and help ease the shock of entering a new culture,"[100] then Italian Americans have been well served by the culinary traditions which they brought with them as they crossed the Atlantic. In many ways, what has happened to foodways epitomizes the general processes of folklore retention and adaptation that have charac-terized developments in most of Italian culture in America.

A few food traditions—especially those whose exotic nature hindered their acceptance by mainstream society—remain close to what they were in Italy and continue to reflect the *campanilismo* and loyalty to *famiglia* that have been such strong factors in Italian and Italian-American life. Some foods such as most pasta dishes have evolved to fit the tastes of mainstream Americans and of Italians who have become Americanized. Others—pizza, for example—often bear little trace of their origins and may be as much the product of interethnic amalgamation as of Italian traditional cuisine.

When social observer Charlotte Adams described Italian life in New York City for readers of *Harper's* in 1881, shortly after the beginning of the mass immigration of the late nineteenth century, she noted,

> I fail to find that Italians here retain their national habits of enjoyment or their love of feast-day finery.... [T]he indifferentism and stolidity of the country react upon them. There seems to be little of the open-air cooking, the polenta and fish stalls, the soup and macaroni booths, that breed conviviality in the Italian streets.

They apparently eat in their own homes, after the New World fashion.[101]

Perhaps Adams was accurate in her assessment of how quickly specific immigrant families she observed had changed their ways. But the data of Italian-American folklore suggest otherwise. Even several generations away from the Italian homeland, the descendants of the men and women who braved the Atlantic crossing continue to use folk speech, proverbs, rites of passage and calendar customs, games and storytelling, music and dance, and even foodways to express their ethnicity—their sense of themselves as Americans who retain and celebrate distinctive qualities rooted in the mountain valleys of Lombardy, the beaches of Campania, the rugged hills of Calabria, the *paesi* whose cultures nourished their ancestors.

Notes

Chapter One. Setting the Scene

1. Interviews with Lucia Peek (Campanian, third generation), 19 January 1991, in Jonesboro, Arkansas; with Sara Vittone (southern Italian, second generation), 16 June 1990, in Masontown, Pennsylvania; with Joseph Capello (Piedmontese, first generation), 19 July 1984, in Masontown, Pennsylvania; and with Mamie Jo DiMarco Chauvin (Sicilian, second generation), 19 March 1991, in Forrest City, Arkansas.

2. An overview of Italian immigration is available in Humbert S. Nelli, "Italians," in *Harvard Encyclopedia of American Ethnic Groups*, ed. Stephan Thernstrom (Cambridge: Harvard Univ. Press, 1980), 545-49.

3. Nathan Glazer and Daniel Patrick Moynihan, *Beyond the Melting Pot, The Negroes, Puerto Ricans, Jews, Italians, and Irish of New York City*, 2nd edition (Cambridge: MIT Press, 1970), 182.

4. The precise proportions of southerners among Italian immigrants during the first four years of this century are as follows: for 1901, 83.23 percent; for 1902, 84.7 percent; for 1903, 83.97 percent; and for 1904, 81.28 percent. See G.E. DiPalma Castiglione, "Italian Immigration into the United States 1901-04," *American Journal of Sociology* 11, no. 2 (September 1905), 185.

5. Joseph Lopreato, *Italian Americans* (New York: Random House, 1970), 33.

6. Phyllis H. Williams, *South Italian Folkways in Europe and America, A Handbook for Social Workers, Visiting Nurses, School Teachers, and Physicians* (1938; reprint, New York: Russell and Russell, 1969), 1.

7. Lopreato, 102.

8. Salvatore J. LaGumina, *The Immigrants Speak, Italian Americans Tell Their Story* (New York: Center for Migration Studies, 1979), 83 (from the memoir of Sicilian Joseph Zappulla).

9. Williams, 17.

10. Lopreato, 104. See also Richard Gambino, *Blood of My Blood, The Dilemma of the Italian-Americans* (Garden City, NY: Doubleday, 1974), 65; and Fred L. Gardaphe, ed., *Italian-American Ways* (New York: Harper and Row, 1989), 87.

11. Marie Hall Ets, *Rosa, The Life of an Italian Immigrant* (Minneapolis: Univ. of Minnesota Press, 1970), 209. For the concept of *forestieri* which informs Cavilleri's comments, see Glazer and Moynihan, 184.

12. Humbert S. Nelli, "Italians in Urban America: A Study in Ethnic Adjustment," *International Migration Review* 1, no. 3 (Summer 1967): 52.

13. Rev. Enrico C. Sartorio, *Social and Religious Life of Italians in America* (Boston: Christopher, 1918), 18.

14. Samuel L. Baily, "The Adjustment of Italian Immigrants in Buenos Aires and New York, 1870-1914," *American Historical Review* 88 (1983): 291.

15. Caroline F. Ware, *Greenwich Village 1920-1930, A Comment on American Civilization in the Post-War Years* (1935; reprint, New York: Harper and Row, 1965), 153-54.

16. James Cascaito and Douglas Radcliff-Umstead, "An Italo-English Dialect," *American Speech* 50 (1975): 6; and Gary Mormino, "'We Worked Hard and Took Care of Our Own': Oral History and Italians in Tampa," *Labor History* 23 (Summer 1982): 397.

17. Carla Bianco, *The Two Rosetos* (Bloomington: Indiana Univ. Press, 1974); interview with Pearl Malpezzi (Piedmontese, first generation), 17 July 1984, in Mason-town, Pennsylvania; and Patrick B. Mullen, *I Heard the Old Fishermen Say, Folklore of the Texas Gulf Coast* (Austin: Univ. of Texas Press, 1978), 78.

18. Glenna Matthews, "An Immigrant Community in Indian Territory," *Labor History* 23 (1982): 387.

19. Dino Cinel, "The Seasonal Emigrations of Italians in the Nineteenth Century: From Internal to International Destinations," *Journal of Ethnic Studies* 10, no. 1 (1982): 43-68; Bianco, 7; Robert F. Foerster, *The Italian Immigration of Our Times* (Cambridge: Harvard Univ. Press, 1919): 23-43; and Rudolph J. Vecoli, Foreword to Ets, viii.

20. Michael La Sorte, *La Merica, Images of Italian Greenhorn Experience* (Philadelphia: Temple Univ. Press, 1985), 120-24; Angelo M. Pellegrini, *Americans by Choice* (New York: Macmillan, 1956), 139-46; and Judith E. Smith, *Family Connections, A History of Italian and Jewish Immigrant Lives in Providence, Rhode Island 1900-1940* (Albany: State Univ. of New York Press, 1985), 105.

21. Lopreato, 40.

22. Humbert S. Nelli, "Italians in Urban America," 39-40.

23. Charlotte Adams, "Italian Life in New York," *Harper's* 62 (1881), 680.

24. Lopreato, 101-03. See also Leonard Covello, *The Social Background of the Italo-American School Child, A Study of the Southern Italian Family Mores and Their Effect on the School Situation in Italy and America* (Leiden: E. J. Brill, 1967), 15-33.

25. Marion Benasutti, *No Steady Job for Papa* (New York: Vanguard, 1966), 3.

26. Bruno Roselli, "An Arkansas Epic," *Century* 77 (1920): 378.

27. Philip A. Buscemi, "The Sicilian Immigrant and His Language Problems," *Sociology and Social Research* 12 (1927): 140.

28. Interview with Albina Malpezzi (Piedmontese, second generation), 25 November 1988, in Jonesboro, Arkansas.

29. Jerre Mangione, *Mount Allegro, A Memoir of Italian American Life* (1943; reprint, New York: Columbia Univ. Press, 1981): 3-4.

30. Jerry Della Femina and Charles Sopkin, *An Italian Grows in Brooklyn* (Boston: Little, Brown, 1978), 43.

31. Interview with Christopher Hodgkins (Calabrian, third generation), 17 July 1990, in Columbus, Ohio.

32. William Foote Whyte, *Street Corner Society, The Social Structure of an Italian Slum*, 2nd edition (Chicago: Univ. of Chicago Press, 1955), 148.

33. Elizabeth Mathias, "The Italian-American Funeral: Persistence Through Change," *Western Folklore* 33 (1974): 39.

34. Joseph Napoli, *A Dying Cadence, Memories of a Sicilian Childhood* (NP: NP, 1986), 59.

35. Leonardo Sciascia, *La Sicilia come metafora* (Milan: Mondadori, 1979), quoted in LaSorte, 133. See also Gambino, 65.

36. LaGumina, 116 (from the memoir of Clara Corica Grillo).

37. Nelli, "Italians in Urban America," 39-40.

38. Donald Tricarico, "The Restructuring of Ethnic Community: The Italian Neighborhood in Greenwich Village," *Journal of Ethnic Studies* 11, no. 2 (1983): 65; and Ware, 156.

39. Foerster, 398-99.

40. Rudolph J. Vecoli, Introduction to *Italian Immigrants in Rural and Small Town America, Essays from the Fourteenth Annual Conference of the American Italian Historical Association,* ed. Rudolph J. Vecoli (Staten Island, NY: American Italian Historical Association, 1987), 4.

41. David C. Estes, "Across Ethnic Boundaries: St. Joseph's Day in a New Orleans Afro-American Spiritual Church," *Mississippi Folklore Register* 21 (1987): 9-22.

42. Carla Bianco, "Migration and Urbanization of a Traditional Culture: An Italian Experience," in *Folklore in the Modern World,* ed. Richard M. Dorson (The Hague: Mouton, 1978), 59.

43. Gambino, 19.

44. Pauline N. Barrese, "Southern Italian Folklore in New York City," *New York Folklore Quarterly* 21 (1965): 193; and Gambino, 20.

45. Barrese, 193.

46. Gambino, 226.

47. Valentine Belfiglio, "Sicilian Houstonians in Transition," in *Italian Americans in Transition, Proceedings of the XXI Annual Conference of the American Italian Historical Association,* ed. Joseph V. Scelsa, Salvatore J. LaGumina, and Lydio Tomasi (Staten Island, NY: American Italian Historical Association, 1990), 40-41.

48. Corinne Azen Krause, *Grandmothers, Mothers, and Daughters: Oral Histories of Three Generations of Ethnic American Women* (Boston: Twayne, 1991), 21.

49. Krause, 36.

50. John Ciardi, "The Patois,"*Saturday Review/World,* 1 June 1974: 34.

51. An annotated listing of eighty-six of these sources is available in Robert A. Georges and Stephen Stern, comps., *American and Canadian Immigrant and Ethnic Folklore, An Annotated Bibliography* (New York: Garland, 1982), 275-92.

52. Surveys of this body of literature are Rose Basile Green, *The Italian-American Novel, A Document of the Interaction of Two Cultures* (Madison, NJ: Fairleigh Dickinson Univ. Press, 1974); and Olga Peragallo, *Italian American Authors and Their Contribution to American Literature* (New York: S. F. Vanni, 1949).

53. Our organizational scheme derives loosely from that suggested in Roger D. Abrahams, "The Complex Relations of Simple Forms," in *Folklore Genres,* ed. Dan Ben-Amos (Austin: Univ. of Texas Press, 1976), 193-214.

54. Pietro Di Donato, *Three Circles of Light* (New York: Julian Messner, 1960), 32-33.

Chapter Two. Conversation

1. Peter J. Venturelli, "Institutions in an Ethnic District," *Human Organization* 41 (1982): 33.

2. Hermann W. Haller, "Italian Speech Varieties in the United States and the Italian-American Lingua Franca," *Italica* 64 (1987): 393.

3. Hermann W. Haller, "Italian-American Speech Varieties," in *Geolinguistic Perspectives, Proceedings of the International Conference Celebrating the Twentieth Anniversary of the American Society of Geolinguistics, 1985*, ed. Jesse Levitt, Leonard R. N. Ashley, and Kenneth H. Rogers (Lanham, VA: Univ. Press of America, 1987), 259.

4. Herbert H. Vaughan, "Italian and Its Dialects as Spoken in the United States," *American Speech* 1, no. 8 (May 1926): 431-32.

5. Michael La Sorte, *La Merica, Images of Italian Greenhorn Experience* (Philadelphia: Temple Univ. Press, 1985), 159.

6. Ibid., 160.

7. James Cascaito and Douglas Radcliff-Umstead, "An Italo-English Dialect," *American Speech* 50 (Spring/Summer1975): 6, 10.

8. Lawrence Biondi, *The Italian-American Child: His Sociolinguistic Acculturation* (Washington: Georgetown Univ. Press, 1975), 36.

9. Anthony M. Gisolfi, "Italo-American: What It Has Borrowed from American English and What It Is Contributing to the American Language," *Commonweal*, 21 July 1939: 311-12; and Anthony M. Turano, "The Speech of Little Italy," *American Mercury* 26 (July 1932): 358. Other sources which include extensive vocabularies of Italglish include La Sorte, 182-88; Arthur Livingston, "La Merica Sanemagogna," *The Romanic Review* 9 (1918): 225-26; and Vaughan, 432-34. See also John Ciardi, "The Patois," *Saturday Review/World*, 1 June 1974: 34.

10. *The Italians of New York, A Survey Prepared by Workers of the Federal Writers' Project, Works Progress Administration in the City of New York* (1938; reprint, New York: Arno, 1969), 169; and Turano, 357.

11. *The Italians of New York*, 169; and Turano, 358.

12. Ibid., both sources.

13. Gisolfi, 312; and H. L. Mencken, *The American Language, An Inquiry into the Development of English in the United States*, 4th edition (New York: Alfred A. Knopf, 1937), 643-44.

14. Interview with Sam Gennuso (Sicilian, second generation), 26 May 1989, in Jonesboro, Arkansas. Richard M. Dorson characterized stories of this sort, usually told by people who are not members of the folk group, as "a new form of American folklore" when he published his findings from a field trip to Michigan's Upper Peninsula. Of the eighty-four texts he published, four dealt with "mispronunciations" by Italian Americans. See his "Dialect Stories of the Upper Peninsula: A New Form of American Folklore," *Journal of American Folklore* 61 (1948): 145-46.

15. Pascal D'Angelo, *Son of Italy* (1924; reprint, New York: Arno, 1975), 71.

16. Rev. Enrico C. Sartorio, *Social and Religious Life of Italians in America* (Boston: Christopher, 1918), 52-53.

17. Carla Bianco, *The Two Rosetos* (Bloomington: Indiana Univ. Press, 1974): 74.

18. Cascaito and Radcliff-Umstead, 9.

19. Interview with Sam Gennuso.

20. Robert E. Park and Herbert A. Miller, *Old World Traits Transplanted* (New York: Harper, 1921), 103-4, and La Sorte, 132-33.

21. Jerry Della Femina and Charles Sopkin, *An Italian Grows in Brooklyn* (Boston: Little, Brown, 1978), 11.

22. Collected from Albina Malpezzi (Piedmontese, second generation), April 1990, in Jonesboro, Arkansas; and Pearl Malpezzi (Piedmontese, first generation), June 1990, in Masontown, Pennsylvania.

23. Cascaito and Radcliff-Umstead, 11, 15.

24. A. G. Zallio, "The Piedmontese Dialects in the United States," *American Speech* 2, no. 12 (September 1927): 501-2.

25. Joe Vergara, *Love and Pasta: A Recollection* (New York: Harper and Row, 1968), 70.

26. Pauline N. Barrese, "Southern Italian Folklore in New York City," *New York Folklore Quarterly* 21 (1965): 185.

27. Collected 11-12 July 1990 in Masontown, Pennsylvania.

28. Cascaito and Radcliff-Umstead, 9; La Sorte, 162; and Joseph Napoli, *A Dying Cadence, Memories of a Sicilian Childhood* (NP: NP, 1986), 101.

29. LaSorte, 168.

30. Interview with Christopher Hodgkins (Calabrian, third generation), 17 July 1990, in Columbus, Ohio.

31. Interview with Frances Gueri Byrd (southern Italian, second generation), 23 May 1990, in Jonesboro, Arkansas.

32. Interview with Joseph Capello (Piedmontese, first generation), 19 July 1984, in Masontown, Pennsylvania.

33. Elizabeth Mathias, "The Italian-American Funeral: Persistence Through Change," *Western Folklore* 33 (1974): 44.

34. Marc L. Miller and John Van Maanen, "'Boats Don't Fish, People Do': Some Ethnographic Notes on the Federal Management of Fisheries in Gloucester," *Human Organization* 38 (Winter 1979): 379-80. See also William Foote Whyte, *Street Corner Society, The Social Structure of an Italian Slum,* 2nd edition (Chicago: Univ. of Chicago Press, 1955), xviii, 149.

35. Mathias, 47n. See also Richard Gambino, *Blood of My Blood, The Dilemma of the Italian-Americans* (Garden City, NY: Doubleday, 1974), 34.

36. Hermann W. Haller, "Between Standard Italian and Creole: An Interim Report on Language Patterns in an Italian-American Community," *WORD* 32, no. 3 (December 1981): 184; and Haller, "Italian-American Speech Varieties," 261.

37. Haller, "Italian Speech Varieties in the United States," 397.

38. Elizabeth Mathias, "Italian-American Culture and Games: The Minnesota Iron Range and South Philadelphia," in *Play as Context, 1979 Proceedings of the Association for the Anthropological Study of Play,* ed. Alyce Taylor Cheska (West Point, NY: Leisure Press, 1981), 78.

39. La Sorte, 153-54.

40. Corinne Azen Krause, *Grandmothers, Mothers, and Daughters: Oral Histories of Three Generations of Ethnic American Women* (Boston: Twayne, 1991), 58.

41. Interview with Sara Rao Vittone (southern Italian, second generation), 16 June 1990, in Masontown, Pennsylvania.

42. Napoli, 62.

43. Gambino, 55-56.

44. Interview with Lucia Peek (Campanian, third generation), 19 January 1991, in Jonesboro, Arkansas.

45. Bianco, 28.

46. Mangione, 140.

47. Frances M. Barbour, "Some Foreign Proverbs in Southern Illinois," *Midwest Folklore* 4 (1954): 164.

48. Carla Bianco, "Migration and Urbanization of a Traditional Culture: An Italian Experience," in *Folklore in the Modern World*, ed. Richard M. Dorson (The Hague: Mouton, 1978), 56; and Angelo M. Pellegrini, *Americans by Choice* (New York: Macmillan, 1956), 56.

49. Pellegrini, 20. See also Peter Seitel, "Proverbs: A Social Use of Metaphor," in *Folklore Genres*, ed. Dan Ben-Amos (Austin: Univ. of Texas Press, 1976), 125-43.

50. Gambino, 85.

51. Constantine M. Panunzio, *The Soul of an Immigrant* (New York: Macmillan, 1928), 278. Variants of this proverb in the Sicilian dialect may be found in Gambino, 2; Fred L. Gardaphe, ed., *Italian-American Ways* (New York: Harper and Row, 1989), 29; and Virginia Yans-McLauglin, *Family and Community: Italian Immigrants in Buffalo, 1880-1930* (1971; reprint, Chicago: Univ. of Illinois Press, 1982), 18.

52. Manuel D. Ramirez, "Italian Folklore from Tampa, Florida. Series no. 2: Proverbs," *Southern Folklore Quarterly* 13 (1949): 121-32.

53. For example, see Phyllis H. Williams, *South Italian Folkways in Europe and America, A Handbook for Social Workers, Visiting Nurses, School Teachers, and Physicians* (1938; reprint, New York: Russell and Russell, 1969), 8.

54. Joe Vergara reports this proverb in *Love and Pasta, A Recollection* (New York: Harper and Row, 1968), 168.

55. For a related text in the dialect of Roseto Valfortore, Apulia, see Bianco, "Migration and Urbanization," 56.

56. See also the use of this proverb in Marion Benasutti's novel *No Steady Job for Papa* (New York: Vantage, 1966), 164.

57. A slightly different version of this proverb appears in Richard Gambino's novel *Bread and Roses* (New York: Seaview Books, 1981), 403.

58. Charles Speroni, "Five Italian Wellerisms," *Western Folklore* 7 (1948): 55.

59. Gambino, *Blood of My Blood*, 126.

Chapter Three. Customs: The Life Cycle

1. Arnold Van Gennep, *The Rites of Passage*, trans. Monika B. Vizedom and Gabrielle L. Caffee (Chicago: Univ. of Chicago Press, 1960).

2. Victor W. Turner, *The Ritual Process, Structure and Anti-Structure* (Chicago: Aldine, 1969).

3. M. Estellie Smith, "Folk Medicine Among the Sicilian-Americans of Buffalo, New York," *Urban Anthropology* 1, no. 1 (1972): 104.

4. Robert Anthony Orsi, *The Madonna of 115th Street, Faith and Community in Italian Harlem, 1880-1950* (New Haven: Yale Univ. Press, 1985), 82; and James R. Foster, "Brooklyn Folklore," *New York Folklore Quarterly* 13 (1957): 90.

5. Giuseppe Cautela, "Italian Funeral," *American Mercury* 15 (1928): 202.

6. Richard Gambino, *Blood of My Blood, The Dilemma of the Italian-Americans* (Garden City, NY: Doubleday, 1974), 203; and Wayland D. Hand, Anna Casetta, and Sondra B. Thiederman, eds., *Popular Beliefs and Superstitions, A Compendium of American Folklore from the Ohio Collection of Newbell Niles Puckett* (Boston: G. K. Hall, 1981), 8 (items no. 188, 195), 10 (no. 252).

7. Hand, Casetta, and Thiederman, 12 (item no. 303); and Phyllis H. Williams, *South Italian Folkways in Europe and America, A Handbook for Social Workers, Visiting Nurses, School Teachers, and Physicians* (1938; reprint, New York: Russell and Russell, 1969), 177-78.

8. Catherine Harris Ainsworth, *Italian-American Folktales* (Buffalo: Clyde Press, 1977), 34-35; Carla Bianco, *The Two Rosetos* (Bloomington: Indiana Univ. Press, 1974), 109; Michael Brunetti, "Italian Folklore Collected from Mrs. Stephanie Nappi," *New York Folklore Quarterly* 28 (1972): 259-60; Louis Jones, "Italian Werewolves," *New York Folklore Quarterly* 6 (1950): 133; and Bob Zappacosta, "Italian Beliefs," *West Virginia Folklore* 12, no. 2 (Winter 1962): 23.

9. Hand, Casetta, and Thiederman, 276 (item no. 6933), 1082 (no. 25728).

10. Ibid., 47(item no. 1148).

11. Brunetti, 259; and Hand, Casetta, and Thiederman, 46 (item no. 1125), 51 (no. 1239).

12. Hand, Casetta, and Thiederman, 26 (items no. 688, 691, 703).

13. Bianco, 108; Brunetti, 259; Hand, Casetta, and Thiederman, 38 (item no. 953), 40 (nos. 993, 996, 997), 41 (nos. 1013, 1016, 1022, 1023); Dorothy Gladys Spicer, "The Immigrant Mother as Seen by a Social Worker," *Hygeia* 4, no. 6 (June 1926): 321; Caroline F. Ware, *Greenwich Village 1920-1930, A Comment on American Civilization in the Post-War Years* (1935; reprint, New York: Harper and Row, 1965), 174; Williams, 87, 103; and Zappacosta, 23.

14. Barbara J. Taft McNaughton, "Calabrian Folklore from Giovanna," *Journal of the Ohio Folklore Society*, n. s., 3, no. 1 (Spring 1974): 26-27.

15. McNaughton, 27.

16. Ware, 191. Through questionnaires Ware found that fifty-four percent of Italian Americans in Greenwich Village over the age of thirty-five believed in prenatal marking, while thirty-one percent of those younger than thirty-five subscribed to the belief.

17. Jo Pagano, *Golden Wedding* (1943; reprint, New York: Arno, 1975), 138-39.

18. Hand, Casetta, and Thiederman, 92 (items no. 2237, 2239), 94 (no. 2278).

19. Gambino, 203-4.

20. Idwal Jones, "Evviva San Francisco," *American Mercury* 12 (1927): 152.

21. Hand, Casetta, and Thiederman, 44 (no. 1092).

22. Gambino, 197; Hand, Casetta, and Thiederman, 94 (item no. 2293); and Williams, 35-36.

23. Marie Hall Ets, *Rosa: The Life of an Italian Immigrant* (Minneapolis: Univ. of Minnesota Press, 1970), 181; and Hand, Casetta, and Thiederman, 155 (item no. 3752).

24. Dorothy Gladys Spicer, "Health Superstitions of the Italian Immigrant," *Hygeia* 4, no. 5 (May 1926): 269.

25. Pietro Di Donato, *Christ in Concrete* (Indianapolis: Bobbs-Merrill, 1939), 51.

26. Elizabeth Ewen, *Immigrant Women in the Land of Dollars, Life and Culture on the Lower East Side 1890-1925* (New York: Monthly Review Press, 1985), 132.

27. Hand, Casetta, and Thiederman, 22 (item no. 585).

28. Di Donato, 52, 58. See also Bianco, 110-11.

29. Spicer, "Health Superstitions," 269.

30. Hand, Casetta, and Thiederman, 76 (item no. 1848), 78 (no. 1880), 80 (no. 1938), 82 (no. 1999), 152 (no. 3693).

31. Lucas Longo, *The Family on Vendetta Street* (Garden City, NY: Doubleday, 1968), 50.

32. Louis Guida, "The Rocconi-Fratesi Family: Italianata in the Arkansas Delta," in *Hogs in the Bottom, Family Folklore in Arkansas,* ed. Deirdre LaPin (Little Rock: August House, 1982), 94.

33. Interview with Mamie Jo DiMarco Chauvin (Sicilian, second generation), 19 March 1991, in Forrest City, Arkansas.

34. Jerre Mangione, *Mount Allegro, A Memoir of Italian American Life* (1943; reprint, New York: Columbia Univ. Press, 1981), 167.

35. Hand, Casetta, and Thiederman, 52 (items no. 1272, 1273, 1275).

36. Ibid., 54 (item no. 1319), 62 (no. 1504).

37. Interview with Albina Malpezzi (Piedmontese, second generation), 25 November 1988, in Jonesboro, Arkansas; Ainsworth, 52; and Hand, Casetta, and Thiederman, 107 (item no. 2621).

38. Interview with Etta Ferraro Goodwin (Campanian, second generation), August 1991, in Peace Dale, Rhode Island (interviewed by Lucia Peek).

39. Williams, 104.

40. Ainsworth, 46-47.

41. Interview with Albina Malpezzi; Hand, Casetta, and Thiederman, 71 (item no. 1700); and Joseph Napoli, *A Dying Cadence, Memories of a Sicilian Childhood* (NP: NP, 1986), 5.

42. Jane Voiles, "Genoese Folkways in a California Mining Camp," *California Folklore Quarterly* 3 (1944): 215.

43. Interview with Pearl Malpezzi (Piedmontese; first generation), 19 July 1984, in Masontown, Pennsylvania. Malpezzi also provided the written transcription and translation of the song.

44. Interview with Sam Gennuso (Sicilian, second generation), 26 May 1989, in Jonesboro, Arkansas. Gennuso provided the written transcription and collaborated with his sisters, Louise Gennuso and Antoinette Giglio, in translating the song.

45. Ware, 174.

46. Interview with Mamie Jo DiMarco Chauvin.

47. Bartolomeo J. Palisi, "Patterns of Social Participation in a Four-Generation Sample of Italian-Americans," *Sociological Quarterly* 7 (1966): 176.

48. Salvatore J. LaGumina, *The Immigrants Speak, Italian Americans Tell Their Story* (New York: Center for Migration Studies, 1979), 117-18 (from the memoir of Clara Corica Grilla).

49. Elizabeth Mathias and Richard Raspa, *Italian Folktales in America, The Verbal Art of an Immigrant Woman* (Detroit: Wayne State Univ. Press, 1985), 281.

50. Virginia Yans-McLaughlin, *Family and Community: Italian Immigrants in Buffalo, 1880-1930* (1971; reprint, Chicago: Univ. of Chicago Press, 1982), 93.

51. Yans-McLaughlin, 82.

52. Charles W. Churchill, *The Italians of Newark, A Community Study* (1942; reprint, New York: Arno, 1975), 79, 81.

53. Corinne Azen Krause, *Grandmothers, Mothers, and Daughters: Oral Histories of Three Generations of Ethnic American Women* (Boston: Twayne, 1991), 19.

54. Interview with Joanne Terranella Burleson (Sicilian, third generation), 14 March 1990, in Jonesboro, Arkansas.

55. Krause, 27.

56. Hand, Casetta, and Thiederman, 545 (item no. 13658).

57. Smith, 103.

58. Napoli, 59.

59. Krause, 30.

60. Yans-McLaughlin, 256.

61. Jerilyn Mankins, "More Italian Beliefs," *West Virginia Folklore* 12, no. 2 (Winter 1962): 29. See also Bianco, 111.

62. Hand, Casetta, and Thiederman, 518 (item no. 13069), 519 (no. 13083), 539 (no. 13517).

63. James R. Foster, "Brooklyn Folklore," *New York Folklore Quarterly* 13 (1957): 90.

64. Mangione, 134.

65. Grace Leonore Pitts, "The Italians of Columbus—A Study in Population," *Annals of the American Academy of Political and Social Science* 19 (1902): 157.

66. Orsi, 114; and Williams, 47-48, 86. See also Bianco, 113.

67. Hand, Casetta, and Thiederman, 590 (items no. 14648, 14649), 1078-79 (nos. 25645, 25668).

68. Rocco Fumento, *Tree of Dark Reflection* (New York: Knopf, 1962), 86; and Hand, Casetta, and Thiederman, 268 (item no. 6743). For auspicious and inauspicious wedding days among Italian Americans, see Bianco, 113.

69. Marion Benasutti, *No Steady Job for Papa* (New York: Vanguard, 1966), 190.

70. Judith Goode, Janet Theophano, and Karen Curtis, "A Framework for the Analysis of Continuity and Change in Shared Sociocultural Rules for Food Use: The Italian-American Pattern," in *Ethnic and Regional Foodways in the United States, The Performance of Group Identity*, ed. Linda Keller Brown and Kay Mussell (Knoxville: Univ. of Tennessee Press, 1984), 78; and Guida, 94.

71. Churchill, 34.

72. C. Richard King, "Old Thurber," in *Singers and Storytellers*, ed. Mody C. Boatright, Wilson M. Hudson, and Allen Maxwell (Dallas: Southern Methodist Univ. Press, 1961), 110.

73. Interview with Frances Gueri Byrd (southern Italian, second generation), 23 May 1990, in Jonesboro, Arkansas; interview with Lucia Peek (Campanian, third generation), 19 January 1991, in Jonesboro, Arkansas; Hand, Casetta, and Thiederman, 610 (item no. 15049); Lorenzo Madalena, *Confetti for Gino* (Garden City, NY: Doubleday, 1959), 86; Pagano, 87; and Williams, 100.

74. Interview with Lucia Peek; interview with Ray Ferraro (Campanian, second generation), August 1991, in Macomb, Illinois (interviewed by Lucia Peek).

75. Interview with Frances Byrd.

76. Pietro DiDonato, *Christ in Concrete* (Indianapolis: Bobbs-Merrill, 1939), 249-60.

77. Churchill, 35; Fred L. Gardaphe, ed., *Italian-American Ways* (New York: Harper and Row, 1989), 32; Longo, 135-36; Joe Vergara, *Love and Pasta, A Recollection* (New York: Harper and Row, 1968), 125-26; and Ware, 191.

78. Hand, Casetta, and Thiederman, 611 (items no. 15064, 15069).

79. Guida 93; and Hand, Casetta, and Thiederman, 615 (item no. 15139), 1079 (no. 25684).

80. Interview with Mamie Jo DiMarco Chauvin; Bianco, 116-18; Elizabeth Mathias, "The Italian-American Funeral: Persistence Through Change," *Western Folklore* 33 (1974): 36-37; and Williams, 199-200.

81. Mathias, 49-50.

82. Hand, Casetta, and Thiederman, 1126 (item no. 26695), 1127 (no. 26712), 1129 (nos. 26748, 26749, 26759), 1132 (no. 26832), 1133 (nos. 26843, 26847, 26848), 1144 (nos. 27121, 27122, 27125), 1149 (no. 27250), 1154 (nos. 27355, 27356), 1157 (no. 27407), 1158 (nos. 27452, 27453), 1159 (nos. 27467, 27468), 1163 (no. 27559), 1170 (no. 27740), 1176 (nos. 27864, 27870), 1177 (nos. 27886, 27891, 27896), 1178 (nos. 27898, 27903), 1179 (no. 27915), 1190 (nos. 28162, 28163), 1191 (nos. 28167, 28186, 28187). See also Di Donato, 72; and Antonia Pola, *Who Can Buy the Stars?* (New York: Vantage, 1957), 184-85.

83. Dan G. Hoffman, "Stregas, Ghosts, and Werewolves," *New York Folklore Quarterly* 3 (1947): 327-28.

84. Cautela, 203.

85. Interview with Marie Marchese (Sicilian, second generation), 12 April 1991, in North Little Rock, Arkansas; Churchill, 36; and David Steven Cohen, *The Folklore and Folklife of New Jersey* (New Brunswick: Rutgers Univ. Press, 1983), 199.

86. Cohen, 199.

87. Interview with Lucia Peek; Churchill, 36; and Rose Grieco, "They Who Mourn," *Commonweal*, 27 March 1953: 630.

88. Donald Tricarico, "The Restructuring of Ethnic Community: The Italian Neighborhood in Greenwich Village," *Journal of Ethnic Studies* 11, no. 2 (1983): 67.

89. Interview with Ray Ferraro.

90. William Foote Whyte, *Street Corner Society, The Social Structure of an Italian Slum*, 2nd edition (Chicago: Univ. of Chicago Press, 1955), 201-02.

91. Interview with Mamie Jo DiMarco Chauvin.

92. Mathias, 50.

93. Daniel David Cowell, "Funerals, Family, and Forefathers: A View of Italian-American Funeral Practices," *Omega* 16, no. 1 (1985-86): 73.

94. Hand, Casetta, and Thiederman, 1224 (items no. 28913, 28915, 28917), 1225 (nos. 28942, 28946), 1226 (nos. 28963, 28970); Mathias, 37n; and Williams, 209.

95. Interview with Mamie Jo DiMarco Chauvin.

96. Cowell, 79.

97. Zappacosta, 23-24. See also Hand, Casetta, and Thiederman, 263 (item no. 6615), 1231 (nos. 29074, 29075).

98. Bianco, 119; Cowell, 80; Hand, Casetta, and Thiederman, 1215 (items no. 28718, 28722), 1217 (no. 28766), 1218 (nos. 28770, 28776); and Mathias, 50.

99. Tina DeRosa, *Paper Fish* (Chicago: Wine Press, 1980), 24.

100. Dorothy Noyes, *Uses of Tradition, Arts of Italian Americans in Philadelphia* (Philadelphia: Philadelphia Folklore Project, 1989), 60-65.

Chapter Four. Customs: The Traditional Calendar

1. Interview with Mamie Jo DiMarco Chauvin (Sicilian, second generation), 19 March 1991, in Forrest City, Arkansas.

2. Michael LaSorte, *La Merica, Images of Italian Greenhorn Experience* (Philadelphia: Temple Univ. Press, 1985), 136.

3. Interview with Ray Ferraro (Campanian, second generation), August 1991, in Macomb, Illinois (interviewed by Lucia Peek).

4. Interview with Etta Ferraro Goodwin (Campanian, second generation), August 1991, in Peace Dale, Rhode Island (interviewed by Lucia Peek).

5. Linda Brandi Cateura, *Growing Up Italian, How Being Brought Up as an Italian-American Helped Shape the Characters, Lives, and Fortunes of Twenty-Four Celebrated Americans* (New York: William Morrow, 1987), 122 (from the memoir of Alphonse D'Amato).

6. Valentine J. Belfiglio, "Italians in Small Town and Rural Texas," in *Italian Immigrants in Rural and Small Town America, Essays from the Fourteenth Annual Conference of the American Italian Historical Association,* ed. Rudolph J. Vecoli (Staten Island, NY: American Italian Historical Association, 1987), 46.

7. Richard Gambino, *Blood of My Blood, The Dilemma of the Italian-Americans* (Garden City, NY: Doubleday, 1974), 20-21.

8. Judith E. Smith, *Family Connections: A History of Italian and Jewish Immigrant Lives in Providence, Rhode Island 1900-1940* (Albany: State Univ. of New York Press, 1985), 103-4.

9. Interview with Etta Ferraro Goodwin.

10. Interview with Albina Malpezzi (Piedmontese, second generation), 25 November 1988, in Jonesboro, Arkansas.

11. Rocco Fumento, *Tree of Dark Reflection* (New York: Alfred A. Knopf, 1962), 24.

12. Interview with Joanne Terranella Burleson (Sicilian, second generation), 6 November 1990, in Jonesboro, Arkansas.

13. Ibid.

14. Ibid.

15. Interview with Sara Rao Vittone (southern Italian, second generation), 16 June 1990, in Masontown, Pennsylvania.

16. Cateura, 184 (from the memoir of Michael Andretti).

17. Corinne Azen Krause, *Grandmothers, Mothers, and Daughters, Oral Histories of Three Generations of Ethnic American Women* (Boston: Twayne, 1991), 25.

18. Interview with Marie Marchese (Sicilian, second generation), 12 April 1991, in North Little Rock, Arkansas.

19. Helen Barolini, *Festa, Recipes and Recollections of Italian Holidays* (New York: Harcourt Brace Jovanovich, 1988), 13, 523; Juliana Bova, "Eel for Christmas— An Italian Tradition," *Pennsylvania Folklife* 39, no. 2 (Winter 1989-90): 82; Cateura, 36 (from the memoir of Eleanor Smeal); Toni F. Fratto, "Cooking in Red and White," *Pennsylvania Folklife* 19, no. 3 (1970): 12; Judith Goode, Janet Theophano, and Karen

Curtis, "A Framework for the Analysis of Continuity and Change in Shared Sociocultural Rules for Food Use: The Italian-American Pattern," in *Ethnic and Regional Foodways in the United States: The Performance of Group Identity*, ed. Linda Keller Brown and Kay Mussell (Knoxville: Univ. of Tennessee Press, 1984), 77; Wayland D. Hand, Anna Casetta, and Sondra B. Thiederman, eds., *Popular Beliefs and Superstitions, A Compendium of American Folklore from the Ohio Collection of Newbell Niles Puckett* (Boston: G. K. Hall, 1981), 670 (item no. 16413); and Lydia Q. Pietropaoli, "The Italians Came Up Watertown Way," *New York Folklore Quarterly* 29, no. 1 (1973): 76.

20. David Steven Cohen, *The Folklore and Folklife of New Jersey* (New Brunswick: Rutgers Univ. Press, 1983), 181.

21. Fumento, 40. See also Pietro Di Donato, *Three Circles of Light* (New York: Julian Messner, 1960), 83.

22. Gambino, 22-23.

23. Interview with Etta Ferraro Goodwin. See also Bova, 82; and Hand, Casetta, and Thiederman, 656 (item no. 16111).

24. Louis Guida, "The Rocconi-Fratesi Family: Italianata in the Arkansas Delta," in *Hogs in the Bottom, Family Folklore in Arkansas*, ed. Deirdre LaPin (Little Rock: August House, 1982), 95.

25. Interview with Sam Gennuso (Sicilian, second generation), 26 May 1989, in Jonesboro, Arkansas; and interview with Joanne Terranella Burleson (Sicilian, second generation), 14 March 1990, in Jonesboro, Arkansas.

26. Hand, Casetta, and Thiederman, 656 (item 16125).

27. Bova, 83; and Hand, Casetta, and Thiederman, 670 (items no. 16417-19).

28. Janes Voiles, "Genoese Folkways in a California Mining Camp," *California Folklore Quarterly* 3 (1944): 216.

29. Bova, 84.

30. Carla Bianco, *The Two Rosetos* (Bloomington: Indiana Univ. Press, 1974), 207.

31. Bova, 83; Cateura, 184 (from the memoir of Michael Andretti); Dorothy Noyes, *Uses of Tradition, Arts of Italian Americans in Philadelphia* (Philadelphia: Philadelphia Folklore Project, 1989), 17; and Pietropaoli, 76-77.

32. Bova, 83; and Pietropaoli, 77. See also Pauline N. Barrese, "Southern Italian Folklore in New York City," *New York Folklore Quarterly* 21 (1965): 189.

33. Salvatore J. LaGumina, *The Immigrants Speak, Italian Americans Tell Their Story* (New York: Center for Migration Studies, 1979), 39.

34. C. Richard King, "Old Thurber," in *Singers and Storytellers*, ed. Mody C. Boatright, Wilson M. Hudson, and Allen Maxwell (Dallas: Southern Methodist Univ. Press, 1961), 110-11.

35. Telephone interview with Augustina Lovoi (Sicilian, second generation), 16 March 1991.

36. Interview with Etta Goodwin Ferraro; and Barolini, 114.

37. Barolini, 142-43.

38. Bianco, 209.

39. Barbara Corrado Pope suggests a parallel between the Brooklyn procession and the *Processione dei Misteri*, which takes place in Trapani, Sicily. The Brooklyn event, she argues, represents considerable modification of the twenty-four-hour observance in Sicily. See "The Origins of South Italian Good Friday Processions," in *Italian*

Americans Celebrate Life, Their Arts and Popular Culture, ed. Paola A. Sensi Isolani and Anthony Julian Tamburri (NP: American Italian Historical Association, 1990), 155-68.

40. Kay F. Turner, "The Virgin of Sorrows Procession: A Brooklyn Inversion," *Folklore Papers of the University Folklore Association* 9 (1980): 2-5.

41. Joseph Sciorra, "Religious Processions in Italian Williamsburg," *Drama Review* 29 (1985): 69-71.

42. Jerre Mangione, *Mount Allegro, A Memoir of Italian American Life* (1943; reprint, New York: Columbia Univ. Press, 1981): 100-01.

43. Voiles, 215-16.

44. Michael De Capite, *Maria* (New York: John Day, 1943), 34-35.

45. Interview with Ray Ferraro; Richard A. Raspa, "Exotic Foods Among Italian-Americans in Mormon Utah: Food as Nostalgic Enactment of Identity," in Brown and Mussell, 192; and Gene P. Veronesi, *Italian Americans and Their Communities in Cleveland* (Cleveland: Cleveland State Univ., 1977), 289.

46. Fratto, 11; and Donald Tricarico, "The Restructuring of Ethnic Community: The Italian Neighborhood in Greenwich Village," *Journal of Ethnic Studies* 11, no. 2 (1983): 66.

47. Interview with Ray Ferraro; and interview with Lucia Peek, (Campanian, third generation), 19 January 1991, in Jonesboro, Arkansas. See also Fratto, 11; and Gambino, 23.

48. Interview with Lucia Peek. See also Bianco, 210; Guida, 95; and Joe Vergara, *Love and Pasta, A Recollection* (New York: Harper and Row, 1968), 170.

49. Interview with Ray Ferraro.

50. One of the most thorough descriptions and analyses of Saint Joseph's Day customs is Kay Turner and Suzanne Seriff, "'Giving an Altar': The Ideology of Reproduction in a St. Joseph's Day Feast," *Journal of American Folklore,* 100 (1987): 446-60.

51. Charles Speroni, "The Observance of Saint Joseph's Day Among Sicilians of Southern California," *Southern Folklore Quarterly* 4 (1940): 135-36.

52. Interview with Augustina Lovoi.

53. Interview with Marie Marchese.

54. Ibid. See also Barolini, 144, 146; and Vergara, 170-71.

55. Interview with Marie Marchese.

56. Lyle Saxon, Edward Dreyer, and Robert Tallant, comps., *Gumbo-Ya-Ya, A Collection of Louisiana Folk Tales* (1945; reprint, New York: Bonanza, ND), 93.

57. Interview with Sam Marchese (Sicilian, second generation), 12 April 1991, North Little Rock, Arkansas.

58. *New Orleans Times-Picayune,* 18 March 1972.

59. Speroni, 137-38.

60. Interview with Marie Marchese.

61. Interview with Mamie Jo DiMarco Chauvin.

62. Saxon, Dreyer, and Tallant, 104; and Catherine Harris Ainsworth, *Italian-American Folktales* (Buffalo: Clyde Press, 1977), 156.

63. Interview with Marie Marchese. See also Barolini, 143; and Speroni, 139.

64. Valentine Belfiglio, "Sicilian Houstonians in Transition," in *Italian Americans in Transition, Proceedings of the XXI Annual Conference of the American Italian*

Historical Association, ed. Joseph V. Scelsa, Salvatore J. LaGumina, and Lydio Tomasi (Staten Island, NY: American Italian Historical Association, 1990), 41.

65. Belfiglio, "Italians in Small Town and Rural Texas," 37.

66. Interview with Sam Gennuso.

67. Saxon, Dreyer, and Tallant, 99.

68. Barolini, 111.

69. Interview with Mamie Jo DiMarco Chauvin.

70. David C. Estes, "Across Ethnic Boundaries: St. Joseph's Day in a New Orleans Afro-American Spiritual Church," *Mississippi Folklore Register* 21 (1987): 9-22.

71. "St. Joe's Parade Hails Lombardi, Italians Celebrate Feast with March, Spaghetti." *New Orleans Times-Picayune,* 19 March 1972. Donna Partridge of Little Rock, Arkansas, provided some information on Saint Joseph's Day parades in a telephone conversation on 8 February 1991.

72. Jacob A. Riis, "Feast-Days in Little Italy," *The Century Magazine* 58 (1899): 494.

73. Reprinted as "Italian Festivals in New York," *The Chautauquan* 34 (1901): 228-29.

74. Phyllis A. Williams, *South Italian Folkways in Europe and America, A Handbook for Social Workers, Visiting Nurses, School Teachers, and Physicians* (1938; reprint, New York: Russell and Russell, 1969), 149.

75. *The Italians of New York, A Survey Prepared by Workers of the Federal Writers' Project, Works Progress Administration in the City of New York* (1939; reprint, New York: Arno, 1969), 87.

76. Bruce B. Giuliano, *Sacro o Profano? A Consideration of Four Italian-Canadian Religious Festivals,* Canadian Centre for Folk Culture Studies Paper no. 17 (Ottawa: National Museums of Canada, 1976), 13-27.

77. Philip M. Rose, *The Italians in America* (New York: George H. Doran, 1922), 74.

78. Charles W. Churchill, *The Italians of Newark, A Community Study* (1942; reprint, New York: Arno, 1975), 39. See also *The Italians of New York,* 88-89; and Robert E. Park and Herbert A. Miller, *Old World Traits Transplanted* (New York: Harper, 1921).

79. Dorothy Gladys Spicer, "Health Superstitions of the Italian Immigrant," *Hygeia* 4, no. 5 (May 1926): 268.

80. Generalized descriptions of *festa* behavior appear in Laurence Biondi, *The Italian-American Child: His Sociolinguistic Acculturation* (Washington: Georgetown Univ. Press, 1975), 32-33; Noyes, 54-57; and especially Sciorra, 65-81. Book-length treatments of specific *feste* include Robert Anthony Orsi, *The Madonna of 115th Street, Faith and Community in Italian Harlem, 1880-1950* (New York: Columbia Univ. Press, 1985); and Richard M. Swiderski, *Voices, An Anthropologist's Dialogue with an Italian-American Festival* (Bowling Green, OH: Popular Press, 1987). Fictional treatments of *feste* appear in Pietro Di Donato, *Three Circles of Light* (New York: Julian Messner, 1960), 110-15; Lucas Longo, *The Family on Vendetta Street* (Garden City, NY: Doubleday, 1968), 12-13; and Anthony Mancini, *Minnie Santangelo's Mortal Sin* (New York: Coward, McCann, and Geoghegan, 1975), 169-70, 179-80. Some accounts of specific *feste* are Churchill, 100-101 (Saint Gerardo); "Festa," *New Yorker* 5 October 1957: 34-36 (Saint Gennaro); Fred L. Gardaphe, ed., *Italian-American Ways* (New

York: Harper and Row, 1989), 79-81 (Our Lady of Mount Carmel); and Vergara, 14-15 (Saint Gennaro).

81. Riis, 491-94; and Williams, 151. Park and Miller (p. 155) include a description of a "flight of angels" from a manuscript written by Marie Leavitt dealing with Sicilians in Chicago.

82. I. Sheldon Posen and Joseph Sciorra, "Brooklyn's Dancing Tower," *Natural History* 92 (June 1983): 30-37; I. Sheldon Posen, "Storing Contexts: The Brooklyn *Giglio* as Folk Art," in *Folk Art and Art Worlds,* ed. John Michael Vlach and Simon J. Bronner (Ann Arbor, MI: UMI Research Press, 1986), 171-91; and Joseph Sciorra, "'O Giglio e Paradiso': Celebration and Identity in an Urban Ethnic Community," *Urban Resources* 5, no. 3 (1989): 15-20, 44-46. We are also grateful to Wayne Narey for sharing his observations of the 1991 enactment of this *festa.*

83. Donald E. Byrne, Jr., "The Race of the Saints: An Italian Religious Festival in Jessup, Pennsylvania," *Journal of Popular Culture* 19, no. 3 (Winter 1985): 119-30.

84. Mildrick Urick, "The San Rocco Festival at Aliquippa, Pennsylvania: A Transplanted Tradition," *Pennsylvania Folklife* 19, no. 1 (Autumn 1969): 20.

85. Vergara, 16.

86. Charles Speroni, "California Fishermen's Festivals," *Western Folklore* 14 (1955): 80-88.

87. Biondi, 32.

88. Orsi, 55.

89. John Alexander Williams, "Italian Regionalism and Pan-Italian Traditions," *Folklife Center News* 11, no. 3 (Summer 1989): 10.

90. Bianco, 29; and Donald E. Byrne, Jr., "Maria Assunta: Berwick's Italian Religious Festival," *Pennsylvania Folklife* 30 (1981): 126-27.

91. Among sources treating the religious and integrative significance of *feste* are those by Giuliano, Orsi, Sciorra, and Swiderski. For ways in which *feste* have evolved in this country, see Dorothy Noyes, "The Changing Role of the Italian-American Religious Festival," in *Italian-American Traditions: Family and Community* (Philadelphia: Balch Institute for Ethnic Studies, 1985), 13-17.

92. *The Italians of New York,* 216.

93. Charles Speroni, "The Development of the Columbus Day Pageant of San Francisco," *Western Folklore* 7 (1948): 328.

94. "Big Crowd Cheers Columbus Parades," *New York Times* 13 October 1909: 7.

95. Speroni, "The Development of the Columbus Day Pageant," 326-27. For photographs of the 1989 San Francisco Columbus Day festivities, see Ken Light, "Christopher Columbus Lands at San Francisco Harbor, September 1989," *Folklife Center News* 11, no. 4 (Fall 1989): 8-9.

96. Noyes, *Uses of Tradition,* 58; and John Alexander Williams, 11-12.

97. *Montreal River Miner,* 8 October 1909; quoted in Paul A. Sturgul, "Italians on the Gogebic Iron Range," in *Italian Immigrants in Rural and Small Town America, Essays from the Fourteenth Annual Conference of the American Italian Historical Association,* ed. Rudolph J. Vecoli (Staten Island, NY: American Italian Historical Association, 1987), 174.

98. Krause, 25.

99. Interview with Etta Ferraro Goodwin.

100. Shari Rhodes, "Italian Culture in Northeast Arkansas," videotape in the Arkansas State University Folklore Archives.

101. Hand, Casetta, and Thiederman, 657 (items no. 16131, 16132), 658 (no. 16146), 659 (nos. 16161, 16162, 16165), 659 (no. 16174), 826 (nos. 19947, 19960).

102. Hand, Casetta, and Thiederman, 831 (items no. 20074, 20082), 832 (no. 20083).

103. Voiles, 216.

104. Ainsworth, 3; and Hand, Casetta, and Thiederman, 1268 (nos. 29861, 29862).

Chapter Five. Folk Supernaturalism

1. Giuseppe Cautela, "Italian Funeral," *American Mercury* 15 (October 1928): 204-5.

2. "Religion of Lucky Pieces, Witches and the Evil Eye," *World Outlook* 3 (October 1917): 24.

3. Corinne Azen Krause, *Grandmothers, Mothers, and Daughters, Oral Histories of Three Generations of Ethnic American Women* (Boston: Twayne, 1991), 35.

4. Joseph Napoli, *A Dying Cadence, Memories of a Sicilian Childhood* (NP: NP, 1986), 33.

5. Herbert J. Gans, *The Urban Villagers, Group and Class in the Life of Italian-Americans* (New York: Free Press, 1962), 111; Philip M. Rose, *The Italians in America* (New York: George H. Doran, 1922), 99; Nicholas John Russo, "Three Generations of Italians in New York City: Their Religious Acculturation," *International Migration Review* 3, no. 2 (Spring 1969): 4-5; Rudolph J. Vecoli, "Cult and Occult in Italian-American Culture, The Persistence of a Religious Heritage," in *Immigrants and Religion in Urban American*, ed. Randall M. Miller and Thomas D. Marzik (Philadelphia: Temple Univ. Press, 1977), 34-37; Rudolph J. Vecoli, "Prelates and Peasants: Italian Immigrants and the Catholic Church," *Journal of Social History* 2 (Spring 1969): 217-68; and Caroline F. Ware, *Greenwich Village 1920-1930, A Comment on American Civilization in the Post-War Years* (1935; reprint, New York: Harper and Row, 1965), 311.

6. Humbert S. Nelli, "Italians in Urban America: A Study in Ethnic Adjustment," *International Migration Review* 1, no. 3 (Summer 1967): 47.

7. Judith E. Smith, *Family Connections, A History of Italian and Jewish Immigrant Lives in Providence, Rhode Island, 1900-1940* (Albany: State Univ. of New York Press, 1985), 145-52.

8. Salvatore J. LaGumina, *The Immigrants Speak, Italian Americans Tell Their Story* (New York: Center for Migration Studies, 1979), 122 (from the memoir of Clara Corica Grillo).

9. Charles W. Churchill, *The Italians of Newark, A Community Study* (1942; reprint New York: Arno, 1975), 110; and Russo 12. See Garibaldi M. LaPolla, *The Fire in the Flesh* (1931; reprint, New York: Arno, 1975), 221-22, for prayers to Saint Biagio when someone is ill.

10. Joseph Sciorra, "Yard Shrines and Sidewalk Altars of New York's Italian-Americans," in *Perspectives in Vernacular Architecture III*, ed. Thomas Carter and Bernard L. Herman (Columbia: Univ. of Missouri Press, 1989), 185-98; Fred L. Gardaphe, ed., *Italian-American Ways* (New York: Harper and Row, 1989), 88-89;

Dorothy Noyes, *Uses of Tradition, Arts of Italian Americans in Philadelphia* (Philadelphia: Philadelphia Folklore Project, 1989), 34-37; Vecoli, "Cult and Occult in Italian-American Culture," 27-28; and Vecoli, "Prelates and Peasants," 228-29.

11. Rev. Enrico C. Sartorio, *Social and Religious Life of Italians in America* (Boston: Christopher, 1918), 103.

12. Krause, 26.

13. Nelli, 49.

14. Churchill, 110; and Phyllis H. Williams, *South Italian Folkways in Europe and America, A Handbook for Social Workers, Visiting Nurses, School Teachers, and Physicians* (1938; reprint, New York: Russell and Russell, 1969), 136

15. Carla Bianco, *The Two Rosetos* (Bloomington: Indiana Univ. Press, 1974), 85-86; and Williams, 186.

16. Dorothy Gladys Spicer, "The Immigrant Mother as Seen by a Social Worker," *Hygeia* 4, no. 6 (June 1926): 319.

17. Recent theoretical and ethnographic works on the evil eye include Lawrence Di Stasi, *Mal Occhio (Evil Eye), The Underside of Vision* (San Francisco: North Point Press, 1981); Alan Dundes, ed., *The Evil Eye: A Folklore Casebook* (New York: Garland, 1981); and Clarence Maloney, ed., *The Evil Eye* (New York: Columbia Univ. Press, 1976).

18. Ware, 193.

19. Gans, 114; Louis C. Jones, "The Evil Eye Among European-Americans," in Dundes, ed., *The Evil Eye*, 151 (originally published in 1951); Richard Swiderski, "From Folk to Popular: Plastic Evil Eye Charms," in Maloney, ed., *The Evil Eye*, 40; and Donald Tricarico, "Guido: Fashioning an Italian-American Youth Style," *Journal of Ethnic Studies* 19, no. 1 (Spring 1991): 44.

20. A variant holds that a possessor of the evil eye may afflict others by giving them bunches of grapes. See Jane Voiles, "Genoese Folkways in a California Mining Camp," *California Folklore Quarterly* 3 (1944): 212.

21. Michael Buonanno, "Becoming White: Notes on an Italian-American Explanation of Evil Eye," *New York Folklore* 10 (1984): 42; and Williams, 142.

22. Michael Brunetti, "Italian Folklore Collected from Mrs. Stephanie Nappi," *New York Folklore Quarterly* 28 (1972): 258-59; Wayland D. Hand, Anna Casetta, and Sondra B. Thiederman, eds., *Popular Beliefs and Superstitions, A Compendium of American Folklore from the Ohio Collection of Newbell Niles Puckett* (Boston: G. K. Hall, 1981), 1076 (item no. 25619); Jones, 152; and Williams, 142, 153.

23. Jones, 159.

24. Ware, 190.

25. Bianco, 94; Di Stasi, 39; Richard Gambino, *Blood of My Blood, The Dilemma of the Italian-Americans* (Garden City, NY: Doubleday, 1974), 204-5; Hand, Casetta, and Thiederman, 1331 (item no. 3236); Joe Vergara, *Love and Pasta: A Recollection* (New York: Harper and Row, 1968), 72; and Williams, 95, 102-3.

26. Interview with Albina Malpezzi (Piedmontese, second generation), 25 November 1988, in Jonesboro, Arkansas.

27. Interview with Frances Gueri Byrd (southern Italian, second generation), 23 May 1990, in Jonesboro, Arkansas.

28. Jones, 156.

29. Carla Bianco, *The Two Rosetos* (Bloomington: Indiana Univ. Press, 1974), 100; and Buonanno, 44-46.

30. Hand, Casetta, and Thiederman, 1077 (item no. 25628); and M. Estellie Smith, "Folk Medicine Among the Sicilian-Americans of Buffalo, New York," *Urban Anthropology* 1, no. 1 (1972): 101.

31. Di Stasi, 25; Hand, Casetta, and Thiederman, 84 (item no. 2053), 108 (no. 2638), 133 (nos. 3250, 3251), 134 (nos. 3264, 3265), 158 (no. 3839), 1056 (no. 25233), 1080 (no. 25699); and M. Estellie Smith, 101.

32. Gambino, 204; Hand, Casetta, and Thiederman, 1069 (no. 25471), 1081-1082 (nos. 25709, 25710); Jones, 155; Jerre Mangione, *Mount Allegro, A Memoir of Italian American Life* (1943; reprint, New York: Columbia Univ. Press, 1981), 101-2; Lydia Q. Pietropaoli, "The Italians Came Up Watertown Way," *New York Folklore Quarterly* 29 (1973): 75; Vergara, 71; and Williams, 143-44.

33. Pietro Di Donato, *Three Circles of Light* (New York: Julian Messner, 1960), 22; Gambino, 204; Hand, Casetta, and Thiederman, 1072 (item no. 25543), 1077 (nos. 25632, 25633); and Jones, 156.

34. Jones, 156.

35. Brunetti 258-59; Tina DeRosa, *Paper Fish* (Chicago: Wine Press, 1980), 59; Di Donato, 158; Di Stasi, 29; Gambino, 200; Hand, Casetta, and Thiederman, 1078 (item no. 25657); Peter Hartman and Karyl McIntosh, "Evil Eye Beliefs Collected in Utica, New York," *New York Folklore* 4 (1978): 61-62; Jones, 153-54; M. Estellie Smith, 96-97; and especially Swiderski, 30-34.

36. Gambino, 200; and Mangione, 103-4.

37. Pauline N. Barrese, "Southern Italian Folklore in New York City," *New York Folklore Quarterly* 21 (1965): 186; Brunetti, 258-59; Charles W. Churchill, *The Italians of Newark, A Community Study* (1942; reprint, New York: Arno, 1975), 108; Di Stasi, 28; Gambino, 200, 204; Wayland D. Hand, "The Evil Eye in Its Folk Medical Aspects: A Survey of North America," in Dundes, ed., *The Evil Eye,* 175 (originally published in 1976); Hand, Casetta, and Thiederman, 130 (item no. 3184), 131 (no. 3185), 132 (no. 3218), 137 (nos. 3337, 3339), 892 (nos. 21452-55, 21457, 21458), 1072 (no. 25523), 1073 (no. 25551), 1078 (nos. 25648-56, 25661), 1079-80 (nos. 25662, 25667, 25670, 25682, 25688-90, 25694, 25695); Hartman and McIntosh 61-62, 64, 68; Jones, 154; Krause, 26; Elizabeth Mathias, "The Italian-American Funeral: Persistence Through Change," *Western Folklore* 33 (1974): 44n; Patrick B. Mullen, *I Heard the Old Fishermen Say, Folklore of the Texas Gulf Coast* (Austin: Univ. of Texas Press, 1978), 76; M. Estellie Smith, 101; Swiderski, 34-38; Vergara, 72-74; Voiles, 212-13; Ware, 190; Williams, 143; and Bob Zappacosta, "Italian Beliefs," *West Virginia Folklore* 12, no. 2 (Winter 1962): 21.

38. Marie Hall Ets, *Rosa: The Life of an Italian Immigrant* (Minneapolis: Univ. of Minnesota Press, 1970), 159; Gambino, 204-5; Hand, Casetta, and Thiederman, 132 (items no. 3214, 3226), 1061 (no. 25327); Karyl McIntosh, "Folk Obstetrics, Gynecology, and Pediatrics in Utica, New York," *New York Folklore* 4 (1978): 56; Jones, 153; and Spicer, 319.

39. Interview with Frances Gueri Byrd.

40. Angelo P. Bertocci, "Memoir of My Mother," *Harper's,* June 1937: 12.

41. Catherine Harris Ainsworth, *Italian-American Folktales* (Buffalo: Clyde Press, 1977), 29-30; Jerry Della Femina and Charles Sopkin, *An Italian Grows in*

Brooklyn (Boston: Little, Brown, 1978), 75; Di Stasi, 19; Hand, Casetta, and Thiederman, 109 (item no. 2655), 393-94 (nos. 9955, 9956, 9959, 9961-63, 9965, 9967), 1077 (nos. 25626, 25627); Hartman and McIntosh, 62-63; and Mangione, 34.

42. Brunetti, 258-59; Buonanno, 41; Di Donato, 172; Di Stasi, 21-22; Hand, Casetta, and Thiederman, 131-32 (items no. 3205, 3206), 394 (nos. 9968-71), 395 (nos. 9976, 9977), 1070 (no. 25492), Hartman and McIntosh, 65; Jones, 160; and Pietropaoli, 75.

43. Voiles, 213.

44. Jerilyn Mankins, "More Italian Beliefs," *West Virginia Folklore* 12, no. 2 (Winter 1962): 29.

45. Jones, 160.

46. Hand, Casetta, and Thiederman, 1171 (item no. 27768); and Jones, 165.

47. Ainsworth, 29; David Steven Cohen, *The Folklore and Folklife of New Jersey* (New Brunswick: Rutgers Univ. Press, 1983), 57; Di Stasi, 30-31; Hand, Casetta, and Thiederman, 1082 (items no. 25729-25730); Hartman and McIntosh, 64; and Jones, 161.

48. Di Stasi, 31, 32.

49. Williams, 155, 156.

50. Bianco, 96-97; Di Stasi, 21-22; and Hand, Casetta, and Thiederman, 1082-83 (items no. 25731, 25732, 25734, 25736-38, 25740-42, 25745-49).

51. Jones, 167-68 (no italics in original).

52. Hand, Casetta, and Thiederman, 1081 (item no. 25724); and Jones, 166-67.

53. Hand, Casetta, and Thiederman, 1083 (item no. 25750); and Vergara, 71-72.

54. Della Femina and Sopkin, 76.

55. Ainsworth, 31; Jones, 164-65; and Voiles, 212.

56. Jones, 165.

57. Ibid., 165.

58. Ainsworth, 34-35; Bianco, 93; Brunetti, 259; Hand, Casetta, and Thiederman, 1124 (items no. 26661, 26662); Louis C. Jones, "Italian Werewolves," *New York Folklore Quarterly* 6 (1950): 133-36; Anthony Navarra, "Old Tales and New Tongues," *New York Folklore Quarterly* 18 (1962): 14; and Williams, 170.

59. Brunetti, 259-60.

60. Jones, "Italian Werewolves," 136.

61. Ainsworth, 69; and Navarra, 14.

62. Ets, 176.

63. Della Femina and Sopkin, 62.

64. Mangione, 237.

65. Michael La Sorte, *La Merica, Images of Italian Greenhorn Experience* (Philadelphia: Temple Univ. Press, 1985), 92-93.

66. Barrese, 186; Raymond De Capite, *The Coming of Fabrizze* (New York: David McKay, 1960), 202; Gambino, 204; and Hand, Casetta, and Thiederman, 651 (items no. 16002, 16004), 652 (nos. 16007, 16008), 654 (no. 16067), 722-23 (nos. 17969, 17974, 17986, 17992), 879 (no. 21153), 1296 (no. 30516).

67. Hand, Casetta, and Thiederman, 671 (item no. 16451), 674 (no. 16501), 679 (nos. 16646, 16648), 680 (no. 16659), 681 (no. 16690), 683 (nos. 16745, 16746), 1319 (nos. 31063, 31069-71), 1511 (no. 35763).

68. Ibid., 638 (item no. 15693), 705 (no. 17272), 808 (nos. 19514-16), 809 (no. 19520), 900 (nos. 21667, 21677, 21678), 987 (no. 23613), 1477 (no. 34918), 1478 (no. 34935), 1518 (nos. 35863, 35864); and Vergara, 147-48.

69. Hand, Casetta, and Thiderman, 926 (items no. 22240, 22241), 929 (nos. 22311, 22313), 938 (no. 22498).

70. Pietro Di Donato, *Christ in Concrete* (Indianapolis: Bobbs-Merrill, 1939), 20; and Hand, Casetta, and Thiederman, 651 (items no. 16002, 16004), 652 (no. 16007, 16008), 693 (no. 16977).

71. Gambino, 204; and Hand, Casetta, and Thiederman, 299 (items no. 7498, 7500), 879 (no. 21149), 1311 (no. 30860), 1315 (nos. 30964, 30966).

72. Hand, Casetta, and Thiederman, 720 (items no. 17661, 17662), 898 (no. 21617), 899 (no. 21643), 900 (no. 21654), 1023 (no. 24508), 1032 (no. 24719).

73. Ibid., 839 (items no. 20261, 20262), 906 (no. 21835).

74. Ibid., 646 (item no. 15889), 995 (nos. 17034-37); and Mullen, 80.

75. Hand, Casetta, and Thiederman, 1484 (item no. 35089), 1486 (no. 35145), 1495 (nos. 35371-73, 35376); and Mullen, 79-81.

76. Donald Tricarico, "The Restructuring of Ethnic Community: The Italian Neighborhood in Greenwich Village," *Journal of Ethnic Studies* 11, no. 2 (1983): 68.

77. Elizabeth Mathias and Angelamaria Varesano, "The Dynamics of Religious Reactivation: A Study of a Charismatic Missionary to Southern Italians in the United States," *Ethnicity* 5 (1978): 301-11.

Chapter Six. Folk Medicine

1. "Calling on the Devil to Cure Disease," *Journal of American Folklore* 5 (1892): 238. The newspaper in which this account first appeared is not specified.

2. Corinne Azen Krause, *Grandmothers, Mothers, and Daughters: Oral Histories of Three Generations of Ethnic American Women* (Boston: Twayne, 1991), 26.

3. Dorothy Gladys Spicer, "Health Superstitions of the Italian Immigrant," *Hygeia* 4, no. 5 (May 1926): 268.

4. Robert Anthony Orsi, *The Madonna of 115th Street, Faith and Community in Italian Harlem, 1880-1950* (New Haven: Yale Univ. Press, 1985), 132; M. Estellie Smith, "Folk Medicine Among the Sicilian-Americans of Buffalo, New York," *Urban Anthropology* 1, no. 1 (1972): 95; and Spicer, 268-69.

5. Smith, 94.

6. Ibid., 87.

7. Pauline N. Barrese, "A Child of the Thirties," *New York Folklore Quarterly* 25 (1969): 134; Jerry Della Femina and Charles Sopkin, *An Italian Grows in Brooklyn* (Boston: Little Brown, 1978), 75; Wayland D. Hand, Anna Casetta, and Sondra B. Thiederman, eds., *Popular Beliefs and Superstitions, A Compendium of American Folklore from the Ohio Collection of Newbell Niles Puckett* (Boston: G. K. Hall, 1981), 256 (items no. 6411, 6420), 257 (no. 6431), 266 (no. 6707), 269 (no. 6770), 270 (nos. 6798, 6804).

8. Hand, Casetta, and Thiederman, 258 (items no. 6472, 6483), 259 (no. 6489), 262 (nos. 6580, 6596), 263 (nos. 6605, 6617), 264 (no. 6652).

9. Phyllis H. Williams, *South Italian Folkways in Europe and America, A Handbook for Social Workers, Visiting Nurses, School Teachers, and Physicians* (1938; reprint, New York: Russell and Russell, 1969), 164.

10. Marie Hall Ets, *Rosa, The Life of an Italian Immigrant* (Minneapolis: Univ. of Minnesota Press, 1970), 12.

11. Hand, Casetta, and Thiederman, 278 (item no. 6972).

12. Williams, 175.

13. Interview with Joanne Terranella Burleson (Sicilian, third generation), 14 March 1990, in Jonesboro, Arkansas; and Hand, Casetta, and Thiederman, 345 (item no. 8654).

14. Interview with Albina Malpezzi (Piedmontese, second generation), 25 November 1988, in Jonesboro, Arkansas.

15. Phylis Cancilla Martinelli, "Pioneer Paisani in Globe, Arizona," in *Italian Immigrants in Rural and Small Town America, Essays from the Fourteenth Annual Conference of the American Italian Historical Association*, ed. Rudolph J. Vecoli (Staten Island, NY: American Italian Historical Association, 1987), 163.

16. Interview with Albina Malpezzi; also collected from Sara Rao Vittone (southern Italian, second generation), 12 July 1989, in Masontown, Pennsylvania; and interview with Pearl Malpezzi (Piedmontese, first generation), 17 July 1984, in Masontown, Pennsylvania. See also Carla Bianco, *The Two Rosetos* (Bloomington: Indiana Univ. Press, 1974), 22, 51, 101; and Hand, Casetta, and Thiederman, 102 (item no. 2490), 414 (no. 10529); and Martinelli, 163. For the use of camomile in Italian-American fiction, see Marion Benasutti, *No Steady Job for Papa* (New York: Vanguard, 1966), 161; and Lucas Longo, *The Family on Vendetta Street* (Garden City, NY: Doubleday, 1968), 184.

17. Hand, Casetta, and Thiederman, 326 (item no. 8145), 423 (no. 10766). See also Benasutti, 161.

18. Interview with Pearl Malpezzi; Bianco, 22, 51, 101; and Hand, Casetta, and Thiederman, 116 (item no. 2831), 372 (no. 9392).

19. Angelo M. Pellegrini, *Americans by Choice* (New York: Macmillan, 1956), 56.

20. Vincent Panella, *The Other Side, Growing Up Italian in America* (Garden City, NY: Doubleday, 1979), 188.

21. Benasutti 161; Hand, Casetta, and Thiederman, 122 (items no. 2959, 2960, 2940.61), 122 (no. 2982), 331 (no. 8281), 346 (no. 8686), 373 (no. 9395), 401 (no. 10158), 432-33 (no. 11012), 444-45 (nos. 11313, 11314), 453 (no. 11525); and Joseph Napoli, *A Dying Cadence, Memories of a Sicilian Childhood* (NP: NP, 1986), 47.

22. John Fante, *Wait Until Spring, Bandini* (1938; reprint, Santa Barbara: Black Sparrow, 1983), 18.

23. Interview with Etta Ferraro Goodwin (Campanian, second generation), August 1991, in Peace Dale, Rhode Island (interviewed by Lucia Peek).

24. Interview with Pearl Malpezzi, 19 July 1984; and Hand, Casetta, and Thiederman, 348 (item no. 8727), 349 (no. 8729), 406 (no. 10307). See also Michael De Capite, *Maria* (New York: John Day, 1943), 105; and Garibaldi M. Lapolla, *The Fire in the Flesh* (1931; reprint, New York: Arno, 1975), 297.

25. Bianco, 152.

26. Hand, Casetta, and Thiederman, 309-310 (items no. 7708, 7709, 7712).

27. Ibid., 313 (item no. 7810), 314 (no. 7817). For the use of the same procedure to cure pneumonia, see Richard Gambino, *Blood of My Blood, The Dilemma of the Italian-Americans* (Garden City, NY: Doubleday, 1974), 202.

28. Hand, Casetta, and Thiederman, 327 (item no. 8180), 328 (nos. 8191, 8193).

29. Barrese, 134; and Hand, Casetta, and Thiederman, 346 (item no. 8677), 347 (nos. 8696, 8707), 348 (nos. 8722, 8731, 8737), 350 (nos. 8779, 8792), 351 (8796).

30. Hand, Casetta, and Thiederman, 358 (items no. 8995, 8999, 9009), 404 (nos. 10231, 10235, 10248).

31. Ibid., 361 (items no 9086, 9100).

32. Ibid., 106 (item no. 2598), 364-65 (nos. 9165, 9186, 9211), 366 (nos. 9216, 9232, 9233); and Panella, 70.

33. Mari Tomasi, *Like Lesser Gods* (Milwaukee: Bruce, 1949), 130; and Hand, Casetta, and Thiederman, 369 (items no. 9288, 9297), 372 (nos. 9371, 9375).

34. Hand, Casetta, and Thiederman, 457 (items no. 11637, 11643), 458 (nos. 11656, 11658).

35. Ibid., 377 (items no. 9535, 9536); and Jane Voiles, "Genoese Folkways in a California Mining Camp," *California Folklore Quarterly* 3 (1944): 215.

36. Interview with Pearl Malpezzi, 17 July 1984; and Hand, Casetta, and Thiederman, 373 (item no. 9412), 374 (no. 9427).

37. Gambino, 202-03; Hand, Casetta, and Thiederman, 389 (item no. 9848, 9899), 391 (no. 9911); and Jerre Mangione, *Mount Allegro, A Memoir of Italian American Life* (1943; reprint New York: Columbia Univ. Press, 1981), 31.

38. Barrese, 135; and Hand, Casetta, and Thiederman, 330 (item no. 8245).

39. Pietro Di Donato, *Christ in Concrete* (Indianapolis: Bobbs-Merrill, 1939), 110.

40. Richard Gambino, *Bread and Roses* (New York: Seaview, 1981), 134; and Hand, Casetta, and Thiederman, 116 (item no. 2834), 469 (nos. 11951, 11954).

41. Bronislaw Malinowski, "The Role of Magic and Religion," in *Reader in Comparative Religion, An Anthropological Approach,* ed. William A. Lessa and Evon Z. Vogt, 2nd edition (New York: Harper and Row, 1965), 106.

42. Rev. Enrico C. Sartorio, *Social and Religious Life of Italians in America* (Boston: Christopher, 1918), 101-02.

43. Interview with Marie Marchese (Sicilian, second generation), 12 April 1991, in North Little Rock, Arkansas.

44. Angelo P. Bertocci, "Memoir of My Mother," *Harper's* 175 (June 1937): 16.

45. Dorothy Gladys Spicer, "The Immigrant Mother as Seen by a Social Worker," *Hygeia* 4, no. 6 (June 1926): 320.

46. Bob Zappacosta, "Italian Beliefs," *West Virginia Folklore* 12, no. 2 (Winter 1962): 19.

47. Interview with Pearl Malpezzi, 17 July 1984.

48. Voiles, 214.

49. Ibid., 213.

50. Smith, 98-99.

51. Hand, Casetta, and Thiederman, 1084 (item no. 25771).

52. Bianco, 90-93, 208; Hand, Casetta, and Thiederman, 135 (item no. 3287), 1094 (nos. 29939, 29940, 25942), 1096 (nos. 25977, 25978, 25980), 1112 (no. 26360), 1113 (no. 26405), 1114 (nos. 26408, 26409); Lydia Q. Pietropaoli, "The Italians Came Up

Watertown Way," *New York Folklore Quarterly* 29 (1973): 75; Williams, 156-57; and Zappacosta, 18-19, 21-22.

53. Alice Hamilton, "Witchcraft in West Polk Street," *American Mercury* 10 (January 1927): 71-72.

54. Hamilton, 73.

55. Sartorio, 101.

56. Hamilton, 74.

57. Interview with Mamie Jo DiMarco Chauvin (Sicilian, second generation), 19 March 1991, in Forrest City, Arkansas.

Chapter Seven. Recreation and Games

1. George Sessions Perry, "Your Neighbors, the Pomaricos," *Saturday Evening Post,* 6 November 1948: 151. See also Dorothy Noyes, *Uses of Tradition, Arts of Italian Americans in Philadelphia* (Philadelphia: Philadelphia Folklore Project, 1989), 58-59.

2. Herbert J. Gans, *The Urban Villagers, Group and Class in the Life of Italian-Americans* (New York: Free Press, 1962), 116.

3. Robert E. Park and Herbert A. Miller, *Old World Traits Transplanted* (New York: Harper, 1921), 129.

4. Gene P. Veronesi, *Italian-Americans and Their Communities in Cleveland* (Cleveland: Cleveland State Univ., 1977), 176, 304-5.

5. Glenna Matthews, "An Immigrant Community in Indian Territory," *Labor History* 23 (1982): 383.

6. *Masontown Sesqui-Centennial Celebration, 1798-1948* (NP: NP, 1948), 40.

7. Rudolph J. Vecoli, "Italians on Minnesota's Iron Range," in *Italian Immigrants in Rural and Small Town America, Essays from the Fourteenth Annual Conference of the American Italian Historical Association,* ed. Rudolph J. Vecoli (Staten Island, NY: American Italian Historical Association, 1987), 187.

8. Veronesi, 176.

9. Park and Miller, 129. The quotation is from F. O. Beck, writing in the *Bulletin of the Department of Public Welfare, Chicago.*

10. Matthews, 383.

11. Phylis Cancilla Martinelli, "Pioneer Paesani in Globe, Arizona," in Vecoli, ed., *Italian Immigrants in Rural and Small Town America,* 167.

12. Charlotte Kimball, "An Outline of Amusements Among Italians in New York," *Charities* 5 (18 August 1900): 3.

13. Interview with Pearl Malpezzi (Piedmontese, first generation), 19 July 1984, in Masontown, Pennsylvania.

14. Interview with Sam Gennuso (Sicilian, second generation), 26 May 1989, in Jonesboro, Arkansas.

15. Wayland D. Hand, Anna Casetta, and Sondra B. Thiederman, eds., *Popular Beliefs and Superstitions, A Compendium of American Folklore form the Ohio Collection of Newbell Niles Puckett* (Boston: G. K. Hall, 1981), 1487 (item no. 35193).

16. Pauline N. Barrese, "Southern Italian Folklore in New York City," *New York Folklore Quarterly* 21 (1965): 186-87; and C. Richard King, "Old Thurber," in *Singers and Storytellers,* ed. Mody C. Boatright, Wilson M. Hudson, and Allen Maxwell (Dallas: Southern Methodist Univ. Press, 1961), 111.

17. Interview with Guido Malpezzi (Tuscan, second generation), August 1990, in Masontown, Pennsylvania; Richard Gambino, *Blood of My Blood, The Dilemma of the Italian-Americans* (Garden City, NY: Doubleday, 1974), 138; Elizabeth Mathias, "The Game as Creator of the Group in an Italian-American Community," *Pennsylvania Folklife* 23, no. 4 (1974): 23-24; and Elizabeth Mathias, "Italian-American Culture and Games: The Minnesota Iron Range and South Philadelphia," in *Play as Context, 1979 Proceedings of the Association for the Anthropological Study of Play*, ed. Alyce Taylor Cheska (West Point, NY: Leisure Press, 1981), 82-83.

18. Mathias, "Italian-American Culture and Games," 82-83.

19. Barrese, 186.

20. Irvin L. Child, *Italian or American? The Second Generation in Conflict* (New Haven: Yale Univ. Press, 1943), 25.

21. Angelo Valenti, *Golden Gate* (1939; reprint New York: Arno, 1975), 161.

22. Interview with Joseph Capello (Piedmontese, first generation), 12 November 1982, in Jonesboro, Arkansas.

23. Sue Samuelson and Ray Kepner, "Bocce Ball Meets Hacky-Sack: A Western Pennsylvania Independence Day Gathering," *Keystone Folklore* 3, no. 2 (1984): 32.

24. Vecoli, 189.

25. Marie Hall Ets, *Rosa, The Life of an Italian Immigrant* (Minneapolis: Univ. of Minnesota Press, 1970), 222; *The Italians of New York, A Survey Prepared by Workers of the Federal Writers' Project, Works Progress Administration in the City of New York* (1938; reprint, New York: Arno, 1975), 210; and Mathias, "Italian-American Culture and Games," 83.

26. For descriptions of *morra*, see Valentine J. Belfiglio, "Italians in Small Town and Rural Texas," in Vecoli, ed., *Italian Immigrants in Rural and Small Town America*, 46; Carla Bianco, *The Two Rosetos* (Bloomington: Indiana Univ. Press, 1974), 211-21; Gambino, 139; Fred L. Gardaphe, "From Oral Tradition to Written Word: Toward an Ethnographically Based Literary Criticism," in *From the Margin, Writings in Italian Americana*, ed. Anthony Julian Tamburri, Paolo A. Giordano, and Fred L. Gardaphe (West Lafayette, IN: Purdue Univ. Press, 1991), 298; Salvatore J. LaGumina, *The Immigrants Speak, Italian Americans Tell Their Story* (New York: Center for Migration Studies, 1979), 121 (from the memoir of Clara Corica Grillo); Mathias, "Italian-American Culture and Games," 83-84; Lydia Q. Pietropaoli, "The Italians Came Up Watertown Way," *New York Folklore Quarterly* 29 (1973): 76; Clement L. Valetta, "Friendship and Games in Italian-American Life," *Keystone Folklore Quarterly* 15 (1970): 181-82; Joe Vergara, *Love and Pasta, A Recollection* (New York: Harper and Row, 1968), 82-83; and Phyllis A. Williams, *South Italian Folkways in Europe and America, A Handbook for Social Workers, Visiting Nurses, School Teachers, and Physicians* (1938; reprint New York: Russell and Russell, 1969), 108. Fictional accounts of the game appear in Fred L. Gardaphe, "Mora Amore," in Tamburri, Giordano, and Gardaphe, eds., *From the Margin*, 102-9; and Mari Tomasi, *Like Lesser Gods* (Milwaukee: Bruce, 1949), 51.

27. Interview with Joseph Capello.

28. Martinelli, 167.

29. Mathias, "Italian-American Culture and Games," 83-84; and Valetta, 181-82.

30. William Foote Whyte, *Street Corner Society, The Social Structure of an Italian Slum*, 2nd edition (Chicago: Univ. of Chicago Press, 1955), 70.

31. Interview with Pearl Malpezzi.

32. Gardaphe, "From Oral Tradition to Written Word," 298-99.

33. Interview with Joseph Capello.

34. For example, see Mildred Urick, "The San Rocco Festival at Aliquippa, Pennsylvania: A Transplanted Tradition," *Pennsylvania Folklife* 19, no. 1 (Autumn 1969): 21.

35. Mathias, "Italian-American Culture and Games," 85-87; and Vergara, 83-84. For a fictional treatment of *passatella*, see Garibaldi M. Lapolla, *The Fire in the Flesh* (1931; reprint, New York: Arno, 1975), 21, 95, 117, 146, 158, 210, 313.

36. Charles W. Churchill, *The Italians of Newark, A Community Study* (1942; reprint, New York: Arno, 1975), 143.

37. Kimball, 4.

38. Jerry Della Femina and Charles Sopkin, *An Italian Grows in Brooklyn* (Boston: Little, Brown, 1978), 54; Lucas Longo, *The Family on Vendetta Street* (Garden City, NY: Doubleday, 1968), 117-18; Jerre Mangione, *Mount Allegro, A Memoir of Italian American Life* (1943; reprint, New York: Columbia Univ. Press, 1981), 14-15; and John Scarne, *Scarne's Encyclopedia of Games* (New York: Harper and Row, 1973), 371-72.

39. Mangione, 120; and Scarnes, 368-71.

40. Barrese, 187; and Vergara, 78-80.

41. Vergara, 81.

42. Donald Tricarico, "Guido: Fashioning an Italian-American Youth Style," *Journal of Ethnic Studies* 19, no. 1 (Spring 1991): 44-47.

Chapter Eight. Stories and Storytelling

1. Elizabeth Mathias and Richard Raspa, *Italian Folktales in America, The Verbal Art of an Immigrant Woman* (Detroit: Wayne State Univ. Press, 1985): 256.

2. Mathias and Raspa, 250.

3. Ibid., 37-45.

4. Anthony Navarra, "Old Tales and New Tongues," *New York Folklore Quarterly* 18 (1962): 14.

5. Carla Bianco, *The Two Rosetos* (Bloomington: Indiana Univ. Press, 1974), 213-14 (ellipses in the original). Bianco suggests that one of the major ways in which Italian Americans in Roseto, Pennsylvania, differ from those in other communities in the United States is in their preservation of traditional storytelling occasions. She was able to record 512 *märchen* and related story forms during her research there.

6. Ibid., 73. For the Tuscan *veglia*, see Alessandro Falassi, *Folklore by the Fireside, Text and Context of the Tuscan* Veglia (Austin: Univ. of Texas Press, 1980).

7. Linda Brandi Cateura, *Growing Up Italian, How Being Brought Up as an Italian-American Helped Shape the Characters, Lives, and Fortunes of Twenty-Four Celebrated Americans* (New York: William Morrow, 1987), 136 (from the memoir of Daniela Gioseffi).

8. Bianco, 77; and Jerre Mangione, *Mount Allegro, A Memoir of Italian American Life* (1943; reprint, New York: Columbia Univ. Press, 1981), 301.

9. Leonard Roberts, "Folktales from the Italian Alps," *Tennessee Folklore Society Bulletin* 22 (1956): 99-100.

10. Antti Aarne and Stith Thompson, *The Types of the Folktale, A Classification and Bibliography,* second revision (Helsinki: Academia Scientiarum Fennica, 1964), 178-79.

11. Leonard Roberts, "More Folktales from the Italian Alps," *Tennessee Folklore Society Bulletin* 23 (1957): 104-6. See Aarne and Thompson, 362.

12. Roberts, "Folktales from the Italian Alps," 102-3. The story includes several motifs and related motifs catalogued in Stith Thompson, *Motif-Index of Folk-Literature, A Classification of Narrative Elements in Folktales, Ballads, Myths, Fables, Mediaeval Romances, Exempla, Fabliaux, Jest-Books and Local Legends,* revised edition (Bloomington: Indiana Univ. Press, 1955-58). See D1506, "Magic object cures deafness" (2: 255); D1618, "Magic weeping object" (2: 288); D1625, "Statue weeps" (2: 290); and F954, "Dumb person brought to speak" (3: 243).

13. Roberts, "More Folktales from the Italian Alps," 100-104. Some elements in this story resemble motifs included in D. P. Rotunda, *Motif-Index of the Italian Novella in Prose* (1942; reprint, New York: Haskell House, 1973), especially H94.8*, "Recognition by medallion (plaque)" (20); and N530, "Discovery of treasure" (153).

14. Ruth Ann Musick, "Italian Folk Tales Told by Rocco Pantalone, of Fairmont," *West Virginia Folklore* 11, no. 1 (Fall 1960): 9-11.

15. Thompson, 3:398, 3:504.

16. Musick, 12-14.

17. Melia Rose Maiolo, "Italian Tales Told in Shinnston," *West Virginia Folklore* 8, no. 1 (Fall 1957): 8-12. See Aarne and Thompson, 299. See also motif K1911.5, "Penniless bride pretends to wealth" in Thompson, 4: 453.

18. Maiolo, 12-14. See Aarne and Thompson, 410.

19. Rosemary Agonito, "Il Paisano, Immigrant Italian Folktales of Central New York," *New York Folklore Quarterly* 23 (1967): 57-59. See Aarne and Thompson, 117; and Thompson, 3: 287.

20. Agonito, 63-64. See Aarne and Thompson, 350-51.

21. Robert A. Orsi, "The Fault of Memory: 'Southern Italy' in the Imagination of Immigrants and the Lives of Their Children in Italian Harlem, 1920-1945," *Journal of Family History* 15 (1990): 141.

22. Interview with Pearl Malpezzi (Piedmontese, first generation), 17 July 1984, in Masontown, Pennsylvania.

23. Interview with Christopher Hodgkins (Calabrian, third generation), 17 July 1990, in Columbus, Ohio.

24. Louis Guida, "The Rocconi-Fratesi Family: Italianata in the Arkansas Delta," in *Hogs in the Bottom, Family Folklore in Arkansas,* ed. Deirdre LaPin (Little Rock: August House, 1982), 86.

25. Interview with Joseph Capello (Piedmontese, first generation), 19 July 1984, in Masontown, Pennsylvania. Cf. the migration stories from written sources surveyed in Michael La Sorte, *La Merica, Images of Italian Greenhorn Experience* (Philadelphia: Temple Univ. Press, 1985), 3-60. An analysis of Joseph Capello's storytelling style may be found in William M. Clements, "The 'Man of Words' in Masontown, Pennsylvania: Two Approaches to Verbal Performance," *Western Folklore* 48 (1989): 169-77.

26. Interview with Pearl Malpezzi.

27. Interview with Joanne Terranella Burleson (Sicilian, third generation), 14 March 1990, in Jonesboro, Arkansas. The fictional crime family in *The Godfather* come from Corleone, Sicily, and have taken the name of the community as their surname.

28. Interview with Joseph Capello. For other examples of narratives about visits to Italy, see Bianco, 66-69. The importance of going to Italy for return visits even during the peak years of immigration is evident from the vignettes in Lewis E. Macbrayne, "The Judgment of the Steerage," *Harper's* 117 (1908): 489-99, which describes the experiences of Italian and Portuguese returnees.

Chapter Nine. Drama, Music, and Dance

1. Caroline Singer, "An Italian Saturday," *Century* 101 (1921): 592.

2. Charlotte Kimball, "An Outline of Amusements Among Italians in New York," *Charities* 5, no. 12 (18 August 1900): 5-6. A brief description of attending one installment of Roland's saga performed by puppets in Brooklyn appears in Stewart Culin, "Italian Marionette Theatre in Brooklyn, N. Y.," *Journal of American Folklore* 3 (1890): 155-57.

3. W[illiam] W[ells] N[ewell], "Italian Marionettes in Boston," *Journal of American Folklore* 7 (1894): 153.

4. Emelise Aleandri and Maxine Schwartz Seller, "Italian-American Theatre," in *Ethnic Theatre in the United States*, ed. Maxine Schwartz Seller (Wesport, CT: Greenwood, 1983), 256.

5. Elisabeth Irwin, "Where the Players Are Marionettes and the Age of Chivalry Is Born Again in a Little Italian Theater in Mulberry Street," *The Craftsman* 12 (1907): 667.

6. Ibid., 668.

7. Ibid., 668-69. See also the turn-of-the-century description of the New York City puppet theater in Hutchins Hapgood, "The Italian Theater of New York," reprinted in *A Documentary History of Italian Americans*, ed. Wayne Moquin and Mark Van Doren (New York: Praeger, 1974), 317-18, and the analysis of contemporary puppet drama in Sicily in Michael Buonanno, "The Palermitan Epic: Dialogism and the Inscription of Social Relations," *Journal of American Folklore* 103 (1990): 324-33.

8. Bruno Roselli, "An Arkansas Epic," *Century Illustrated* 77 (1920): 384.

9. Robert F. Foerster, *The Italian Emigration of Our Times* (Cambridge: Harvard Univ. Press, 1919), 396-97.

10. Lois Adler, "The Manteo Family's Sicilian Puppets," *Drama Review* 20, no. 2 (June 1976): 27.

11. Ibid., 28-29. For a description of Aggrippino Manteo's puppet theater in the 1930s, see *The Italians of New York, A Survey Prepared by Workers of the Federal Writers' Project, Works Progress Administration in the City of New York* (1938; reprint, New York: Arno, 1969), 200.

12. Salvatore Primeggia and Joseph A. Varacalli, "Southern Italian Comedy: Old to New World," in *Italian Americans in Transition, Proceedings of the XXI Annual Conference of the American Italian Historical Association*, ed. Joseph V. Scelsa, Salvatore J. LaGumina, and Lydio Tomasi (Staten Island, NY: American Italian Historical Association, 1990), 244-45.

13. Aleandri and Seller, 266. For Migliacci, see also Giuseppe Cautela, "The Italian Theatre in New York," *American Mercury* 12 (1927): 109-10; Michael La Sorte, *La Merica, Images of Italian Greenhorn Experience* (Philadelphia: Temple Univ. Press, 1985), 174; and Primeggia and Varacalli, 246-47.

14. Michael Schlesinger, "Italian Music in New York," *New York Folklore* 14, nos. 3-4 (Summer-Fall 1988): 130.

15. Anna L. Chairetakis, Notes to *Cantate con Noi, Choral Songs from Istria and the Alps and Vintage Popular Music from South-Central Italy* (Global Village Music GVM #678, 1986), 3.

16. Anna L. Chairetakis, Notes to *Chesta E la Voci Ca Canuscite, This Is the Voice You Know: Southern Italian Mountain Music from Calabria, Campania, Basilicata and Abruzzi* (Global Village Music GVM #675, 1986), 10,14.

17. Elizabeth Mathias and Richard Raspa, *Italian Folktales in America, The Verbal Art of an Immigrant Woman* (Detroit: Wayne State Univ. Press, 1985), 37-45.

18. Cautela, 106.

19. Rose Grieco, "They Who Mourn," *Commonweal,* 27 March 1953: 629.

20. Chairetakis, *Cantate con Noi,* 4.

21. Sung by Antoinette Giglio (Sicilian, second generation) to Sam Gennuso in September 1991. Transcribed and translated by Giglio and Gennuso.

22. Collected by Clara Regnoni-Macera, March 1962, in Boulder, Colorado, and first published as "Il Magg" ("Welcome, May"), *Colorado Folksong Bulletin* 1, no. 3 (November 1962): 32-33. Republished in Clara Regnoni-Macera, "The Song of May," *Western Folklore* 23 (1964): 23-24.

23. Collected by Ben Gray Lumpkin, December 1952, in Santa Fe, New Mexico, and first published as "La Monaca Sposa" in *Colorado Folksong Bulletin* 1, no. 2 (April 1962): 24-25.

24. Collected in December 1961 in Santa Fe, New Mexico, and first published as "The Cat on the Mountain" in *Colorado Folksong Bulletin* 1, no. 3 (November 1962): 30.

25. Collected in August 1962 in Lafayette, Colorado, and first published as "Spazzacamino: The Chimney Sweep," in *Colorado Folksong Bulletin* 1, no. 3 (November 1962): 31. A couple of lines in translation and some account of this song's appeal appear in Angelo M. Pellegrini, *Americans by Choice* (New York: Macmillan, 1965), 85, 160.

26. Phyllis H. Williams, *South Italian Folkways in Europe and America, A Handbook for Social Workers, Visiting Nurses, School Teachers, and Physicians* (1938; reprint, New York: Russell and Russell, 1969), 44.

27. Chairetakis, *Cantate con Noi,* 11.

28. Charles W. Churchill, *The Italians of Newark, A Community Study* (1942; reprint, New York: Arno, 1975): 145. See also Anthony Mancini, *Minnie Santangelo's Mortal Sin* (New York: Coward, McCann, and Geoghegan, 1975), 90, where *stornelli* are referred to as "Sunday songs" and regarded as "not merely folk songs but a contest, a good natured competition with neighbors."

29. Garibaldi M. Lapolla, *The Fire in the Flesh* (1931; reprint, New York: Arno, 1975), 136.

30. Chairetakis, *Chesta E la Voci Ca Canuscite* 9, 12, 16-17.

31. Manuel D. Ramirez, "Italian Folklore from Tampa, Florida: Introduction," *Southern Folklore Quarterly* 5 (1941): 105-6. For information on the bawdy implications of the song, see Richard Gambino, *Blood of My Blood, The Dilemma of the Italian-Americans* (Garden City, NY: Doubleday, 1974), 170.

32. Schlesinger, 131.

33. John Alexander Williams, "Italian Regionalism and Pan-Italian Traditions," *Folklife Center News* 11, no. 3 (Summer 1989): 12.

34. Churchill, 146.

35. Reported by Daniel D'Angelo of North Tonawanda, New York, in 1969 and first published in Catherine Harris Ainsworth, *Italian-American Folktales* (Buffalo: Clyde Press, 1977), 15.

36. Anthony T. Rauche, "The Tarantella: Musical and Ethnic Identity for Italian-Americans," in Joseph V. Scelsa et al., eds., *Italian Americans in Transition*, 189-97.

37. Gambino, 141-42. For a *tarantella* at a wedding, see Pietro Di Donato, *Christ in Concrete* (Indianapolis: Bobbs-Merrill, 1939), 264-69.

Chapter Ten. Foodways

1. Irvin L. Child, *Italian or American? The Second Generation in Conflict* (New Haven: Yale Univ. Press, 1943), 141.

2. Interview with Christoper Hodgkins (Calabrian, third generation), 17 July 1990, in Columbus, Ohio.

3. Salvatore J. LaGumina, *The Immigrants Speak, Italian Americans Tell Their Story* (New York: Center for Migration Studies, 1979): 37 (from the memoir of Bruna Pieracci).

4. James Cascaito and Douglas Radcliff-Umstead," An Italo-English Dialect," *American Speech* 50 (1975): 14.

5. Joe Vergara, *Love and Pasta, A Recollection* (New York: Harper and Row, 1968), 39.

6. Richard Gambino, *Blood of My Blood, The Dilemma of the Italian-Americans* (Garden City, NY: Doubleday, 1974), 16; and Herbert J. Gans, *The Urban Villagers, Group and Class in the Life of Italian-Americans* (New York: Free Press, 1962), 33.

7. Frederick O. Bushee, "Italian Immigrants in Boston," in *A Documentary History of Italian Americans*, ed. Wayne Moquin and Charles Van Doren (New York: Praeger, 1974), 52. The piece was originally published in the April 1897 issue of *Arena*.

8. For example, see Lucy H. Gillett, "Factors Influencing Nutrition Work Among Italians," *Journal of Home Economics* 14 (January 1922): 14-19; and Gertrude Gates Mudge, "Italian Dietary Adjustments," *Journal of Home Economics* 15 (April 1923): 181-85.

9. Dorothy Gladys Spicer, "Health Superstitions of the Italian Immigrant," *Hygeia* 4, no. 5 (May 1926): 266; and Phyllis H. Williams, *South Italian Folkways in Europe and America, A Handbook for Social Workers, Visiting Nurses, School Teachers, and Physicians* (1938; reprint, New York: Russell and Russell, 1969), 61-62.

10. Elizabeth Ewen, *Immigrant Women in the Land of Dollars, Life and Culture on the Lower East Side 1890-1925* (New York: Monthly Review Press, 1985), 175.

11. Child, 197.

12. Interview with Christoper Hodgkins.

13. Rocco Fumento, *Tree of Dark Reflection* (New York: Alfred A. Knopf, 1962): 61.

14. Richard Raspa," Exotic Foods Among Italian-Americans in Mormon Utah: Food as Nostalgic Enactment of Identity," in *Ethnic and Regional Foodways in the United States, The Performance of Identity,* ed. Linda Keller Brown and Kay Mussell (Knoxville: Univ. of Tennessee Press, 1984), 191.

15. Ibid., 189-92.

16. Gambino, 16.

17. Williams, 122.

18. John Alexander Williams, "Italian Regionalism and Pan-Italian Traditions," *Folklife Center News* 11, no. 3 (Summer 1989): 13.

19. Ibid., 12.

20. Grace Leonore Pitts, "The Italians of Columbus—A Study in Population," *Annals of the American Academy of Political and Social Science* 19 (1902): 158.

21. Interview with Sam Gennuso (Sicilian, second generation), 26 May 1989, in Jonesboro, Arkansas. See also Jerre Mangione, *Mount Allegro, A Memoir of Italian American Life* (1943; reprint New York: Columbia Univ. Press, 1981), 132.

22. Jerry Della Femina and Charles Sopkin, *An Italian Grows in Brooklyn* (Boston: Little, Brown, 1978), 22; and Louis Guida, "The Rocconi-Fratesi Family: Italianata in the Arkansas Delta," in *Hogs in the Bottom, Family Folklore in Arkansas,* ed. Deirdre LaPin (Little Rock: August House, 1982), 97-98.

23. Guido D'Agostino, *Olives on the Apple Tree* (1940; reprint, New York: Arno, 1975), 296.

24. Interview with Sara Rao Vittone (southern Italian, second generation), 16 June 1990, in Masontown, Pennsylvania.

25. Bushee, 51; Ralph Corsel, *Up There the Stars* (New York: Citadel, 1968), 83; Michael De Capite, *Maria* (New York: John Day, 1943), 4; and Lorenzo Madalena, *Confetti for Gino* (Garden City, NY: Doubleday, 1959), 40.

26. C. Richard King, "Old Thurber," in *Singers and Storytellers,* ed. Mody C. Boatright, Wilson M. Hudson, and Allen Maxwell (Dallas: Southern Methodist Univ. Press, 1961), 111. See also Madalena, 40.

27. Interview with Sara Rao Vittone.

28. Carla Bianco, *The Two Rosetos* (Bloomington: Indiana Univ. Press, 1974), 99; Wayland D. Hand, Anna Casetta, and Sondra B. Thiederman, eds., *Popular Beliefs and Superstitions, A Compendium of American Folklore from the Ohio Collection of Newbell Niles Puckett* (Boston: G. K. Hall, 1981), 630 (item no. 15498), 631 (nos. 15521-23), 633 (no. 15562), 635-36 (nos. 15628, 15631, 15632, 15640), 1031 (nos. 24677, 24678); Mangione, 132-33; and Joseph Napoli, *A Dying Cadence, Memories of a Sicilian Childhood* (NP: NP, 1986), 54.

29. Hand, Casetta, and Thiederman, 635 (item no. 15624), 666 (nos. 16330, 16331), 833 (nos. 20108, 20111, 20112).

30. Mangione, 132-33.

31. Gene P. Veronesi, *Italian Americans and Their Communities of Cleveland* (Cleveland: Cleveland State Univ., 1977), 284.

32. Pauline N. Barrese, "Southern Italian Folklore in New York City," *New York Folklore Quarterly* 21 (1965): 184.

33. Interview with Ray Ferraro (Campanian, second generation), August 1991, in Macomb, Illinois (interviewed by Lucia Peek).

34. Leonard Covello (with Guido D'Agostino), *A Teacher in the Urban Community: A Half Century in City Schools* (Totowa, NJ: Littlefied, Adams, 1970), 71; and Angelo Valenti, *Golden Gate* (1939; reprint, New York: Arno, 1975), 106.

35. Vergara, 38.

36. Judith Goode, Janet Theophano, and Karen Curtis, "A Framework for the Analysis of Continuity and Change in Shared Sociocultural Rules for Food Use: The Italian-American Pattern," in *Ethnic and Regional Foodways in the United States,* ed. Brown and Mussell, 74-75.

37. George Sessions Perry, "Your Neighbors, the Pomaricos," *Saturday Evening Post,* 6 November 1948: 148.

38. Napoli, 53; and Valenti, 201.

39. Mari Tomasi, *Like Lesser Gods* (Milwaukee: Bruce, 1949), 183-84.

40. Interview with Sara Rao Vittone.

41. Toni Fratto, "Cooking in Red and White," *Pennsylvania Folklife* 19, no. 3 (1970): 5-6.

42. Interview with Frances Gueri Byrd (southern Italian, third generation), 23 May 1990, in Jonesboro, Arkansas.

43. Interview with Mamie Jo DiMarco Chauvin (Sicilian, second generation), 19 March 1991, in Forrest City, Arkansas; and Fratto 6.

44. Linda Brandi Cateura, *Growing Up Italian, How Being Brought Up as an Italian-American Helped Shape the Characters, Lives, and Fortunes of Twenty-Four Celebrated Americans* (New York: William Morrow, 1987), 143 (from the memoir of John Ciardi); Vincent Panella, *The Other Side, Growing Up Italian in America* (Garden City, NY: Doubleday, 1979), 22; Tomasi, 44-45; and Vergara, 32.

45. Gambino, 22; and Hand, Casetta, and Thiederman, 643 (item no. 15804).

46. Interview with Sam Gennuso.

47. Interview with Sam Gennuso.

48. Goode, Theophano, and Curtis, 75.

49. Interview with Frances Gueri Byrd; interview with Joanne Terranella Burleson (Sicilian, third generation), 14 March 1990, in Jonesboro, Arkansas; Cateura, 44 (from the memoir of Joseph Bernardin); and Guida, 97.

50. Interview with Pearl Malpezzi (Piedmontese, first generation), 19 July 1984, in Masontown, Pennsylvania.

51. Interview with Joseph Capello (Piedmontese, first generation), 12 November 1982, in Jonesboro, Arkansas. Cf. Veronesi, 285.

52. For example, see Marion Benasutti, *No Steady Job for Papa* (New York: Vanguard, 1966), 5, 74.

53. Cateura, 44 (from the memoir of Joseph Bernardin); and Valenti, 98.

54. LaGumina, 36-37 (from the memoir of Bruna Pieracci).

55. Phyllis H. Williams, 52-53.

56. Phylis Cancilla Martinelli, "Pioneer Paesani in Globe, Arizona," in *Italians in Rural and Small Town America, Essays from the Fourteenth Annual Conference of the American Italian Historical Association,* ed. Rudolph J. Vecoli (Staten Island, NY: American Italian Historical Association, 1987), 162.

57. Interview with Joseph Capello.

58. Fratto, 5; and Antonia Pola, *Who Can Buy the Stars?* (New York: Vantage, 1957), 159.

59. Cateura, 44 (from the memoir of Joseph Bernardin).

60. Phyllis H. Williams, 121.

61. Veronesi, 240.

62. Gambino, 23; and Veronesi, 289.

63. Lydia Q. Pietropaoli, "The Italians Came Up Watertown Way," *New York Folklore Quarterly* 29 (1973): 67.

64. Giorgio Lolli, Emidio Serianni, Grace M. Golder, and Pierpaolo Luzzatto-Fegiz, *Alcohol in Italian Culture, Food and Wine in Relation to Sobriety Among Italians and Italian-Americans* (Glencoe, IL: Free Press, 1958), 63.

65. Interview with Pearl Malpezzi. See also Gambino, 135.

66. Gambino, 24.

67. Lolli and others, 131. See also Ben James Simboli, "Acculturated Italian-American Drinking Behavior," in *The American Experience with Alcohol, Contrasting Cultural Perspectives,* ed. Linda A. Bennett and Genevieve M. Ames (New York: Plenum, 1985), 61-76.

68. Interview with Frances Gueri Byrd; Gambino, 24; and Mangione, 24.

69. Benasutti, 148.

70. Interview with Joseph Capello.

71. Della Femina and Sopkin, 21.

72. Gambino, 136.

73. Andrew Rolle, *The Italian Americans, Troubled Roots* (Norman: Univ. of Oklahoma Press, 1980), 44.

74. Mangione, 28.

75. Interview with Joseph Capello. For more on Capello's winemaking, see William M. Clements, "Winemaking and Personal Cosmology: A Piedmontese-American Example," *New York Folklore* 16, nos. 1-2 (1990): 17-24. Other descriptions of Italian-American winemaking appear in Corinne Azen Krause, *Grandmothers, Mothers, and Daughters, Oral Histories of Three Generations of Ethnic American Women* (Boston: Twayne, 1991), 25; Napoli, 39; and Nat Scammacca, *Bye Bye America, Memories of a Sicilian-American* (New York: Cross-Cultural Communications, 1986), 26-27.

76. Hand, Casetta, and Thiederman, 1396 (item no. 32900).

77. Catherine Harris Ainsworth, *Italian-American Folktales* (Buffalo: Clyde Press, 1977), 37; Hand, Casetta, and Thiederman, 629 (item no. 15461); and Napoli, 39.

78. Rose Grieco, "Wine and Fig Trees," *Commonweal,* 4 June 1954: 221-23.

79. Helen Barolini, *Festa, Recipes and Recollections of Italian Holidays* (New York: Harcourt Brace Jovanovich, 1988), 17.

80. Carla Bianco, "Migration and Urbanization of a Traditional Culture: An Italian Experience," in *Folklore in the Modern World,* ed. Richard M. Dorson (The Hague: Mouton, 1978), 61. See also Bianco, *The Two Rosetos,* 134-35.

81. Fratto, 4.

82. Judith E. Smith, *Family Connections, A History of Italian and Jewish Immigrant Lives in Providence, Rhode Island 1900-1940* (Albany: State Univ. of New York Press, 1985), 41.

83. Vergara, 34-35.

84. Raspa, 189. See also Gambino, 36.

85. John Alexander Williams, "From Backyard Garden to Agribusiness: Italian-American Foodways in the West," *Folklife Center News* 11, no. 2 (Spring 1989): 5.

86. Interview with Sara Rao Vittone.

87. Scammacca, 25. See also Gambino, 36.

88. Bruno Roselli, "An Arkansas Epic," *Century Illustrated* 77 (1920): 382.

89. John A. Williams, "From Backyard Garden to Agribusiness," 5.

90. William Boelhower, *Through a Glass Darkly, Ethnic Semiosis in American Literature* (New York: Oxford Univ. Press, 1987), 114.

91. Bianco, *The Two Rosetos,* 22.

92. Raspa, 189.

93. Interview with Joseph Capello. See also Hand, Casetta, and Thiederman, 1372 (item no. 32318), 1373 (no. 32324), 1374 (nos. 32341, 32356), 1389 (no. 32735).

94. *The Italians of New York, A Survey Prepared by Workers of the Federal Writers' Project, Works Progress Administration in the City of New York* (1938; reprint, New York: Arno, 1969), 71.

95. John A. Williams, "From Backyard Garden to Agribusiness," 5.

96. Interview with Pearl Malpezzi; and Barolini, 277.

97. Interview with Pearl Malpezzi.

98. Interview with Christopher Hodgkins.

99. Fratto, 10; and Tomasi, 139.

100. Susan Kalcik, "Ethnic Foodways in America: Symbol and Performance of Identity," in *Ethnic and Regional Foodways in the United States,* ed. Brown and Mussell, 37.

101. Charlotte Adams, "Italian Life in New York," *Harper's* 62 (1881): 682.

Bibliography

Aarne, Antti, and Stith Thompson. *The Types of the Folktale, A Classification and Bibliography.* Second revision. Helsinki: Academia Scientiarum Fennica, 1964.

Abrahams, Roger D. "The Complex Relations of Simple Forms." In *Folklore Genres,* edited by Dan Ben-Amos, 193-214. Austin: Univ. of Texas Press, 1976.

Adams, Charlotte. "Italian Life in New York." *Harper's* 62 (1881): 676-84.

Adler, Lois. "The Manteo Family's Sicilian Puppets." *Drama Review* 20, no. 2 (June 1976): 25-30.

Agonito, Rosemary. "Il Paisano, Immigrant Italian Folktales of Central New York." *New York Folklore Quarterly* 23 (1967): 52-64.

Ainsworth, Catherine Harris. *Italian-American Folktales.* Buffalo, NY: Clyde Press, 1977.

Aleandri, Emelise, and Maxine Schwartz Seller. "Italian-American Theatre." In *Ethnic Theatre in the United States,* edited by Maxine Schwartz Seller, 237-76. Westport, CT: Greenwood, 1983.

Baily, Samuel L. "The Adjustment of Italian Immigrants in Buenos Aires and New York, 1870-1914." *American Historical Review* 88 (1983): 281-305.

Barbour, Frances M. "Some Foreign Proverbs in Southern Illinois." *Midwest Folklore* 4 (1954): 161-64.

Barolini, Helen. *Festa, Recipes and Recollections of Italian Holidays.* New York: Harcourt Brace Jovanovich, 1988.

Barrese, Pauline N. "A Child of the Thirties." *New York Folklore Quarterly* 25 (1969): 129-36.

——. "Southern Italian Folklore in New York City." *New York Folklore Quarterly* 21 (1965): 184-93.

Belfiglio, Valentine J. "Italians in Small Town and Rural Texas." In *Italian Immigrants in Rural and Small Town America*, edited by Rudolph J. Vecoli, 31-49. Staten Island, NY: American Italian Historical Association, 1987.

———. "Sicilian Houstonians in Transition." In *Italian Americans in Transition, Proceedings of the XXI Annual Conference of The American Italian Historical Association*, edited by Joseph V. Scelsa, Salvatore J. LaGumina, and Lydio Tomasi, 39-47. Staten Island, NY: American Italian Historical Association, 1990.

Ben-Amos, Dan, ed. *Folklore Genres*. Austin: Univ. of Texas Press, 1976.

Benasutti, Marion. *No Steady Job for Papa*. New York: Vanguard, 1966.

Bertocci, Angelo P. "Memoir of My Mother." *Harper's* 175 (June 1937): 8-19.

Bianco, Carla. "Migration and Urbanization of a Traditional Culture: An Italian Experience." In *Folklore in the Modern World*, edited by Richard M. Dorson, 55-63. The Hague: Mouton, 1978.

———. *The Two Rosetos*. Bloomington: Indiana Univ. Press, 1974.

"Big Crowd Cheers Columbus Parade." *New York Times*, 13 October 1909: 7.

Biondi, Lawrence. *The Italian-American Child: His Sociolinguistic Acculturation*. Washington: Georgetown Univ. Press, 1975.

Boelhower, William. *Through a Glass Darkly, Ethnic Semiosis in American Literature*. New York: Oxford Univ. Press, 1987.

Bova, Juliana. "Eel for Christmas—An Italian Tradition." *Pennsylvania Folklife* 39, no. 2 (Winter 1989-90): 82-85.

Brown, Linda Keller, and Kay Mussell, eds., *Ethnic and Regional Foodways in the United States: The Performance of Group Identity*. Knoxville: Univ. of Tennessee Press, 1984.

Brunetti, Michael. "Italian Folklore Collected from Mrs. Stephanie Nappi." *New York Folklore Quarterly* 28 (1972): 257-62.

Buonanno, Michael. "Becoming White: Notes on an Italian-American Explanation of Evil Eye." *New York Folklore* 10, nos. 1-2 (Winter/Spring 1984): 39-53.

———. "The Palermitan Epic: Dialogism and the Inscription of Social Relations." *Journal of American Folklore* 103 (1990): 324-33.

Buscemi, Philip A. "The Sicilian Immigrant and His Language Problems." *Sociology and Social Research* 12 (November 1927): 137-43.

Bushee, Frederick O. "Italian Immigrants in Boston." In *A Documentary History of Italian Americans,* edited by Wayne Moquin and Charles Van Doren, 49-54. New York: Praeger, 1974.

Byrne, Donald E., Jr. "Maria Assunta: Berwick's Italian Religious Festival." *Pennsylvania Folklife* 30 (1981): 123-41.

———. "The Race of the Saints: An Italian Religious Festival in Jessup, Pennsylvania." *Journal of Popular Culture* 19 (Winter 1985): 119-30.

"Calling on the Devil to Cure Disease." *Journal of American Folklore* 5 (1892): 238.

Cascaito, James, and Douglas Radcliff-Umstead. "An Italo-English Dialect." *American Speech* 50 (1975): 5-17.

Castiglione, G. E. DiPalma. "Italian Immigration into the United States 1901-04." *American Journal of Sociology* 11, no. 2 (September 1905): 183-206.

"The Cat on the Mountain." *Colorado Folksong Bulletin* 1, no. 3 (November 1962): 30.

Cateura, Linda Brandi. *Growing Up Italian: How Being Brought Up as an Italian-American Helped Shape the Characters, Lives, and Fortunes of Twenty-Four Celebrated Americans.* New York: William Morrow, 1987.

Cautela, Giuseppe. "Italian Funeral." *American Mercury* 15 (October 1928): 200-206.

———. "The Italian Theatre in New York." *American Mercury* 12 (September 1927): 106-12.

Chairetakis, Anna L. Notes to *Cantate con Noi, Choral Songs from Istria and the Alps and Vintage Popular Music from South-Central Italy.* Global Village Music GVM #678, 1986.

———. Notes to *Chesta E la Voci Ca Canuscite, This Is the Voice Your Know: Southern Italian Mountain Music from Calabria, Cam-*

pania, Basilicata and Abruzzi. Global Village Music GVM #675, 1986.

Child, Irvin L. *Italian or American? The Second Generation in Conflict.* New Haven: Yale Univ. Press, 1943.

Churchill, Charles W. *The Italians of Newark, A Community Study.* 1942. Reprint. New York: Arno, 1975.

Ciardi, John. "The Patois." *Saturday Review/World,* 1 June 1974: 34.

Cinel, Dino. "The Seasonal Emigrations of Italians in the Nineteenth Century: From Internal to International Destinations." *Journal of Ethnic Studies* 10, no.1 (1982): 43-68.

Clements, William M. "The 'Man of Words' in Masontown, Pennsylvania: Two Approaches to Verbal Performance." *Western Folklore* 48 (1989): 169-77.

——. "Winemaking and Personal Cosmology: A Piedmontese-American Example." *New York Folklore* 16, nos. 1-2 (1990): 17-24.

Cohen, David Steven. *The Folklore and Folklife of New Jersey.* New Brunswick: Rutgers Univ. Press, 1983.

Corsel, Ralph. *Up There the Stars.* New York: Citadel, 1968.

Covello, Leonard. *The Social Background of the Italo-American School Child, A Study of the Southern Italian Family Mores and Their Effect on the School Situation in Italy and America.* Leiden: E. J. Brill, 1967.

—— (with Guido D'Agostino). *A Teacher in the Urban Community: A Half Century in City Schools.* Totowa, NJ: Littlefield, Adams, 1970.

Cowell, Daniel David. "Funerals, Family, and Forefathers: A View of Italian-American Funeral Practices." *Omega* 16, no. 1 (1985-86): 69-85.

Culin, Stewart. "Italian Marionette Theatre in Brooklyn, N.Y." *Journal of American Folklore* 3 (1890): 155-57.

D'Agostino, Guido. *Olives on the Apple Tree.* 1940. Reprint. New York: Arno, 1975.

D'Angelo, Pascal. *Son of Italy.* 1924. Reprint. New York: Arno, 1975.

De Capite, Michael. *Maria.* New York: John Day, 1943.

De Capite, Raymond. *The Coming of Fabrizze.* New York: David McKay, 1960.

Della Femina, Jerry, and Charles Sopkin. *An Italian Grows in Brooklyn.* Boston: Little, Brown, 1978.

DeRosa, Tina. *Paper Fish.* Chicago: Wine Press, 1980.

Di Donato, Pietro. *Christ in Concrete.* Indianapolis: Bobbs-Merrill, 1939.

———. *Three Circles of Light.* New York: Julian Messner, 1960.

Di Stasi, Lawrence. *Mal Occhio (Evil Eye), The Underside of Vision.* San Francisco: North Point Press, 1981.

Dorson, Richard M. "Dialect Stories of the Upper Peninsula: A New Form of American Folklore." *Journal of American Folklore* 61 (1948): 113-50.

Dundes, Alan, ed. *The Evil Eye: A Folklore Casebook.* New York: Garland, 1981.

Estes, David C. "Across Ethnic Boundaries: St. Joseph's Day in a New Orleans Afro-American Spiritual Church." *Mississippi Folklore Register* 21 (1987): 9-22.

Ets, Marie Hall. *Rosa: The Life of an Italian Immigrant.* Minneapolis: Univ. of Minnesota Press, 1970.

Ewen, Elizabeth. *Immigrant Women in the Land of Dollars, Life and Culture on the Lower East Side 1890-1925.* New York: Monthly Review Press, 1985.

Falassi, Alessandro. *Folklore by the Fireside, Text and Context of the Tuscan Veglia.* Austin: Univ. of Texas Press, 1980.

Fante, John. *Wait Until Spring, Bandini.* 1938. Reprint. Santa Barbara: Black Sparrow, 1983.

"Festa." *New Yorker,* 5 October 1957: 34-36.

Foerster, Robert F. *The Italian Emigration of Our Times.* Cambridge: Harvard Univ. Press, 1919.

Foster, James R. "Brooklyn Folklore." *New York Folklore Quarterly* 13 (1957): 83-91.

Fratto, Toni F. "Cooking in Red and White." *Pennsylvania Folklife* 19, no. 3 (1970): 2-15.

Fumento, Rocco. *Tree of Dark Reflection.* New York: Alfred A. Knopf, 1962.

Gambino, Richard. *Blood of My Blood, The Dilemma of the Italian-Americans.* Garden City, NY: Doubleday, 1974.

———. *Bread and Roses.* New York: Seaview Books, 1981.

Gans, Herbert J. *The Urban Villagers, Group and Class in the Life of Italian-Americans.* New York: Free Press, 1962.

Gardaphe, Fred L. "From Oral Tradition to Written Word: Toward an Ethnographically Based Literary Criticism." In *From the Margin, Writings in Italian Americana,* edited by Anthony Julian Tamburri et al., 294-306. West Lafayette, IN: Purdue Univ. Press, 1991.

———, ed. *Italian-American Ways.* New York: Harper and Row, 1989.

———. "Mora Amore." In *From the Margin, Writings in Italian Americana,* edited by Anthony Julian Tamburri et al., 102-9.

Georges, Robert A., and Stephen Stern, comps. *American and Canadian Immigrant and Ethnic Folklore, An Annotated Bibliography.* New York: Garland, 1982.

Gillett, Lucy H. "Factors Influencing Nutrition Work Among Italians." *Journal of Home Economics* 14 (January 1922): 14-19.

Gisolfi, Anthony M. "Italo-American: What It Has Borrowed from American English and What It Is Contributing to the American Language." *Commonweal,* 21 July 1939: 311-13.

Giuliano, Bruce B. *Sacro o Profano? A Consideration of Four Italian-Canadian Religious Festivals,* Canadian Centre for Folk Culture Studies Paper no. 17. Ottawa: National Museums of Canada, 1976.

Glazer, Nathan, and Daniel Patrick Moynihan. *Beyond the Melting Pot, The Negroes, Puerto Ricans, Jews, Italians, and Irish of New York City.* 2nd edition. Cambridge: MIT Press, 1970.

Goode, Judith, Janet Theophano, and Karen Curtis. "A Framework for the Analysis of Continuity and Change in Shared Sociocultural Rules for Food Use: The Italian-American Pattern." In *Ethnic and Regional Foodways,* edited by Linda Keller Brown and Kay Mussell, 66-88. Knoxville: Univ. of Tennessee Press, 1984.

Green, Rose Basile. *The Italian-American Novel, A Document of the Interaction of Two Cultures.* Madison, NJ: Fairleigh Dickinson Univ. Press, 1974.

Grieco, Rose. "They Who Mourn." *Commonweal,* 27 March 1953: 628-30.

———. "Wine and Fig Trees." *Commonweal,* 4 June 1954: 221-23.

Guida, Louis. "The Rocconi-Fratesi Family: Italianata in the Arkansas Delta." In *Hogs in the Bottom, Family Folklore in Arkansas,* edited by Deirdre LaPin, 85-99. Little Rock: August House, 1982.

Haller, Hermann W. "Between Standard Italian and Creole: An Interim Report on Language Patterns in an Italian-American Community." *WORD* 32, no. 3 (December 1981): 181-91.

———. "Italian-American Speech Varieties." In *Geolinguistic Perspectives, Proceedings of the International Conference Celebrating the Twentieth Anniversary of the American Society of Geolinguistics, 1985,* edited by Jesse Levitt, Leonard R. N. Ashley, and Kenneth H. Rogers, 259-66. Lanham, VA: Univ. Press of America, 1987.

———. "Italian Speech Varieties in the United States and the Italian-American Lingua Franca." *Italica* 64 (1987): 393-409.

Hamilton, Alice. "Witchcraft in West Polk Street." *American Mercury* 10 (January 1927): 71-75.

Hand, Wayland D. "The Evil Eye in Its Folk Medical Aspects: A Survey of North America." In *The Evil Eye: A Folklore Casebook,* edited by Alan Dundes, 169-80. New York: Garland, 1981.

———, Anna Casetta, and Sondra B. Thiederman, eds. *Popular Beliefs and Superstitions, A Compendium of American Folklore from the Ohio Collection of Newbell Niles Puckett.* Boston: G. K. Hall, 1981.

Hapgood, Hutchins. "The Italian Theater of New York." In *A Documentary History of Italian Americans,* edited by Wayne Moquin and Charles Van Doren, 317-20. New York: Praeger, 1974.

Hartman, Peter, and Karyl McIntosh. "Evil Eye Beliefs Collected in Utica, New York." *New York Folklore* 4 (1978): 61-69.

Hoffman, Dan G. "Stregas, Ghosts, and Werewolves." *New York Folklore Quarterly* 3 (1947): 325-28.

Irwin, Elisabeth. "Where the Players Are Marionettes and the Age of Chivalry Is Born Again in a Little Italian Theater in Mulberry Street." *The Craftsman* 12 (1907): 667-69.

Isolani, Paola A. Sensi, and Anthony Julian Tamburri, eds. *Italian Americans Celebrate Life: Their Arts and Popular Culture.* NP: American Italian Historical Association, 1990.

"Italian Festivals in New York." *The Chautauquan* 34 (1901): 228-29.

The Italians of New York, A Survey Prepared by Workers of the Federal Writers' Project, Works Progress Administration in the City of New York. 1938. Reprint. New York: Arno, 1969.

Jones, Idwal. "Evviva San Francisco." *American Mercury* 12 (October 1927): 151-58.

Jones, Louis C. "The Evil Eye Among European-Americans." In *The Evil Eye: A Folklore Casebook,* edited by Alan Dundes, 150-68. New York: Garland, 1981.

———. "Italian Werewolves." *New York Folklore Quarterly* 6 (1950): 133-38.

Kalčik, Susan. "Ethnic Foodways in America: Symbol and Performance of Identity." In *Ethnic and Regional Foodways in the United States: The Performance of Group Identity,* edited by Linda Keller Brown and Kay Mussell, 37-65. Knoxville: Univ. of Tennessee Press, 1984.

Kimball, Charlotte. "An Outline of Amusements Among Italians in New York." *Charities* 5, no. 12 (18 August 1900): 1-8.

King, C. Richard. "Old Thurber." In *Singers and Storytellers,* edited by Mody C. Boatright, Wilson M. Hudson, and Allen Maxwell, 107-14. Dallas: Southern Methodist Univ. Press, 1961.

Krause, Corinne Azen. *Grandmothers, Mothers, and Daughters: Oral Histories of Three Generations of Ethnic American Women.* Boston: Twayne, 1991.

LaGumina, Salvatore J. *The Immigrants Speak, Italian Americans Tell Their Story.* New York: Center for Migration Studies, 1979.

LaPolla, Garibaldi M. *The Fire in the Flesh.* 1931. Reprint. New York: Arno, 1975.

La Sorte, Michael. *La Merica, Images of Italian Greenhorn Experience.* Philadephia: Temple Univ. Press, 1985.

Light, Ken. "Christopher Columbus Lands at San Francisco Harbor." *Folklife Center News* 11, no. 4 (Fall 1989): 8-9.

Livingston, Arthur. "La Merica Sanemagogna." *The Romanic Review* 9 (1918): 206-26.

Lolli, Giorgio, Emidio Serianni, Grace M. Golder, and Pierpaolo Luzzatto-Fegiz. *Alcohol in Italian Culture, Food and Wine in Relation to Sobriety Among Italians and Italian-Americans.* Glencoe, IL: Free Press, 1958.

Longo, Lucas. *The Family on Vendetta Street.* Garden City, NY: Doubleday, 1968.

Lopreato, Joseph. *Italian Americans.* New York: Random House, 1970.

Lumpkin, Ben Gray. "La Monaca Sposa." *Colorado Folksong Bulletin* 1, no. 2 (April 1962): 24-25.

Macbrayne, Lewis E. "The Judgment of the Steerage." *Harper's* 117 (1908): 489-99.

Madalena, Lorenzo. *Confetti for Gino.* Garden City, NY: Doubleday, 1959.

Maiolo, Melia Rose. "Italian Tales Told in Shinnston." *West Virginia Folklore* 8, no. 1 (Fall 1957): 8-16.

Malinowski, Bronislaw. "The Role of Magic and Religion." In *Reader in Comparative Religion, An Anthropological Approach,* edited by William A. Lessa and Evon Z. Vogt, 102-12. New York: Harper and Row, 1965.

Maloney, Clarence, ed. *The Evil Eye.* New York: Columbia Univ. Press, 1976.

Mancini, Anthony. *Minnie Santangelo's Mortal Sin.* New York: Coward, McCann, and Geoghegan, 1975.

Mangione, Jerre. *Mount Allegro, A Memoir of Italian American Life.* 1943. Reprint. New York: Columbia Univ. Press, 1981.

Mankins, Jerilyn. "More Italian Beliefs." *West Virginia Folklore* 12, no. 2 (Winter 1962): 24-29.

Martinelli, Phylis Cancilla. "Pioneer Paesani in Globe, Arizona." In *Italian Immigrants in Rural and Small Town America,* edited by Rudolph J. Vecoli, 153-69. Staten Island, NY: American Italian Historical Association, 1987.

Masontown Sesqui-Centennial Celebration, 1798-1948. NP: NP, 1948.

Mathias, Elizabeth. "The Game as Creator of the Group in an Italian-American Community." *Pennsylvania Folklife* 23, no. 4 (1974): 22-30.

——. "Italian-American Culture and Games: The Minnesota Iron Range and South Philadelphia." In *Play as Context, 1979 Proceedings of the Association for the Anthropological Study of Play,* edited by Alyce Taylor Cheska. West Point, NY: Leisure Press, 1981.

——. "The Italian-American Funeral: Persistence Through Change." *Western Folklore* 33 (1974): 35-50.

——, and Richard Raspa. *Italian Folktales in America, The Verbal Art of an Immigrant Woman.* Detroit: Wayne State Univ. Press, 1985.

——, and Angelamaria Varesano. "The Dynamics of Religious Reactivation: A Study of a Charismatic Missionary to Southern Italians in the United States." *Ethnicity* 5 (1978): 301-11.

Matthews, Glenna. "An Immigrant Community in Indian Territory." *Labor History* 23 (1982): 374-94.

McIntosh, Karyl. "Folk Obstetrics, Gynecology, and Pediatrics in Utica, New York." *New York Folkore* 4 (1978): 49-59.

McNaughton, Barbara J. Taft. "Calabrian Folklore from Giovanna." *Journal of the Ohio Folklore Society,* n.s. 3, no. 1 (Spring 1974): 20-28.

Mencken, H. L. *The American Language, An Inquiry into the Development of English in the United States.* 4th edition. New York: Alfred A. Knopf, 1937.

Miller, Marc L., and John Van Maanen. "'Boats Don't Fish, People Do': Some Ethnographic Notes on the Federal Management of Fisheries in Gloucester." *Human Organization* 38 (1979): 377-85.

Moquin, Wayne, and Charles Van Doren, eds. *A Documentary History of Italian Americans*. New York: Praeger, 1974.

Mormino, Gary. "'We Worked Hard and Took Care of Our Own': Oral History and Italians in Tampa." *Labor History* 23 (1982): 395-415.

Mudge, Gertrude Gates. "Italian Dietary Adjustments." *Journal of Home Economics* 15 (April 1923): 181-85.

Mullen, Patrick B. *I Heard the Old Fishermen Say: Folklore of the Texas Gulf Coast*. Austin: Univ. of Texas Press, 1978.

Musick, Ruth Ann. "Italian Folk Tales Told by Rocco Pantalone, of Fairmont." *West Virginia Folklore* 11, no. 1 (Fall 1960): 2-16.

Napoli, Joseph. *A Dying Cadence, Memories of a Sicilian Childhood*. NP: NP, 1986.

Navarra, Anthony. "Old Tales and New Tongues." *New York Folklore Quarterly* 18 (1962): 12-15.

Nelli, Humbert S. "Italians." In *Harvard Encyclopedia of American Ethnic Groups*, edited by Stephan Thernstrom, 545-60. Cambridge: Harvard Univ. Press, 1980.

———. "Italians in Urban America: A Study in Ethnic Adjustment." *International Migration Review* 1, no. 3 (Summer 1967): 38-55.

N[ewell], W[illiam] W[ells]. "Italian Marionettes in Boston." *Journal of American Folklore* 7 (1894): 153.

Noyes, Dorothy. "The Changing Role of the Italian-American Religious Festival." In *Italian-American Traditions: Family and Community*, 13-17. Philadelphia: Balch Institute for Ethnic Studies, 1985.

———. *Uses of Tradition, Arts of Italian Americans in Philadelphia*. Philadelphia: Philadelphia Folklore Project, 1989.

Orsi, Robert Anthony. "The Fault of Memory: 'Southern Italy' in the Imagination of Immigrants and the Lives of Their Children in Italian Harlem, 1920-1945." *Journal of Family History* 15 (1990): 133-47.

———. *The Madonna of 115th Street, Faith and Community in Italian Harlem, 1880-1950*. New Haven: Yale Univ. Press, 1985.

Pagano, Jo. *Golden Wedding*. 1943. Reprint. New York: Arno, 1975.

Palisi, Bartolomeo J. "Patterns of Social Participation in a Four-Generation Sample of Italian-Americans." *Sociological Quarterly* 7 (1966): 167-78.

Panella, Vincent. *The Other Side, Growing Up Italian in America.* Garden City, NY: Doubleday, 1979.

Panunzio, Constantine M. *The Soul of an Immigrant.* New York: Macmillan, 1928.

Park, Robert E., and Herbert A. Miller, *Old World Traits Transplanted.* New York: Harper, 1921.

Pellegrini, Angelo M. *Americans by Choice.* New York: Macmillan, 1956.

Peragallo, Olga. *Italian American Authors and Their Contribution to American Literature.* New York: S.F. Vanni, 1949.

Perry, George Sessions. "Your Neighbors, The Pomaricos." *Saturday Evening Post,* 6 November 1948: 38-39, 144-51.

Pietropaoli, Lydia Q. "The Italians Came Up Watertown Way." *New York Folklore Quarterly* 29, no. 1 (1973): 58-79.

Pitts, Grace Leonore. "The Italians of Columbus—A Study in Population." *Annals of the American Academy of Political and Social Science* 19 (1902): 154-59.

Pola, Antonia. *Who Can Buy the Stars?* New York: Vantage, 1957.

Pope, Barbara Corrado. "The Origins of Southern Italian Good Friday Processions." In *Italian Americans Celebrate Life: Their Arts and Popular Culture,* edited by Paoli A. Sensi Isolani and Anthony Julian Tamburri, 155-68. NP: American Italian Historical Association, 1990.

Posen, I. Sheldon. "Storing Contexts: The Brooklyn *Giglio* as Folk Art." In *Folk Art and Art Worlds,* edited by John Michael Vlach and Simon J. Bronner, 171-91. Ann Arbor, MI: UMI Research Press, 1986.

——, and Joseph Sciorra. "Brooklyn's Dancing Tower." *Natural History* 92 (June 1983): 30-37.

Primeggia, Salvatore, and Joseph A. Varacalli. "Southern Italian Comedy: Old to New World." In *Italian Americans in Transition, Proceedings of the XXI Annual Conference of the Italian American Historical Association,* edited by Joseph V. Scelsa,

Salvatore J. LaGuimina, and Lydio Tomasi, 241-52. Staten Island, NY: American Italian Historical Association, 1990.

Ramirez, Manuel D. "Italian Folklore from Tampa, Florida: Introduction." *Southern Folklore Quarterly* 5 (1941): 101-6.

——. "Italian Folklore from Tampa, Florida. Series No. II: Proverbs." *Southern Folklore Quarterly* 13 (1949): 121-32.

Raspa, Richard. "Exotic Foods Among Italian-Americans in Mormon Utah: Food as Nostalgic Enactment of Identity." In *Ethnic and Regional Foodways: The Performance of Group Identity*, edited by Linda Keller Brown and Kay Mussell, 185-94. Knoxville: Univ. of Tennessee Press, 1984.

Rauche, Anthony T. "The Tarantella: Musical and Ethnic Identity for Italian-Americans." In *Italian Americans in Transition*, edited by Scelsa, LaGuimina, and Tomasi, 189-97.

Regnoni-Macera, Clara. "Il Magg (Welcome, May)." *Colorado Folksong Bulletin* 1.3 (November 1962): 32-33.

——. "The Song of May." *Western Folklore* 23 (1964): 23-26.

"Religion of Lucky Pieces, Witches and the Evil Eye." *World Outlook* 3 (October 1917): 24-25, 28.

Rhodes, Shari. "Italian Culture in Northeast Arkansas." Videotape in Arkansas State University Folklore Archives.

Riis, Jacob A. "Feast-Days in Little Italy." *Century Magazine* 58 (August 1899): 491-99.

Roberts, Leonard. "Folktales from the Italian Alps." *Tennessee Folklore Society Bulletin* 22 (1956): 99-108.

——. "More Folktales from the Italian Alps." *Tennessee Folklore Society Bulletin* 23 (1957): 95-104.

Rolle, Andrew. *The Italian Americans: Troubled Roots.* 1980. Reprint. Norman: Univ. of Oklahoma Press, 1984.

Rose, Philip M. *The Italians in America.* New York: George H. Doran, 1922.

Roselli, Bruno. "An Arkansas Epic." *Century Illustrated* 77 (January 1920): 377-86.

Rotunda, D. P. *Motif-Index of the Italian Novella in Prose.* 1942. Reprint. New York: Haskell House, 1973.

Russo, Nicholas John. "Three Generations of Italians in New York City: Their Religious Acculturation." *International Migration Review* 3, no. 2 (Spring 1969): 3-17.

"St. Joe's Parade Hails Lombardi, Italians Celebrate Feast with March, Spaghetti." *New Orleans Times-Picayune,* 19 March 1972.

Samuelson, Sue, and Ray Kepner. "Bocce Ball Meets Hacky-Sack: A Western Pennsylvania Independence Day Gathering." *Keystone Folklore* 3, no. 2 (1984): 26-35.

Sartorio, Rev. Enrico C. *Social and Religious Life of Italians in America.* Boston: Christopher, 1918.

Saxon, Lyle, Edward Dreyer, and Robert Tallant. *Gumbo Ya-Ya, A Collection of Louisiana Folk Tales.* 1945. Reprint. New York: Bonanza, n.d.

Scammacca, Nat. *Bye Bye America, Memories of a Sicilian-American.* New York: Cross-Cultural Communications, 1986.

Scarne, John. *Scarne's Encyclopedia of Games.* New York: Harper and Row, 1973.

Scelsa, Joseph V., Salvatore J. LaGumina, and Lydio Tomasi, eds. *Italian Americans in Transition, Proceedings of the XXI Annual Conference of the American Italian Historical Association.* Staten Island, NY: American Italian Historical Association, 1990.

Schlesinger, Michael. "Italian Music in New York." *New York Folklore* 14, nos. 3-4 (Summer-Fall 1988): 129-38.

Sciorra, Joseph. "'O Giglio e Paradiso': Celebration and Identity in an Urban Community," *Urban Resources* 5, no. 3 (1989): 15-20, 44-46.

——. "Religious Processions in Italian Williamsburg." *Drama Review* 29 (Fall 1985): 65-81.

——. "Yard Shrines and Sidewalk Altars of New York's Italian-Americans." In *Perspectives in Vernacular Architecture III,* edited by Thomas Carter and Bernard L. Herman, 185-98. Columbia: Univ. of Missouri Press, 1989.

Seitel, Peter. "Proverbs: A Social Use of Metaphor." In *Folklore Genres,* edited by Dan Ben-Amos, 125-43. Austin: Univ. of Texas Press, 1976.

Simbioli, Ben James. "Acculturated Italian-American Drinking Behavior." In *The American Experience with Alcohol: Contrasting Cultural Perspectives,* edited by Linda A. Bennett and Genevieve M. Ames, 61-76. New York: Plenum Press, 1985.

Singer, Caroline. "An Italian Saturday." *Century* 101 (1921): 590-600.

Smith, Judith E. *Family Connections, A History of Italian and Jewish Immigrant Lives in Providence, Rhode Island 1900-1940.* Albany: State Univ. of New York Press, 1985.

Smith, M. Estellie. "Folk Medicine Among the Sicilian-Americans of Buffalo, New York." *Urban Anthropology* 1, no. 1 (1972): 87-106.

"Spazzacamino: The Chimney Sweep." *Colorado Folksong Bulletin* 1, no. 3 (November 1962): 31.

Speroni, Charles. "California Fishermen's Festivals." *Western Folklore* 14 (1955): 77-91.

———. "The Development of the Columbus Day Pageant of San Francisco." *Western Folklore* 7 (1948): 325-35.

———. "Five Italian Wellerisms." *Western Folklore* 7 (1948): 54-55.

———. "The Observance of Saint Joseph's Day Among the Sicilians of Southern California." *Southern Folklore Quarterly* 4 (1940): 135-39.

Spicer, Dorothy Gladys. "Health Superstitions of the Italian Immigrant." *Hygeia* 4, no. 5 (May 1926): 266-69.

———. "The Immigrant Mother as Seen by a Social Worker." *Hygeia* 4, no. 6 (June 1926): 319-21.

Sturgul, Paul A. "Italians on the Gogebic Iron Range." In *Italian Immigrants in Rural and Small Town America,* edited by Rudolph J. Vecoli, 170-78. Staten Island, NY: American Italian Historical Association, 1987.

Swiderski, Richard. "From Folk to Popular: Plastic Evil Eye Charms." In *The Evil Eye,* edited by Clarence Maloney, 28-41. New York: Columbia Univ. Press, 1976.

———. *Voices: An Anthropologist's Dialogue with an Italian-American Festival.* Bowling Green, OH: Popular Press, 1987.

Tamburri, Anthony Julian, Paolo A. Giordano, and Fred L. Gardaphe, eds. *From the Margin, Writings in Italian Americana.* West Lafayette, IN: Purdue Univ. Press, 1991.

Thompson, Stith. *Motif-Index of Folk-Literature, A Classification of Narrative Elements in Folktales, Ballads, Myths, Fables, Mediaeval Romances, Exempla, Fabliaux, Jest-Books and Local Legends.* 6 volumes. Bloomington: Indiana Univ. Press, 1955-58.

Tomasi, Mari. *Like Lesser Gods.* Milwaukee: Bruce, 1949.

Tricarico, Donald. "Guido: Fashioning an Italian-American Youth Style." *Journal of Ethnic Studies* 19, no. 1 (Spring 1991): 41-66.

———. "The Restructuring of Ethnic Community: The Italian Neighborhood in Greenwich Village." *Journal of Ethnic Studies* 11, no. 2 (1983): 61-77.

Turano, Anthony M. "The Speech of Little Italy." *American Mercury* 26 (1932): 356-59.

Turner, Kay F. "The Virgin of Sorrows Procession: A Brooklyn Inversion." *Folklore Papers of the University Folklore Association* 9 (1980): 1-26.

———, and Suzanne Seriff. "'Giving an Altar': The Ideology of Reproduction in a St. Joseph's Day Feast." *Journal of American Folklore* 100 (1987): 446-60.

Turner, Victor W. *The Ritual Process, Structure and Anti-Structure.* Chicago: Aldine, 1969.

Urick, Mildred. "The San Rocco Festival at Aliquippa, Pennsylvania: A Transplanted Tradition." *Pennsylvania Folklife* 19, no. 1 (Autumn 1969): 14-22.

Valenti, Angelo. *Golden Gate.* 1939. Reprint. New York: Arno, 1975.

Valetta, Clement L. "Friendship and Games in Italian-American Life." *Keystone Folklore Quarterly* 15 (1970): 174-87.

Van Gennep, Arnold. *The Rites of Passage.* Trans. Monika B. Vizedom and Gabrielle L. Caffee. Chicago: Univ. of Chicago Press, 1960.

Vaughan, Herbert H. "Italian and Its Dialects as Spoken in the United States." *American Speech* 1, no. 8 (May 1926): 431-35.

Vecoli, Rudolph J. "Cult and Occult in Italian-American Culture: The Persistence of a Religious Heritage." In *Immigrants and Religion in Urban America,* edited by Randall M. Miller and Thomas D. Marzik, 25-47. Philadelphia: Temple Univ. Press, 1977.

———, ed. *Italian Immigrants in Rural and Small Town America. Essays from the Fourteenth Annual Conference of the American Italian Historical Association.* Staten Island, NY: American Italian Historical Association, 1987.

———. "Italians on Minnesota's Iron Range." In *Italian Immigrants in Rural and Small Town America,* edited by Rudolph J. Vecoli, 179-89.

———. "Prelates and Peasants: Italian Immigrants and the Catholic Church." *Journal of Social History* 2 (Spring 1969): 217-68.

Venturelli, Peter J. "Institutions in an Ethnic District." *Human Organization* 41 (Spring 1982): 26-35.

Vergara, Joe. *Love and Pasta, A Recollection.* New York: Harper and Row, 1968.

Veronesi, Gene P. *Italian Americans and Their Communities of Cleveland.* Cleveland: Cleveland State Univ., 1977.

Voiles, Jane. "Genoese Folkways in a California Mining Camp." *California Folklore Quarterly* 3 (1944): 212-16.

Ware, Caroline F. *Greenwich Village 1920-1930, A Comment on American Civilization in the Post-War Years.* 1935. Reprint. New York: Harper and Row, 1965.

Whyte, William Foote. *Street Corner Society, The Social Structure of an Italian Slum.* 2nd edition. Chicago: Univ. of Chicago Press, 1955.

Williams, John Alexander. "From Backyard Garden to Agribusiness: Italian-American Foodways in the West." *Folklife Center News* 11, no. 2 (Spring 1989): 4-6.

———. "Italian Regionalism and Pan-Italian Traditions." *Folklife Center News* 11, no. 3 (Summer 1989): 10-13.

Williams, Phyllis H. *South Italian Folkways in Europe and America, A Handbook for Social Workers, Visiting Nurses, School Teachers, and Physicians.* 1938. Reprint. New York: Russell and Russell, 1969.

Yans-McLauglin, Virginia. *Family and Community: Italian Immigrants in Buffalo, 1880-1930*. 1971. Reprint. Chicago: Univ. of Chicago Press, 1982.

Zallio, A. G. "The Piedmontese Dialects in the United States." *American Speech* 2, no. 12 (September 1927): 501-4.

Zappacosta, Bob. "Italian Beliefs." *West Virginia Folklore* 12, no. 2 (Winter 1962): 18-24.